THE AMERICAN EXPRESS POCKET GUIDE TO
BARCELONA & MADRID

Herbert Bailey Livesey

For Mitchell Beazley:

Mitchell Beazley

The Author
Herbert Bailey Livesey, a native New Yorker, also has a home in
Spain and is a regular visitor to the country. He is the author of
several titles in this series: *New York; Toronto, Montréal & Québec
City;* and *Spain* (which this volume supersedes). He is a novelist
and travel writer, and contributes regularly to *Travel & Leisure*
magazine.

Acknowledgments
The author would like to thank Pilar Vico of the National Tourist
Office of Spain in New York and Iberia Airlines for their
invaluable help.
   The publishers wish to thank the American Express Publishing
Corporation Inc., New York, and Gary Walther, Editor-in-Chief of
Departures, for their co-operation during the production of this
book, and Harry Eyres for his careful reading of the typescript.
   The editor wishes to thank Mike de Mello of Triptych Systems
Limited for his technical assistance during the preparation of the
book.
   The *American Express Travel Guide Series* was conceived
under the direction of Susannah Read, Douglas Wilson, Hal
Robinson and Eric Drewery.

For the series
General Editor   David Townsend Jones
Map Editor   David Haslam
Indexer   Hilary Bird

For this edition
Edited on desktop by   David Townsend Jones
Associate Editor   Sharon Charity
Art editors   Castle House Press
Illustrator   Jeremy Ford (David Lewis Artists), Illustrated Arts,
   Rodney Paull
Gazetteer   Anne Evans

For Mitchell Beazley
Senior Executive Art Editor   Tim Foster
Managing Editor   Alison Starling
Production   Sarah Schuman

Edited and designed by Mitchell Beazley Publishers, part of Reed International
Books, Michelin House, 81 Fulham Road, London SW3 6RB for the American
Express (R) Travel Guide Series

Maps in 2-color and 4-color by Lovell Johns, Oxford, England.
Desktop layout in Ventura Publisher by Castle House Press, Llantrisant, Wales.
Typeset in Garamond and Univers.
Linotronic output through Tradespools Limited, Frome, England.
Produced by Mandarin Offset. Printed and bound in Malaysia.

Contents

How to use this book

How to find it **(1)** For the organization of the book, see CONTENTS on the previous page. **(2)** Wherever possible, sections are arranged alphabetically, with headings appearing in **BLUE CAPITALS**. The headings are followed by addresses, telephone numbers and other practical details printed in *blue italics*. **(3)** Subject headers, similar to those used in telephone directories, appear in **bold black type** in the top corner of each page. **(4)** If you still cannot find it, look in the INDEX (on pages 152-158).

Cross-references These are printed in SMALL CAPITALS, referring the reader to other sections or entries in the book.

Using the maps The full-color maps at the end of the book have a standard grid system, to which the map co-ordinates given throughout the book refer. For example, Montjuïc is on map **3**F3 and the Museo del Prado on map **10**D5. A complete list of street names with their map co-ordinates, which includes all streets that fall within the area of our maps, appears on pages 159-160.

Bold and italic type **Bold type** emphasizes points or topics of interest. As well as being used conventionally for titles, foreign words etc., *italic type* is also used within brackets for addresses, telephone numbers and other practical details.

Abbreviations These include days of the week and months; N, S, E and W (points of the compass); St (Saint); rms (rooms); C (century); measurements; # (road/street no.); pta (peseta); s/n (*sin numero* = no number); and address abbreviations: Av. (Avinguda, Avenida), Bda. (Baixada), C. (Carrer, Calle — usually omitted), Pg. (Passeig), Pge. (Passatge), Pl. (Plaça, Plaza), Po. (Paseo), Pta. (Puerta), Rbla. (Rambla), Rda. (Ronda) and Trav. (Travessera).

Floors The European convention is used: "first floor" means the floor above the ground floor, and so on.

Price categories Price categories for hotels and restaurants are represented by the symbols ☐ ☐ ☐ ☐ and ☐ , which signify cheap, inexpensive, moderately priced, expensive and very expensive, respectively.

These correspond approximately with the following actual prices, valid as of spring 1991, which provide a guideline at the time of printing. Although actual prices will inevitably increase, price categories relative to each other should remain stable.

Price categories	Corresponding to approximate prices	
	for **hotels**	for **restaurants**
	double room with bath; single hardly any cheaper	*meal for one with house wine, service and taxes*
☐ cheap	under 4,000ptas	under 1,000ptas
☐ inexpensive	4,000-9,000ptas	1,000-2,000ptas
☐ moderate	9,000-15,000ptas	2,000-3,500ptas
☐ expensive	15,000-20,000ptas	3,500-5,000ptas
☐ very expensive	over 20,000ptas	over 5,000ptas

Key to symbols

☎	Telephone	⬒	Rooms with private bathroom
✆	Telex	⬓	Secure garage
⊗	Facsimile (fax)	⬛	Luxury hotel
★	Recommended sight	♨	Quiet hotel
✿	Good value (in its class)	⬍	Elevator
i	Tourist information	♿	Facilities for disabled people
⇌	Parking	☐	TV in each room
⛫	Building of architectural interest	☎	Telephone in each room
⊡	Free entrance	🐕	Dogs not allowed
⊠	Entrance fee payable	✿	Garden
⋘	Good view	≋	Swimming pool
✗	Guided tour	⚐	Golf
✷	Special interest for children	⚏	Gym/Fitness facilities
⌂	Hotel	☂	Sauna
⊏	Restaurant	⊟	Mini-bar
☕	Cafeteria	⊏	Simple restaurant
▦	Air conditioning	⬡	Luxury restaurant
☐	Cheap	▭	A la carte available
▯	Inexpensive	▬	Set (fixed-price) menu available
▮	Moderately priced	⬖	Good wines
▰	Expensive	⬟	Open-air dining
▱	Very expensive	⅄	Bar
𝐀𝐄	American Express	⊙	Disco dancing
⬚	Diners Club	⌐	Nightclub
⬛	MasterCard/Eurocard	♪	Live music
VISA	Visa	✾	Dancing

A word from the General Editor

Our authors and editors go to great lengths to ensure that all the information is accurate at the time the *American Express Travel Guides* go to press. However, no travel book can be completely free of error or totally up to date. In Spain, major changes will continue to follow the Olympic Games and Expo '92 long after they are over. Moreover, telephone numbers and opening hours change without warning, and hotels and restaurants come under new management, which may affect their standards.

We are always delighted to receive corrections or suggestions for improvements from our readers, which where appropriate can be incorporated in the next edition.

I am particularly indebted to readers who wrote during the preparation of this book. Please continue to stay in touch — your feedback is very important to our efforts to tailor the series to the very distinctive tastes and requirements of our sophisticated international readership.

Send your comments to me at Mitchell Beazley Publishers, Michelin House, 81 Fulham Road, London SW3 6RB; or, in the US, c/o American Express Travel Guides, Prentice Hall Travel, 15 Columbus Circle, New York, NY 10023.

The publishers regret that they cannot accept any consequences arising from the use of this book or from the information it contains.

David Townsend Jones

5

Another Golden Age

"Now you have two homes" — so goes a Spanish farewell to new friends. But in truth, Spain is a country we know before we first set foot in it. There is a frisson of recognition at every turning, a snippet from a mental scrapbook composed of half-remembered films, travel posters, and meals in Spanish restaurants. The images are sharp. White villages spill down tawny hillsides like heaps of sugar cubes. Whiffs of saffron and burning olive wood drift from tiled foyers and grilled windows. Bent crones in eternal mourning lean from doorways, and guitars strum in the night shadows.

Beyond familiarity, visitors who break away from the iron circle of hall porters, waiters and tour guides may discover an empathy with the land and the people almost as strong as that which they have with their own country. Even on a superficial level, there is much more to Spain than can easily be absorbed. There is the Alhambra of Granada, a magical compound of Moorish palaces and gardens that ranks in stature with the Parthenon. But there is also the Arab mosque at Córdoba, a vast forest of columns and arches with a wildly baroque cathedral dropped in the middle. The Romans left a city in Mérida, an aqueduct in Segovia and a fortress in Tarragona, which equal anything outside Italy. Felipe II left his gloomy Xanadu at El Escorial; and the dictator Franco, his monument of intimidating proportions in the Valley of the Fallen, dedicated to those killed in the Civil War.

From pagan temples compiled of 30-tonne rocks, to Roman bridges still in use, to palaces encrusted with gold plundered from the Americas, to the Surrealism in stone of the visionary Antoni Gaudí, Spain is architecturally unsurpassed. Picasso and Miró have their own museums in Barcelona, in buildings as engaging as the works they house. Their late 20th century successors are seen to best advantage in the exciting Museo de Arte Abstracto Español within the "hanging houses" of Cuenca. And, of course, the Prado in Madrid is a repository for the greatest of pre-20th century Spanish painters.

Most Spaniards regard their cultural heritage with nonchalance, saving their enthusiasm for the numerous local, and often folkloric, music festivals, fairs and fiestas that mark saints' days in every village, town and city. Popular traditions are maintained more strongly in Spain than anywhere else in Europe.

In Barcelona's Plaça de Catalunya you may see children being taught to dance the Catalan *sardana;* or turn a corner in its Gothic Quarter to find an orchestra and choral group performing Handel against the backdrop of a Roman wall. Go to Santander for the swimming and gambling and chance upon recitals held in churches and public squares on summer nights. Pause in a village in Aragón for a cool drink and encounter the strange Lenten ritual in which every male beats a drum continuously for 24 hours. Elsewhere, livestock auctions give an excuse for running bulls through the streets.

Orientation

Spain's population of more than 40 million is spread over 504,780 square kilometers (19,880 square miles) of mountains, plains, both wild and sandy coastlines, and islands that include the Balearics and Canaries. All but two of Spain's 50 provinces bear the same names as their largest cities, and they are gathered into 17 administrative regions, which roughly correspond to the ancient kingdoms of the Moors and early Catholic kings. The capital and largest city is Madrid, at the approximate geographical center, surrounded by a vast arid plateau. Next in size are the industrial seaports of Barcelona in the northeast and Valencia halfway down the east coast.

Castilian Spanish (*Castellano*) is the official language, with its characteristic lisp. Linguists also recognize as distinct tongues the Catalan (*Català*) of the northeast and the Basque (*Euskera*) of the north. The former sounds like a blend of Spanish and French with strong Latin roots; the latter defies classification. Complex dialects persist, such as the Spanish-Portuguese mix spoken in northwest Galicia and the Catalan dialects of Mallorca and Valencia. In resort areas, French and German are often better understood than English.

The people

First impressions are likely to be of the innate Spanish reserve, too often interpreted as hauteur but usually masking an underlying warmth. Persistent friendly inquiry about the history of a region or its typical cuisine cuts through a sometimes dour demeanor, and you may quickly find yourself sharing a glass of wine and discussing family photographs.

More than 97 percent of Spanish people are Catholic, although women are more diligent in observance than their menfolk. From the perspective of most foreigners, Spain is a homogeneous nation. Apart from regional distinctions apparent primarily to natives, ethnic and racial differences are minute, and the only visible minorities are the Gypsies and a growing number of immigrants from sub-Saharan Africa.

Spaniards can be a contentious lot, each man and woman holding strong convictions on family life and politics. Conversation is a primary diversion, so much so that formalized versions of it have been given the name, *tertulia*. It is only slight hyperbole to assert that asking any five Spaniards a question is to ensure the receipt of six opinions. But while pridefulness and unshakable certitude are among a Spaniard's least endearing qualities, they are balanced by a nearly universal generosity of spirit. That hospitable facet of the Spanish character is one of the features that make a visit to Spain so worthwhile.

A brief history

Cave paintings and monolithic structures attest to the presence of Paleolithic people as early as 14000BC. These early inhabitants were replaced by the migrant Iberians, who were in turn superseded by Celts from Central Europe. The Phoenicians founded trading posts on the perimeters of the peninsula, the largest on the site of the present-day city of Cádiz, west of the Gibraltar Strait. The Greeks and Carthaginians followed, establishing colonies along the Mediterranean coast and on the Balearic Islands.

By the 3rdC BC the Carthaginians controlled much of Iberia, a hegemony soon challenged by the Roman Empire. By 201BC the Romans were in control of the east and south coasts, with beachheads along the Atlantic coast. They took another century to impose suzerainty over all but the Basque region. Thereafter, the natives enthusiastically embraced the laws and customs of their conquerors and were rewarded with citizenship and integration into the Empire.

Vandals and Suevi swept across the Pyrenees in the early 5thC AD, swiftly displacing the weakened Roman rulers. In less than a decade, they in turn were routed by the Visigoths. Although the latter eventually lost their territories in Gaul and were

Introduction

periodically beset by attacks from the Byzantines and Franks, they retained control of most of the peninsula until the Arab invasion of 711. A legacy of fervent Catholicism remained to stiffen the Spanish resistance to the alien Muslim Moors (the imprecise catch-all phrase applied to the Berber and Arab enemy). As before, the new invaders conquered all but the stubborn Asturians and Basques. Over the next seven centuries, the gradual Christian Reconquest moved south, aided as often by marriage between monarchs of rival kingdoms and local quarrels among competing Moorish dynasties as by armed conflict.

By 1212, only the emirate of Granada and lesser scattered holdings remained in Moorish hands, but stalemate continued until 1492, when Isabel of Castilla and Fernando of Aragón captured Granada and expelled the Moors from their last stronghold. To this day prayers are offered in Middle Eastern mosques for the return to Islam of its erstwhile Iberian territories. America was discovered the same year, and thereafter the confiscated wealth of the American Indian empires fueled the Golden Age when Spain became one of the greatest powers the world has known.

Carlos I succeeded Fernando. On the death of his maternal grandfather, he also became Holy Roman Emperor, thereby expanding Spain's European territories enormously. But constant warfare dogged his reign and that of his son Felipe II, resulting in the secession of many of these territories, the depletion of the national treasury, and the start of progressive decline under Felipe III and IV. When Carlos II died in 1700, with no natural heir, he left the throne to the Bourbon Felipe of Anjou. That plunged much of Europe into the War of the Spanish Succession.

By the early 19th century, most of the American colonies had been lost. In Spain, Napoleon's brother, Joseph Bonaparte, was installed on the throne, but his brief reign ended when the French were defeated by the British. The country then collapsed into anarchistic bickering, revolts and successive civil wars. An experiment with democracy in 1873 lasted only a year; but the seed was sown, and support began to grow for various radical ideologies. The Spanish-American War of 1898 resulted in the loss of all overseas colonies except Morocco. One positive result of that otherwise hugely demoralizing defeat was the emergence of the so-called "Generation of '98," a literary and intellectual movement that sought to define the Spanish character and culture. It eventually included in its number the authors Ortega y Gasset, Unamuno and Dario, and was to influence significantly the works and thought of their 20th century successors. In Spain itself, uprisings on behalf of separatism and trade unionism were set in motion by the Socialist and Anarcho-Syndicalist movements that began to gain influence in the late 19th century. Time after time, they were brutally suppressed by the army, but continued to flare up through the first two decades of the new century.

One of these, a rebellion in Catalunya in 1923, led directly to the installation of a right-wing dictatorship led by Miguel Primo de Rivera. A respected general who served in several of the now lost overseas colonies, he quashed the revolt and engineered a coup in league with monarchists, the Church and the military. Mounting opposition to his rule brought about his self-imposed exile in 1930.

Alfonso XIII was deposed the next year, when elections brought about the Second Republic. (The First Republic, an earlier experiment in democracy, had lasted less than 18 months, from 1873-1874.) The Second Republic's policies fluctuated from left to right and back in reaction to challenges from both extremes.

Neutrality in World War I sealed Spain's isolation from European affairs. In 1936 a massive military revolt was launched from Morocco, bringing on the tragic Civil War that resulted in more than half a million deaths among civilians and soldiers. General Franco took command of the rebel forces early on, espousing a form of fascism under the rubric of the Falangist party.

Franco's victory in 1939 installed a rightist dictatorship that lasted until his death in 1975. Gradual liberalization in his later years laid the groundwork for the constitutional monarchy that followed. His designated successor, King Juan Carlos, has proved a deft statesman, and his authority has had a moderating influence on the Spanish tendency toward political extremes. Living standards are at their highest ever, the contentious Basques and Catalans now enjoy a measure of autonomy, censorship of the press hardly exists, all ideologies are tolerated, the stranglehold of the conservative clergy on issues of public morality has been loosened, and support for terrorists has shrunk markedly.

Time chart

Origins and conquests

14000- 10000BC	Late Paleolithic people left cave paintings at Altamira and many other locations.
13th- 6thC BC	Original Iberian tribes appeared in Spain, probably having migrated from N Africa.
11thC BC	Phoenicians established trading ports.
10th- 7thC BC	Celts from Central Europe came to Spain across the Pyrenees. Some tribes mixed with resident Iberians to form Celtiberians. The Greeks set up trading settlements in the Balearic Islands and along the SE coast, in competition with the Phoenicians.
6th- 3rdC BC	North African Carthaginians displaced the Greeks and established Cartagena as capital of their colonial empire. They soon conflicted with the Romans and were vanquished in the Second Punic War.
2ndC BC	Roman control expanded over much of Iberia, but was resisted in the NW and the interior until the fall of the Celtiberian city of Numantia in 133BC.
1stC BC- 1stC AD	Spain was divided into three provinces of the Roman Empire. Despite periodic uprisings, the new citizens prospered and assimilated the language, culture and law of their rulers.
2ndC	Christianity spread throughout Spain despite Roman suppression.
5thC	The Romans, unable to stave off the first Hun invaders, enlisted the aid of the Visigothic kings Ataulf and Eurich, who created a fragile unity throughout most of Iberia.
6thC	Although the Visigoths lost Gaul to the Franks in 507, they kept Spain, with Toledo as their capital. Byzantine trading communities occupied parts of the southern coast. The Visigoths declared Christianity the official religion.

Time chart

7thC	The Byzantines were expelled from Spain in 624 and the Suevi were defeated in Galicia. The Church gained control over education and also influenced secular affairs.

The Moors

8thC	The Moors — a term that links several ethnic groups — under general Tariq defeated a Visigothic army in 711 near Jerez de la Frontera, then swept across the country and into Gaul. Galicia, Asturias and the Basque territories resisted the invaders. The rearguard of Charlemagne's retreating Frankish army was destroyed by Basques at Roncesvalles in 778.
10th-12thC	The caliphates, centered at Córdoba, permitted a measure of religious freedom and established schools and libraries. Frequent rebellions in the N caused them to seek assistance from the N African Berber Almoravid sect, and later from the fanatic Almohads, but the Christian monarchs of Asturias, León, Barcelona, Aragón and Castilla continued to gain strength. By 1214, over half the peninsula had been regained by the Catholics and, by 1242, the Moors controlled only the SE kingdom centering on Granada.
13th-14thC	The Granada Emirate enjoyed more than two centuries of prosperity while the Christians were distracted by civil wars in the reconquered territories. The Alhambra was begun.

The Catholic Monarchs

15thC	The kingdoms of Aragón and Castilla were united by the marriage of Fernando II and Isabel in 1469. She established the Inquisition in Castilla in 1478, which was later extended across the rest of the country and led to the expulsion of Jews and Muslims unwilling to convert to Christianity. The infamous Torquemada was named Grand Inquisitor in 1483. The armies of the Catholic king and queen conquered the last Moorish enclave of Granada in 1492, thus unifying the entire nation. That year, Christopher Columbus (Cristóbal Colón) discovered the New World.
1504	Isabel died and Fernando acted as regent of Castilla until his death in 1517. He was succeeded by his grandson Carlos I. With his installation, the expanding empire now incorporated Naples and the islands of Sicily and Sardinia.

The Golden Age

1519	The Golden Age of Spain began with the capture of Mexico by Cortés. Treasure ships returned with cargoes of gold, silver and precious stones. On the death of his Hapsburg grandfather, Carlos I became the Holy Roman Emperor, Carlos V. The Netherlands, Austria and the German principalities were thereby added to the Empire, which at this point encompassed most of Europe as well as the Spanish colonies overseas.
1522-56	Castilian noblemen, known as Comuneros, revolted against increasing centralization of authority by Carlos, but were defeated. Carlos became embroiled in numerous wars over his European territories, causing a serious drain on resources. When he could not suppress the German Reformation launched by Martin Luther, he agreed to allow a measure of

	religious freedom in the affected states. In 1556 he abdicated in favor of his son Felipe II.
1559	Felipe launched the Counter-Reformation. The Inquisition revived persecution of Christian Moors and the remaining Jews.
1563	Construction of the Escorial began.
1568	The Protestant Netherlands revolted against Spanish rule.
1571	Spain lost Tunis to the Turks. Retribution came at the battle of Lepanto, when a naval force, assembled with the aid of the city-states of Venice and Genoa, destroyed the Turkish fleet. The victory gave Spain control of the Mediterranean. In the Pacific, the Philippines were taken.
1580	Felipe forcibly assumed the title of King of Portugal.
1581-88	Despite these successes, the Spanish Empire continued to deteriorate. Spoils from the American colonies diminished, and Spanish treasure ships were harried by English privateers. The Protestants of the Netherlands gained support from Germany and England. The enormously costly Armada set out to invade England but suffered a humiliating defeat through inferior tactics and bad weather, thereby losing command of the sea to England.
1598	Felipe II died, leaving his son, Felipe III, most of his inherited empire, but a depleted treasury.

The decline

1609	Felipe III expelled all remaining Moors and Jews. The Netherlands were declared an independent republic.
1618	The start of the Thirty Years' War drained Spain's power further.
1640	Portugal broke away from Spain.
1659	Spain's participation in the Thirty Years' War ended with the Treaty of the Pyrenees.
1668	In the War of Devolution with France, Spain lost land in France and the Low Countries.
1700	Carlos II died, bequeathing his throne to Felipe, Duke of Anjou (grandson of the Bourbon Louis XIV of France), which resulted in the outbreak of the War of the Spanish Succession in 1701. England and Holland opposed the resulting union of French and Spanish dominions.
1713	The Treaty of Utrecht ended the War of the Spanish Succession, leaving Felipe V only his American and Pacific colonies; Gibraltar was ceded to Britain.
1759	Carlos III ascended the throne, introducing many economic reforms.
1788	Carlos IV turned administration over to an adviser, Manuel de Godoy, whose intrigues drew Spain into the French Revolution and Napoleon's subsequent wars.
1805	Nelson defeated the combined Spanish and French fleets at Trafalgar.
1808	Carlos IV and his son Fernando VII abdicated under pressure from Napoleon, whose brother Joseph Bonaparte became their unpopular successor. An uprising in Madrid precipitated the Peninsular War, known in Spain as the War of Independence.
1812	A liberal constitution was created and approved by the Cortes (Parliament) at Cádiz.

Time chart

1813	Wellington finally drove the French force out of Spain at the decisive Battle of Vitoria. In South America several colonies declared their independence.

19th century unrest

1814	Fernando VII reclaimed the Spanish throne and rejected the 1812 constitution.
1833	Isabel II was proclaimed queen on the death of her father, Fernando VII. The NE provinces supported the claim to the throne of his brother, Don Carlos, in the First Carlist War, but were unsuccessful. The Inquisition was formally terminated.
1845	A new constitution provoked the Second Carlist War.
1868	Isabel II abdicated. The Cortes proclaimed a constitutional monarchy, and in 1870 chose Amadeo of Savoy as king.
1873	Amadeo abdicated. The liberal first Spanish Republic was formed but did not survive, and the Bourbon, Alfonso XII, son of Isabel II, assumed the throne.
1885	Alfonso XII died, leaving María Cristina as regent for his son.
1898	With the end of the Spanish-American War, Spain lost Cuba, Puerto Rico and the Philippines.

The 20th century

1902	16yr-old Alfonso XIII ascended the throne.
1904	A secret pact between Spain and France partitioned Morocco.
1914	Spain remained neutral during World War I, but suffered popular unrest and internal instability.
1921	In Morocco, resentment of European rule sparked the Rif War.
1923	A right-wing dictatorship was founded by General Primo de Rivera. The Cortes was dismissed. Despite a period of prosperity, opposition to restrictive policies grew among intellectuals and workers.
1930	Primo de Rivera was forced into exile.
1931	Alfonso XIII abdicated amid strong antimonarchist feeling. The Second Republic was born with the reconstitution of the Cortes.
1933-35	Primo de Rivera's son, José Antonio, formed the Falangist party. Political factionalism increased.
1936	The Popular Front, a liberal-left coalition, won the national election. José Antonio was imprisoned and his monarchist ally Calvo Sotelo was murdered. The Civil War began. Franco and his troops crossed the Straits of Gibraltar, joining with rebel forces in Sevilla. The Nationalist movement was supported by fascist Italy, Germany and Portugal. The Loyalist Republicans were aided principally by Russia and the International Brigades.
1936-39	The Civil War was marked by its bitterness. Atrocities committed by both sides left a deep-seated legacy of hate.
1939	Barcelona fell in January. The Western democracies recognized the Falange as the legitimate government of Spain. Valencia, the last Loyalist stronghold, surrendered on Mar 30. Franco established a dictatorship that was to last 36yrs.
1940	Recovery began slowly and, after the devastation, suffering was widespread. Authoritarian government

and censorship were imposed.

1941   Spain remained neutral in World War II, although Franco sent the "volunteer" Blue Division to fight for Germany on the Russian front.

1942   Franco re-established the Cortes.

1945-55   An agreement in 1953 to allow the United States to establish air bases in Spain signaled an upturn in international relations. Spain was allowed to join the United Nations in 1955. Recovery, aided by an increase in tourism, progressed slowly, with continuing emphasis on national unity despite the growing interest in regional autonomy.

1956   Spanish Morocco was annexed by independent Morocco, but Spain retained Melilla and Ceuta.

1968   Spain closed the border with Gibraltar.

1969   Juan Carlos, grandson of Alfonso XIII, was named by Franco as his successor.

1970   Although political restrictions were loosened, discontent with the regime was manifest in strikes, protests and increasing terrorist activity.

1975   Franco died on Nov 20. Juan Carlos was proclaimed king.

1976   Prime Minister Suárez formed a center-right coalition.

1978   The death penalty was abolished and divorce permitted.

1980   Autonomy within a Republican framework was granted to Catalunya and the Basque provinces.

1981   A right-wing military coup was attempted, but collapsed after the intercession of Juan Carlos.

1982   The national election brought the Socialists to power under the leadership of Felipe González.

1990   González won re-election for the third time.

1992   Olympic Games at Barcelona, Expo '92 in Sevilla, Quincentenary of Columbus' discovery of the New World.

Architecture

Testimony to Spain's architectural heritage is encountered everywhere, if only in the scavenged fragments of old buildings imbedded in newer walls. Conquerors built upon the remains left by their predecessors or altered structures to suit their own purposes. The common people built according to the dictates of climate and available materials, producing villages that are, in their way, as visually captivating as the palaces of kings.

Prehistory

Ancient structures made of enormous boulders weighing many tons are among the earliest constructions in Spain. They are described as "Cyclopean" after the mythical giants, because the origins of the builders are unknown. The ramparts at Tarragona are laid on a Cyclopean foundation, and the *dolmens* (temple-tombs) near Antequera bear the same label. Bronze Age conical structures of piled stone called *talayots* survive on the island of Menorca, and cave dwellings, which might have been occupied from the same time, can be seen outside Guadix, near Granada. Settlements of the original Iberians, who probably migrated from N Africa between the 13th and 6thC BC, are found in remote parts of Galicia and Aragón.

Architecture

Pre-Roman and Roman (12thC BC–4thC AD)
The Phoenicians, Greeks and Carthaginians preceded the Romans, but left little beyond caches of trinkets and household implements to mark their occupations. The engineering feats of Imperial Rome were more durable. Still surviving are impressive aqueducts in Segovia and outside Tarragona, vestiges of the cities of Itálica near Sevilla and Numantia near Soria, the theater at Sagunto, the bridge at Alcántara, and theater, bridge and other remains at Mérida.

Visigothic (5th-7thC)
The Visigothic legacy was composed less of stone and mortar than of ideas, as in a code of law that persisted into the Middle Ages. Remains can be found, however, particularly in the Visigoths' capital, Toledo. The few intact buildings reflect Byzantine influences: slender braided columns, stone medallions, horseshoe-shaped arches and vaguely Oriental etched traceries.

Early Moorish (8th-11thC)
Characteristic Moorish horseshoe arches, in russet and sand-colored stripes, can be seen to best advantage in the 8thC *mezquita* in Córdoba. The mosque follows a rectangular plan, and many of the supporting pillars were scavenged from Roman, Visigothic and Carthaginian sites. Above the grove of columns are double arches, one on top of the other, and this, despite the darkness, contributes to the sense of structural airiness and fluidity of space.

Pre-Romanesque (8th-11thC)
In Asturias, on the Cantabrian coast, which escaped all but occasional Arab raids, there developed an architectural style that

Left Built in 24BC in the style of the great theaters in Rome, the **Roman theater at Mérida** is remarkably well preserved and one of the finest monuments of this period in Spain.

Below left The superb early Moorish **Mosque at Córdoba** has a vast interior of double-tiered arches in alternating bands of stone and brick.

Below right **Santa María de Naranco** (842-50), with its flat buttress and lofty porch, is a fine example of Asturian architecture.

anticipated the Romanesque. Early churches were stolid, simple, often as wide as they were tall, with rounded arches over the doors and windows, and rich with hints of their Visigothic antecedents.

Middle Moorish (late 11th-13thC)

The relative equanimity of the early caliphates was shattered by the arrival of the puritanical Almoravid and Almohad Arabs, who not only expelled the "decadent" Jews and Christians but destroyed most major Moorish buildings. In place of these they built mosques and minarets of brutally austere brickwork, as in the Giralda in Sevilla. Pointed, more distinctly Eastern arches replaced the horseshoe shape, and wood or plaster ceilings of geometrically ribbed design were gradually introduced.

Mozarabic and Mudejar (11th-15thC)

Mozarabs were Christians living under caliphate rule. When they fled to the N, their architects found favor in the smaller villages of Castilla, such as San Miguel de Escalada, near León. The horseshoe-shaped arch was much in evidence, combining Visigothic and caliphate elements, augmented by pierced stone screens and capitals and corbels carved in floral and bird motifs.

Conversely, the Mudejars were Moors caught up in the Christian Reconquest. Their work is characterized by patterned brick construction set off by bands of ceramic tiles, a style originally developed under the Almohads. This same style spread to the NE and is still preserved in Aragón, far from the administrative center of Sevilla. The *alcázar* of Sevilla was built in the 14thC by Mudejar artisans for the Catholic King Pedro the Cruel. Imitative of parts of the Alhambra in Granada, it lacks that

Right **The Alhambra**, with its ornate stucco and cupolas and arcaded patios, is the pinnacle of Muslim architecture in Spain.

Above The 12thC Almohad **Giralda tower**, with ornate Renaissance belfry.

Right The outstanding Gothic **Toledo cathedral**, begun in 1226.

monument's lyric delicacy but is nevertheless a valuable and accessible lesson in the Moorish heritage. The Alhambra itself is principally 14thC, late Moorish architecture, and is most renowned for the superlative design and decoration of its rooms and courtyards. Some scholars see its arrangements of pillars, arches and reflecting pools as stylized oases of palm trees and springs, evocations of the builders' ancestral desert origins. A palace of dreams, it represents the pinnacle of extant Muslim architecture in Spain, and remains a memorial to 700yrs of Moorish rule.

Romanesque (11th-13thC)

By the mid-11thC, Christianity prevailed throughout Europe, and the architectural idioms that it had encountered coalesced in the Romanesque style. As a prototype already existed in northern Spain, it was here that the style was most readily adopted, most evidently in northern Catalunya. In Romanesque churches, timber ceilings are replaced by rounded groin vaults, interiors are dimly lit (although some have exceptional rose windows), and the whole conveys the impression of massive solidity, emphasizing the fact that these churches frequently had an additional function as fortresses. Campaniles are beautiful, open-arched structures.

Gothic (13th-16thC)

Unlike the Romanesque, which had partly native roots, the Gothic style that first appeared in Paris in the 12thC was alien to Spain. Given the innate conservatism and understandable xenophobia of the Spanish, the new French style was an alarming departure, and it was only accepted grudgingly.

Above The ornate carving of **Isabeline decoration** is often contained in panels and covers entire facades.

Above **El Escorial**, the 16thC monastery-palace built for Philip II, is a massive, austere, rectangular building on five stories with vast corner towers.

Left The flamboyant, undulating facade of **Casa Battló** (1905-7), designed by Gaudí, derives from Art Nouveau, but reflects his highly individual style.

Below **Coca Castle**, a vast 15thC brick fortress, is a magnificent example of Mudejar military architecture.

Buttresses, until now merely vertical pillars flat against outside walls, swept far to the sides to contain the thrust of the much higher vaulting. Light entered through expanses of stained glass so great that in some cathedrals, such as that at León, the structure of the building was threatened. Stone carving was finer, with more detailing, pierced and scrolled into delicate filigrees. Arches were pointed over doorways and in arcading and ribbed vaulting. The best examples are the cathedrals of Barcelona, Toledo, Sevilla and León.

Renaissance and Baroque (16th-18thC)

With the completion of the Reconquest under Fernando and Isabel, the last spasm of Gothic fancy flared in riots of sculptural detailing that incorporated references to military prowess and secular history, as well as theology. The vogue, called Isabeline, was followed by the Plateresque, so called because of the resemblance of its ornamental surface to intricate silverwork. Neither enthusiasm lasted long, for Juan de Herrera then arrived on the scene. An apostle of the comparatively subdued Neoclassical Renaissance style, he is cited by many as Spain's greatest architect. El Escorial, the monastery-palace he designed for his patron, Felipe II, is his signature style. By the 18thC, restraint was cast to the winds in the Baroque excess of voluptuous lines and highly elaborate decorations. At the Rococo extreme was the overblown Churrigueresque style, an amusing example of which can be seen adorning the entrance of the Museo Municipal in Madrid. The facade of the cathedral of Santiago de Compostela is another fine example.

Revivalist (late 18th-19thC)

The predictable reaction to the entertaining but shallow immoderation of Baroque was another return to Classicism. As there was by this time an abundance of churches, many of which had been shamelessly tampered with during the Baroque era, benefactors and municipalities turned to building Greco-Roman fountains and public buildings, particularly in Madrid. This enthusiasm resulted in the intermingling of several styles in a single structure.

El Modernisme (late 19th-early 20thC)

In parallel with the developments of what was known in France as Art Nouveau, and by other labels in Austria and Germany, Catalan architect Antoni Gaudí turned the sinuous lines of the "new art" into a structural form beyond mere surface decoration. In his Casa Milá and Casa Battló in Barcelona, lintels and pediments appear to drip, balconies and towers to melt. Although he was clearly the dominant force in the Catalan architectural movement that came to be known as *El Modernisme,* there were others nearly as inventive. Among them were Salvator Valeri i Puprull, Josep Puig i Cadafalch and Lluis Domènech i Montaner. Domènech designed the Palau de la Música Catalana, a fantastical structure to rival the work of the visionary Gaudí himself, and one of the most enchanting settings for musical performances in all Europe. The *Modernisme* movement flared brightly, but died, for all practical purposes, when Gaudí did, in 1926. Barcelona was left with a legacy in stone that is once again attracting the attention of historians and designers.

Military architecture

Castles in Spain take the traditional medieval form but can also be fortified palaces, monasteries and churches. *Alcazaba, alcázar* and *castillo* are the three major types. The *alcazaba,* introduced by the Moors, was a small fort with a watchtower built directly into a town's defensive walls, rather than standing alone within its own ramparts. The Moors were also responsible for *alcázares*, fortified palaces such as the Alhambra at Granada. Christian *castillos*, usually constructed on strategic mounds, are among the most characteristic sights of rural Spain, particularly on the central plateau, the Meseta. Simple watchtowers and small keeps served as early warning outposts for far larger main fortifications, which had as many protective walls and moats and turrets as the local lord could afford. Many have been maintained and restored, while others have crumbled into heaps and shards. They are seen all over Spain, but are ubiquitous in the heartland, as evidenced in the very name of the region: Castilla.

The arts

Spain's creativity has flourished in explosions of invention springing from periodically fallow terrain. During the Golden Age of the 16th-17thC, when the nation reached the zenith of its power, the celebrated painter Velázquez brought the Renaissance to Madrid while the aging El Greco toiled in relative obscurity in Toledo. Cervantes invented his immortal Don Quixote, attaining an esteemed position in world literature, while the poet and dramatist Lope de Vega, in effect, founded the Spanish theater. However, from then until the late 19thC, only the brooding genius of Goya interrupted the slide into artistic and intellectual mediocrity.

Around the turn of this century, there was a remarkable revival, which produced painters Picasso, Miró and Dalí, composer Manuel de Falla, playwright García Lorca, classical guitarist Andrés Segovia, and important figures in other arts. This cultural surge continues to the present day: witness the bounty of music festivals and special exhibitions all over Spain throughout each year.

Painting and sculpture

Paleolithic artists began the esthetic tradition, with depictions of beasts and hunters painted on the walls of their caves. While those at Altamira are deservedly most famous, examples are found throughout the N and E. Some 9,000yrs later, Celtiberian sculptors produced astonishingly sophisticated portraits in stone. *La Dama de Elche*, discovered in 1897 and now in the Museo Arqueológico in Madrid, dates back to the 5thC BC. It is a bust of a woman, presumably of royal birth, attired in heavy necklaces and an unusual head-dress with large decorative discs over the ears. Reminiscent of eastern Mediterranean cultures of the period, the grand lady teases with a mysterious grace surpassing that of many contemporary Cretan and Grecian sculptures.

The Romans were prolific in their construction of ceremonial buildings, but they also left heroic statuary and large, intricate mosaics, examples of which can be seen at Mérida and at Itálica, near Sevilla. Moorish achievement in the arts was primarily in architecture, although interiors were richly embellished with majolica tiles and reliefs of stylized Arabic script.

In the wake of the Christian Reconquest, accomplished in 1492, French and Italian artistic styles were introduced. Figures in church paintings became more animated, their features and surroundings more finely observed. Works of uncanny similarity to those of the Italian painter Giotto appeared throughout

Catalunya and Aragón, anticipating the Renaissance. In the 16thC, intensive study of anatomy and perspective gave flesh-and-blood life to scenes of passion and religious ardor. The debt of Alonso Berruguete (1486-1561) to Michelangelo is clear in the expressive sculptural poses of his tormented figures. Schools of painting developed in Barcelona, Madrid, Valencia and Sevilla, each drawing on French, Flemish and Italian concepts, but all driven by the Spanish love for the dramatic in life and art.

Profound religious fervor, almost demented in its intensity, provided much of the spiritual impetus for conquest abroad and for the Counter-Reformation. This is reflected in the distorted figures of the later paintings of El Greco (1540-1614). His work was too eccentric for Felipe II, and he was not summoned from his home in Toledo to work in the new Escorial. José de Ribera (1591-1652) worked in pronounced *chiaroscuro*, a style known in Spain as *tenebrismo*.

The wealth from the Americas was concentrated in Sevilla and attracted artists from Italy and northern Europe. Juan de las Roelas (1559-1625) laid the groundwork for the far more important Francisco Zurbarán (1598-1664) and Bartolomé Esteban Murillo (1617-82). The supreme master, Diego Velázquez (1599-1660), was court painter to Felipe IV. His early compositions show the influence of Caravaggio and the Dutch painters, but his later ecclesiastical and court portraits were vehicles for his own sophisticated experiments in liquid light and space.

By the end of the 16thC, portraiture, still life and genre subjects were deemed to be as respectable as the religious themes that had previously dominated. But support for the arts waned with the decline of Spanish power in the late 17thC. The Bourbon kings favored foreigners, most of them innovators of the romantic Classicism engendered by the Baroque. The flaccid landscapes and frolicking wood nymphs of the time are memorable only as a syrupy counterpoint to the ferocious iconoclasm of Francisco Goya (1746-1828).

Goya was Velázquez's equal in technique, but he was incapable of the earlier master's detachment. A political liberal by the standards of his day, he was nonetheless a favorite at the court of Carlos IV. In his 1800 portrait of the royal family, he mimics Velázquez's *Las Meninas*, showing himself at the easel. The king, queen and their children are depicted as caricatures of inanity, but were apparently quite satisfied by the painting. Goya's etchings include biting attacks on corruption and decadence, but neither these nor his outrage over the horrors of the Napoleonic invasions, epitomized in the harrowing scene of the firing squad in *May 3rd, 1808*, harmed his reputation. With age and despair came his macabre, expressionistic scenes painted on the walls of his house. Known as the "Black Paintings," they are now on display in the Prado Museum.

During these centuries of ascendancy and decline Spanish sculpture rarely aspired to greatness, concentrating rather on the polychrome wood sculptures representing saints and martyrs, which are still central elements of popular religious veneration. Complete with real garments and hair, crystal eyes and glass tears, they stand in shrines and chapels throughout Spain, awaiting the festivals and processions in their honor, during which they are carried through the streets.

In the early 20thC, following a century of almost continuous warfare, word of a new wave of Impressionism filtered into Catalunya, a region long attuned to French sensibilities. Manet and Cézanne inspired the Cubism of Juan Gris (1887-1927) and Pablo Picasso (1881-1973). Blessed with a voracious inquisitiveness, great energy, and a life span that extended his productivity over eight decades, Picasso was a dominant figure in the international art community until his death. He worked in every conceivable medium — oil, tempera, collage, stone, metal, ceramics, graphics, textiles, pen and ink — often manipulated or applied by unconventional means. He spent some of his early years in Barcelona, but by 1904 had moved to Paris. After the onset of the Spanish Civil War, he exiled himself permanently in France.

Picasso's younger Catalan contemporaries, Joan Miró (1893-1983) and Salvador Dalí (1904-1989) are both described as Surrealists, but the connection is tenuous. Miró's biomorphic forms dancing across two-dimensional planes are more abstract than figurative, while Dalí's wildly dream-like fantasies are executed with superb draftsmanship and coldly meticulous detail.

A number of artists emerged in the wake of postwar Abstract Expressionism. Their early painting was characterized by subdued earth tones, but their later work has developed into vivid slashes of color and experiments in mixed media. Among the artists of particular note are Antoni Tàpies, Luis Feito, Eduardo Chillida and Antonio Saura. Tàpies now has his own museum in Barcelona, and his and his colleagues' works are displayed to good advantage in the Museo de Arte Abstracto Español in Cuenca.

Literature

The Spanish literary tradition began with a flourish under the Romans. Seneca the Elder (c.60BC-37AD) was born in Córdoba and lived most of his life there. His major surviving works include a history of Rome and collections of orations. His son was Seneca the Stoic, who was also born in Córdoba but spent most of his life in Rome. There he accumulated a substantial fortune while engaging in frequent conspiracies and clandestine romances, activities at pronounced variance with the Stoic philosophy that inspired his numerous essays and plays.

The Moors established centers of scholarship that drew upon the works of Arab scientists and Greek philosophers. Under their relatively tolerant rule, the important Hebrew philosopher Maimonides, born in Córdoba in 1135, was able to produce a vast collection of work that influences Jewish and Christian religious thought to this day.

The exploits of Rodrigo Díaz de Vivar inspired the 12thC epic poem *El Cantar del Mío Cid*, the first significant work in the Castilian language. When Alfonso X ascended the throne in the 13thC, he decreed that Castilian should henceforth be the official tongue, although he himself wrote poetry in Gallego (Galician). Translations of Arabic works, compilations of Spanish history and early efforts at a prose form followed.

With the blossoming of the Golden Age in the 16thC, the stage was set for a true native theater, with roots in the life of the Spanish people. Félix Lope de Vega (1562-1635) is regarded as the father of this school of drama. His astonishingly prolific output included 1,800 plays and numerous epic poems, many of them no doubt inspired by his prodigious appetite for illicit love affairs. His contemporary, Miguel de Cervantes Saavedra (1547-1616), suffered frequent misfortune and was not nearly so prolific. But Cervantes' masterpiece, *Don Quixote de la Mancha*, was in itself sufficient to place him in the company of Tolstoy and Dostoyevsky. Humor, pathos, tragedy and triumph illustrate this moving tale of naive idealism in conflict with corruption and avarice.

Also important during this fruitful period were the richly descriptive poet Luis de Góngora (1561-1627); the satirist, poet and novelist Francisco Quevedo (1580-1645); the dramatists Calderón de la Barca (1600-81) and Tirso de Molina (1584-1648), the latter renowned for his rendering of the story of Don Juan; and the mystic St Teresa of Avila (1515-82), remembered as much for her literary skills as for her piety and organizational ability.

The Romantic movement of the 19thC coincided with similar fashions in painting. The poet Gustavo Adolfo Bécquer (1836-70) was a direct exponent of Romanticism, his work contrasting strongly with the gritty realism of the novelists Pedro de Alarcón (1833-91) and Benito Pérez Galdós (1843-1920). The younger novelist Vicente Blasco Ibáñez (1869-1928) bridged the Realist-Modernist transition and was the first Spanish writer since Cervantes to gain substantial notice outside his country. A prominent antimonarchist who spent years in prison and in exile, he is best known for *The Four Horsemen of the Apocalypse.*

From the Spanish-American War until the Falangist victory in 1939, prose writers and poets alike were swept along by a wave of political and philosophical awareness, expressions of which took all forms, from the near-Existentialist stance of Miguel de Unamuno (1864-1936) to the matter-of-fact observation of the vagaries of life in the work of Pío Baroja y Nessi (1872-1956). Another important voice was that of José Ortega y Gasset (1883-1955) who, in *The Revolt of the Masses,* argued for an intellectual elite to lead the aggrieved working class. The poetry and drama of Federico García Lorca (1898-1936) contain echoes of these political and philosophical concerns but are so powerfully individual that they stand alone. Rich metaphors of violence and primitive sensuality, linked with lyrical images of the countryside around his native Granada, established Lorca as the most remarkable literary figure of this century in Spain.

Although no clear form or new tradition has emerged, the combination of Surrealist and Existentialist influences with the acute sociopolitical perceptions encouraged by Spain's recent history have created a fertile environment for modern Spanish literature. Significant figures include Nobel prize-winner Juan Ramón Jiménez, the dramatist Alejandro Casona and the novelists Camilo José Cela, Carmen Laforet and Juan Goytisolo.

Music

The tradition of combined performance of words and music developed in the 15thC as a form of courtly entertainment during the reign of Fernando and Isabel. One of the most popular of these was written by the dramatist Lope de Vega in 1629. A more specifically musical play was popularized by Calderón de la Barca some 20yrs later. A form of light opera, it came to be known as *zarzuela,* for the palace outside Madrid where it was first performed. Although eclipsed for a time by the more fashionable Italian opera, *zarzuelas* regained popularity in the 19thC, among common citizens as well as royalty.

Spain, probably more than any other European country, has retained a strong tradition of regionally distinct folk music and dance independent of her more formal musical heritage. Characteristic instruments include the oboe of Catalunya, the bagpipes of Galicia and the guitar of Andalucía. Certain traditional forms have acquired widespread popularity, notably flamenco, which evolved from a Gypsy lament into the now familiar show of snapping fingers, pounding feet and swirling movements.

Some reconciliation between the folkloric and classical heritages occurred in the early 20thC, largely as a result of the efforts of Felipe Pedrell, the Catalan musicologist. Pedrell's interest in the folk tradition inspired composers Isaac Albéniz (1860-1909), Manuel de Falla (1876-1946), Enrique Granados (1867-1916) and, a generation later, Joaquín Rodrigo (1902-1990) to incorporate essentially Spanish elements — guitar and dance — in compositions of a conventional European classical style. Falla wrote guitar music especially for Andrés Segovia (1893-1987), who did more than anyone to re-establish the guitar as a serious classical instrument. Segovia commissioned new music for the guitar, adapted such composers as Bach, and resurrected the music of Spanish composers Fernando Sor (1778-1839) and Francisco Tarrega (1852-1909), both supreme contributors to the repertoire of this quintessentially Spanish instrument.

Before you go

Documents required
North Americans and British subjects need only their **passports** for stays of up to 3mths, but they must be valid beyond the end of the planned visit. British nationals may also use the **British Visitor's Passport**, and citizens of most EC member nations may enter with only their **national identity cards**. **Visas** are required for citizens of other countries. Extensions of stays beyond 90 days can be arranged once you are in Spain.

At least, these have been the regulations. In this time of bewilderingly rapid change, nothing stands still for long. By the end of 1992, for example, it is expected that citizens of EC nations will need only common identity cards to pass into Spain. Be certain to check with the nearest Spanish consulate well in advance of a planned trip. Visitors may be asked for evidence that they have the means to return home or that they can support themselves without working while in Spain.

No **vaccinations** are required for entry, but carry a prescription from your own doctor if you require specific medication. An **international driver's license**, **vehicle registration certificate** (logbook), **national identity sticker** and **international insurance certificate** (green card) are required when entering with a private car.

Travel and medical insurance
Medical care is at least satisfactory and often excellent, especially in private clinics. But it is expensive, and medical insurance is strongly recommended. This can be obtained through local tourist offices in Spain, where the special tourist insurance is called **ASTES**, or through your own insurance company or travel agent. Policies are also available to protect against cost incurred by cancellation of your trip.

The **IAMAT** (International Association for Medical Assistance to Travellers) has a list of English-speaking doctors who will call, for a low fixed fee. There are member hospitals and clinics throughout Europe, including Barcelona and Madrid. Membership is free. For further information, write to **IAMAT** (*417 Center St., Lewiston, NY 14092*).

Money

The **peseta** (pta) is the basic unit. It was once divided into 100 centimos, but they have all but disappeared. There are 1, 5, 25, 50, 100, 200 and 500pta coins, and banknotes for 500, 1,000, 5,000 and 10,000ptas. Some of the newer coins are similar in size and appearance to older ones, notably the new 5 and old 200pta, and new 100 and old 500pta pieces, so take care in handing them out. Any amount of foreign currency can be imported. This theoretically applies to pesetas as well, but it is wise to declare amounts over 100,000. That amount can also be freely taken out of the country.

Travelers checks issued by American Express, Thomas Cook, Barclays and Citibank are widely recognized. Make sure you read the instructions included with your travelers checks. It is important also to note separately the serial numbers and the telephone number to call in case of loss. Specialist travelers check companies such as **American Express** provide extensive local refund facilities through their own offices or agents.

Readily accepted **charge and credit cards** are American Express, Diners Club, MasterCard (Eurocard) and Visa. A personal check supported by a **Eurocheque Encashment Card** can be cashed at major banks.

American Express also has a **MoneyGram** (R) money transfer service that makes it possible to wire money worldwide in just minutes, from any American Express Travel Service Office. This service is available to all customers and is not limited to American Express Card members. See USEFUL ADDRESSES in BARCELONA (page 43) and MADRID (page 86).

Customs

The completion of the European Single Market takes place at the end of 1992. Duty- and tax-free shopping will still be available to travelers departing directly for countries outside the European Community, such as the US, and for non-EC citizens a list of duty-free allowances can be obtained at Spanish tourist offices and airports. Within the EC, it is probable that as of January 1, 1993, the sale of goods at duty-free prices will no longer apply, and that no duty will be payable on goods brought into Spain by EC citizens. British residents can obtain information from the **Single Market Unit, HM Customs and Excise** (☎ 071-865 5426).

It is advisable to carry dated receipts for new or more valuable items to avoid the remote possibility of being charged duty. Note that the penalties for possession of illegal "hard" drugs are severe.

Visitors are exempt from paying Value Added Tax (IVA) on purchases above a certain amount, on completion of a simple form and presentation of a passport at the time of purchase. However, to validate the refund, which will be made to you at your home address, or through a charge or credit card, you must present the paperwork and goods at a checkpoint before going through passport control on leaving the country. Leave enough time to do this.

Spanish National Tourist Offices

UK   57-58 St James's St., London SW1A 1LD ☎(071) 499 0901-6
USA   National Tourist Office of Spain, 665 5th Ave., New York, NY 10022 ☎(212) 759 8822

There are also offices in **Chicago** (☎ (312) 641 1842), **San Francisco** (☎ (415) 986 2125) and **Toronto** (☎ (416) 961 3131).

Getting there

By air   The majority of flights from outside western Europe arrive at Barajas airport, even if Madrid is not the intended final destination.

However, both Iberia and TWA have inaugurated a nonstop service between New York and Barcelona, and similar flights from other US cities are anticipated. From the UK and some parts of the Continent there are direct flights to a number of other cities, most notably Barcelona, Málaga, Palma de Mallorca, Santiago de Compostela, Sevilla and Valencia.

By rail   Principal railroad crossing points from France are at opposite ends of the Pyrenees, near Perpignan-Figueres in the E and Biarritz-San Sebastián in the W. Direct services are available from Rome, Paris, Nice and intermediate stations. Speed and superior standards characterize the *Puerta del Sol* express between Paris and Madrid and the *Barcelona Talgo* between Paris and Barcelona. Both leave Paris every evening and arrive early next day. There are also Motorail services from Boulogne to Biarritz and from Paris to Madrid.

By bus   The London-based **Euroways Express Coach Ltd** (☎ *(071) 730-8235*) serves many destinations in Spain, including Madrid and Barcelona.

By road   From France, roads cross into Spain at more than a dozen points. Most approaches twist through mountain passes and it is wise to make these trips during daylight, since border posts are often closed at night. Snow closes some roads in spring and fall as well as winter. An expanding system of toll superhighways (*autopistas*) connects Biarritz to Bilbao, the Atlantic coast to the Mediterranean, and the French border at Perpignan to Murcia in the SE, passing Barcelona, Valencia and Alicante along the way.

By sea   Car ferries ply several routes on weekly or more frequent schedules. Among their routes are Plymouth-Santander, Marseille-Alicante, Marseille-Mallorca and Genoa-Barcelona. Cruise ships usually put in at Cádiz, Málaga, Mallorca, Ibiza and Barcelona.

Climate

May, June, Sept and Oct are the months for the good weather that happens to coincide with many local fiestas and celebrations. Seaside Barcelona tends to be milder than inland Madrid in both summer and winter, but both cities experience frequent spells of rain from late fall to early spring. July and Aug are blazing hot throughout the peninsula except along the Cantabrian Sea (Bay of Biscay). At that time, Sevilla and interior districts of Andalucía routinely boast temperatures of up to 46°C (115°F). In deepest winter, only the waters of the distant Canary Islands are suitable for swimming. Snow falls in the Pyrenees, Picos de Europa, Sierra de Gredos, Sierra de Guadarrama and Sierra Nevada from Oct-Apr.

Clothes

Informality in dress is increasingly the rule. Jeans are everywhere, and skimpy bathing costumes are now the norm on most beaches. While casual clothing is acceptable, simple courtesy demands discretion in churches and religious houses. Raincoats and/or umbrellas are indispensable from Oct-Apr in northern and central parts of the country, but extra-warm clothes are only necessary in winter in the mountains. Men rarely need to wear ties in restaurants.

Getting around

By air

Iberia flights connect major cities. There is a shuttle service between Madrid and Barcelona called the *Puente Aereo* — "Air Bridge" — with flights leaving from early morning to late evening. Aviaco, a domestic carrier, has flights to many smaller cities. The airlines' offices in Madrid are:

Aviaco   Maudes 51 ☎(91) 254 3600
Iberia   Velázquez 130 ☎(91) 262 6731

By rail

Routes and quality of service are being upgraded, especially between Madrid, Barcelona and Sevilla. A new high-speed train called the *AVE* begins service in 1992 between Madrid and Sevilla, cutting that trip from over 6 to under 3hrs. (See SEVILLA.) Other categories of express train are the *Talgo* and slower *Rápido*.

The national rail system is RENFE *(Red Nacional de los Ferrocarriles Españoles)*. It accepts the North American **Eurailpass** and the British **InterRail** pass, but supplements may be payable for sleeping cars. **Discount tickets** are available for young people, families and senior citizens, but under a bewildering number of restrictions and convoluted circumstances. Ask a travel agent to sift through the possibilities.

By road

Roads have greatly improved in recent years, especially those between major cities, but also those leading to previously isolated villages of interest to tourists. The speed limit in built-up areas is 60kph (37mph), on country roads 90kph (56mph), on national highways 100kph (62mph) and on *autopistas* 120kph (75mph). Speed limits are not supposed to be exceeded even when passing other vehicles. Major routes are patrolled by licensed repair trucks, and breakdown assistance usually arrives quickly. Even in small villages, mechanics tend to be competent, but parts for foreign vehicles are not always readily available.

Always use directional signals when overtaking and when turning, and yield to vehicles coming from the right unless road signs dictate otherwise. An exception to this is that cars entering a traffic circle (roundabout) must yield to those already in the circle. Headlights must be adjusted on right-hand-drive cars, and it is illegal to drive without spare light bulbs and a warning triangle in case of breakdowns. Seat belts are compulsory outside city limits. It is forbidden to park facing oncoming traffic, on forks in the road, and in front of public buildings — not that those restrictions deter many Spaniards. Children under 12 must ride in the rear seat unless special seat belts are provided in the front. A new traffic code stipulates that motorcyclists must wear helmets at all times and that it is an offense to wear earphones attached to a cassette player while driving.

Police do not pursue violators of speed limits, preferring to use radar and road blocks. If pulled over, be prepared to produce your driver's license, passport and car rental agreement or registration and insurance papers.

Car rental

To rent a car you must bring a valid driver's license and your passport. An international driving permit is not required. A charge or credit card obviates the need for cash deposits, and comprehensive insurance is strongly advised.

Avis, **Hertz**, **Europcar** and the national rental firm **ATESA** have branches in all major cities and airports. These networks permit rent-it-here-leave-it-there schemes, with drop-off facilities even in other countries. Daily, weekly and unlimited mileage packages are available. North Americans accustomed to the routine availability of air conditioning and automatic drive are cautioned that these are expensive extras. Small private agencies with unfamiliar names exchange lower fees for less protection than the larger firms offer in case of breakdown or accident, and cars must usually be returned to the original depot. Savings, however, can be substantial.

Other transportation
ATESA and other car rental firms provide chauffeur-driven cars. Alternatively, tourist offices in the larger cities have lists of accredited English-speaking guides, some of whom will drive your car while showing you the sights.

On-the-spot information

Public holidays
New Year's Day, Jan 1; Epiphany, Jan 6; St Joseph's Day, Mar 19; Good Friday; Ascension Day; Labor Day, May 1; Corpus Christi; Feast of St John, June 24; Feast of Sts Peter and Paul, June 29; Feast of St James, July 25; Assumption, Aug 15; Hispanic (National) Day, Oct 12; All Saints' Day, Nov 1; Feast of the Immaculate Conception, Dec 8; Christmas Day, Dec 25. In addition, local and regional holidays dot the calendar.

Shops and post offices are usually closed on national holidays, and opening hours are shorter during festivals.

Time zones
Spain lies within a single time zone, 1hr ahead of GMT, except between Apr and Oct when it is 2hrs ahead. It is 6hrs ahead of Eastern Standard Time and from 7-9hrs ahead of the other US time zones.

Banks and currency exchange
Customary business hours for banks are 9am-2pm Mon-Fri and 9am-1pm on Sat, although some reopen their foreign exchange (*cambio*) windows from 5-7pm. Rates are less favorable at most (but not all) hotels and exchange booths in airports, but those at main **American Express** and **Thomas Cook** offices are competitive with banks. See *Money* in BEFORE YOU GO for further details.

Shopping, eating, entertainment and rush hours
Shops are usually open 9.30 or 10am to 1 or 2pm Mon-Sat and 4.30 or 5pm to 7.30 or 8pm Mon-Fri, although a few large **department stores** stay open during the afternoon *siesta*. **Restaurants** serve meals from 1.30-4pm and 9pm-midnight, but in hotels and tourist areas concession is often made to foreign eating habits and dinner is served from 8pm. **Cafeterias** stay open without a break from about 9am-11pm.

Some **discos** have "afternoon hours," 7-9pm, but most are open from 10.30pm. The first show at a **nightclub** may not start until midnight. **Cinemas and theaters** also keep late hours: matinées are at 7pm Mon-Sat and 4.30pm Sun, and evening performances at 10 or 11pm. In large Spanish towns and cities there are **markets** daily, and in smaller places once or twice a week; details can be obtained locally. In cities, avoid the **rush hour** crush of public transportation and the madness of the traffic from 8-10am, 1-2pm, 4-5pm and 7.30-8.30pm.

Communications
Most post offices throughout Spain will keep **mail** marked *lista de correos*. You will need your passport when you collect your mail, but

no charge is made. Post offices normally follow 9am-1pm and 5-7pm hours, but the main post offices in Madrid and Barcelona keep their *lista de correos* windows open until midnight. **Post offices** can be recognized by the word *correos* above the entrance; **mail boxes**, similarly marked, are yellow. Postage stamps (*sellos*) can be bought from tobacco stores (*estancos*) as well as post offices. Mail can also be sent to **American Express** and **Thomas Cook** offices, but to use the service provided by the former, you must have an American Express Card or travelers checks.

Public telephones (*teléfonos públicos*) are found primarily in bars and restaurants. They are coin-operated; simply drop in the coin and dial. For **long-distance calls**, a knowledge of Spanish is essential to deal with intermediate operators. Or, use the hotel operator; surcharges can be high, but some hotels subscribe to **Teleplan**, which limits the extra calling fee to approximately 25 percent.

The **ringing signal** is a slow repeating tone; the **busy (engaged) signal** is a fast repeating tone. All **telephone prefixes (area codes)** within Spain begin with **9** and are followed by the province code number. Information for making **international calls** is given in four languages in any telephone booth under the word *internacional*.

For **telegrams** ☎(91) 232-8800 in Madrid and ☎(93) 317-6898 in Barcelona, or use the **fax, telex and cable** facilities that are standard in larger hotels.

Shops offering **copying services** are widely available: a sign reading *copias* is the usual identification. Secretarial and other services are best obtained through hotels. For larger conferences, the municipal tourist office is a good first source.

Public rest rooms (toilets)

Facilities in railroad stations and bars are not appealing, so use those in restaurants, hotels or museums. Ask for *los servicios, los aseos* or *el baño*, or simply *caballeros* or *señoras*, and tip the attendant about 50ptas.

Electric current

Standard current is 220 volt (50 cycles AC), although many hotel rooms have 110- or 120-volt outlets intended for electric shavers. Two-pin round plugs are standard, making adaptors necessary for appliances bought for use in many other countries. Current converters are unreliable, so battery-powered units can be useful.

Laws and regulations

A **bail bond** guarantees a cash deposit of up to £1,500 (about $2,600) as bail if you are arrested during your trip, in which case the bond money must be reimbursed. The bond will be included in car rentals arranged for US citizens in Spain; but make sure you have one if you are driving a car rented *outside* Spain. British citizens are advised to obtain their bail bond before leaving for Spain, from either the AA or their own insurance company.

If crossing into Spain by car with an unrelated minor, you must have written permission from his or her parents. A written statement is also required when driving a car owned by another person. Fines for speeding and other moving traffic violations must usually be paid on the spot, but police officers will sometimes add the amount of the fine to the car rental form. There are stiff penalties for leaving the scene of an accident or driving while intoxicated.

The laws on narcotics are tough. Possession of illicit hard drugs, even in very small quantities, is a severely punishable offense that can lead to years in prison.

Customs and etiquette

Relatives and good friends kiss each other on both cheeks on meeting, but otherwise Spaniards are more formal in social situations than other Europeans or North Americans. Men and women shake hands in greeting. Ordinarily, only close friends, family and young people use the familiar *tú* form of address, as opposed to the very proper *usted*, and *Señor, Señora* or *Señorita* is a customary address for strangers. Visitors fortunate enough to make friends with Spaniards will soon learn of their characteristic generosity. But take no offense if they do not answer letters; just show up five years later and they will act as if you were there the week before. Children are not sent away to leave adults alone, nor to bed the night of a fiesta simply because the hour approaches midnight. Rather, they are allowed to be present and to occupy the center of attention as long as they behave.

Health concerns and public campaigns against smoking have yet to make significant inroads into entrenched habits, and Spaniards smoke constantly, everywhere, including in the immediate presence of bright red *No Fumar* signs.

Tipping

With some exceptions, restaurant bills no longer include the long-familiar service charge, apparently in a near-unanimous effort to make inflationary prices appear less onerous. Ensure that your bill doesn't adhere to the old practice — the words *servicio incluido* mean that it does. If not, 10-12 percent is adequate in smaller, medium-level restaurants, 15 percent for good service in more elaborate surroundings, and up to 20 percent in such luxurious, world-class surroundings as Madrid's Zalacaín and Barcelona's Neichel. While it isn't rigid practice, most people leave 5-10 percent for drinks or snacks served at a bar.

Small tips of up to 100ptas should be given to doormen, cloakroom attendants, ushers and, perhaps surprisingly, to gas station attendants. A similar amount, for each night stayed in a hotel, is left behind for the chambermaid. Porters in airports and railroad stations have fixed charges of 50-100ptas per bag, and taxi drivers expect about 10 percent of the fare.

Disabled travelers

Few allowances are made yet for handicapped people. Newer, larger hotels are more likely to have rooms with specially modified bathrooms and toilets. Lowered curbs and ramps for wheelchairs are more frequently encountered than they were a few years ago. Guide dogs are permitted everywhere, however, and certain travel agents are familiar with tours that have been specifically designed for disabled people.

Madrid and Barcelona city guides for the disabled are obtainable from **Cruz Roja Española** (*Dr Santero 18, Madrid*) and **ECOM** (*Balmes 311, Barcelona*). For further details contact **SEREM** (*María de Guzmán 52, Madrid*), the official government department for disabled people.

For further information on travel in Europe, and details of tour operators specializing in tours for handicapped people, US residents should write to the **Travel Information Service** (*Moss Rehabilitation Hospital, 12th St. and Tabor Rd., Philadelphia, Pa. 19141*) or to **Mobility International USA** (*PO Box 3551, Eugene, Or. 97403*). Britons should contact **RADAR** (*25 Mortimer St., London W1N 8AB* ☎ *071-637 5400*). For general advice, ask for the leaflet provided by the **National Tourist Office of Spain** in your home country.

Local and foreign publications

Foreign-language newspapers and periodicals are on sale at newsstands and larger hotels in both Barcelona and Madrid. English-speaking residents publish the wan and insular *Iberia Daily Sun* and the glossy magazine *Lookout*, which is growing noticeably more sophisticated and analytical about its host country than the expatriate Costa del Sol readership for which it was originally created. In Madrid, the weekly *Guidepost Magazine* focuses on events of interest to English speakers. Barcelona and Madrid have versions of the *Guía del Ocio* — "Leisure Guide" — which covers current sports, restaurants and entertainment; although printed in Spanish, the listings are not hard to decipher.

Emergency information

Emergency services (Madrid and Barcelona)

Police ☎091
Ambulance ☎227-2021
Fire (*Cuerpo de bomberos*) ☎232-3232

For emergency services elsewhere, call the operator. Emergency telephone numbers are likely to be standardized throughout the EC from January 1993.

Automobile accidents

Summon the police immediately. Call the number in your car rental agreement. Do not admit liability or incriminate yourself. Exchange names, addresses, car details and insurance company details with any other parties involved. In serious accidents, notify your nearest consulate.

Car breakdowns

Use the emergency telephones on *autopistas*. Attract the attention of a patrolling police car. Call the RACE, which has an arrangement with the AAA and the AA.

Lost passport

Notify the police and go to your nearest consulate to obtain emergency documents.

Lost travelers checks

Notify the local police immediately, then follow the instructions provided with your travelers checks, or contact the issuing company's nearest office. Contact your consulate or **American Express** if you are stranded with no money.

Emergency phrases

Help! *¡Socorro!*
There has been an accident. *Ha habido un accidente.*
Where is the nearest telephone/hospital? *¿Donde está el teléfono/hospital más cercano?*
Call a doctor/ambulance! *¡Llame a un doctor/una ambulancia!*
Call the police! *¡Llame a la policía!*

See also EMERGENCY INFORMATION in BARCELONA (page 42) and MADRID (page 85).

Calendar of events

Almost every Spanish town has several of its own annual festivals and fairs. These are some of the better known and nationally celebrated events. See also *Public holidays* in BASIC INFORMATION.

January

‡ New Year's Day. ‡ Jan 2. **Granada**. Celebration of the 1492 Christian Reconquest. ‡ Jan 6. Day of the Kings. Gift-giving and processions. ‡ Jan 17. *Fiesta de San Antonio*. Parades, fireworks and ceremonies blessing domestic animals.

February

‡ Feb 5. Commemoration of Santa Águeda. ‡ Feb 25. Vintage car rally from **Barcelona** to **Sitges**. ‡ Late Feb-early Mar. *Carnaval* in many cities.

March

‡ Mar 12-19. **Valencia**. *Las Fallas*. Parades, bonfires and fireworks. Easter Holy Week. Extensive and solemn celebrations everywhere. ‡ Week after Easter. **Murcia**. Spring festival with parades, flower displays and floats.

April

‡ Mid to late Apr. **Sevilla**. *Feria de Sevilla*, with processions, music and dancing, to welcome the spring. ‡ Sun after Apr 25. Pilgrimage from Tafalla to Ujue. ‡ Late Apr or first week in May. **Jerez de la Frontera**. *Feria del Caballo*. Flamenco competitions.

May

‡ May 1. Labor Day. ‡ First Fri. **Jaca**. Celebration recounting the role of local women in repelling an Arab attack in 795. ‡ May 15-30. **Madrid**. *Fiesta de San Isidro*, with bullfights and other celebrations in honor of patron saint of Madrid. ‡ Late May. **Sitges**. Festival where flowers cover the streets in intricate carpet-like patterns. ‡ Late May-early June. **Pontevedra**. Round-up of wild horses. ‡ Late May-early June, Corpus Christi. Devout processions at **Barcelona** and **Toledo**.

June

‡ June 21-29. **Alicante**. *Hogueras de San Juan*. Parades and bonfires. ‡ June 23-28. **Barcelona**. Festival in Poble Espanyol. ‡ June 24-29. **Burgos**. *Fiesta de San Pedro*. **Segovia**. Festivals associated with San Juan and San Pedro.

Sevilla. Folk-dancing competitions. ‡ Late June-early July. **Granada**. Festival of music and dance.

July

‡ July 6-14. **Pamplona**. *Feria de San Fermín*, with parades, bullfights and the celebrated running of the bulls. ‡ July 15-31. **Santiago de Compostela**. Feast of St James, with religious processions and fireworks. ‡ July 17-31. **Valencia**. Festival of St James, with flower battles and bullfights.

August

‡ First week. **Málaga**. Celebrations involving parades and bullfights. ‡ All month. Cantabrian coast, especially **Bilbao**, **La Coruña** and **San Sebastián**. Festival of Semana Grande, with open-air concerts, plays, bullfights, dancing competitions and films. ‡ Aug 4-9. **Vitoria**. *Fiesta de la Virgen Blanca*. ‡ Aug 10. **El Escorial**. St Lawrence's Day, with bullfights and street celebrations. ‡ Aug 12-15. **Elche**. Mystery play. ‡ Aug 15. Feast of the Assumption.

September

‡ Early Sept. **Jerez de la Frontera**. *Fiesta de la Vendimia*. Colorful festival to celebrate the grape harvest. ‡ First week in Sept. **San Sebastián**. Competitions in Basque sports. ‡ Sept 19. **Oviedo**. *Día de las Américas*, with dancing, parades and bullfights. ‡ Sept 19-26. **Logroño**. Celebrations of the Rioja grape harvest. ‡ Sept 23-24. **Tarragona**. Festival of St Tecla, with folk dancing and human pyramids. ‡ Sept 24-28. **Barcelona**. Catalan festivities, in honor of the Virgen de la Merced, with dancing and bullfights.

October

‡ Oct 7-15. **Avila**. *Feria de Santa Teresa*. ‡ Oct 12. Hispanic Day. ‡ Week of Oct 12. **Zaragoza**. *Fiesta de la Virgen del Pilar*.

November

‡ Nov 1. All Saints' Day.

December

‡ Dec 25. Christmas Day. ‡ Dec 31. New Year's Eve.

When to go

Personal interests dictate vacation choices in Spain just as often as the weather. Skiers find ideal conditions nearly every December-February in the Cantabrian Cordillera, in the Gredos near Madrid and, surprisingly, in the Sierra Nevada to the south. Sometimes skiing is possible as early as October and as late as April. However, those with expectations of a sea warm enough for swimming all year long are too optimistic. Only a few visitors will want to brave the waters of the east and south Mediterranean coasts from November to February. The season along the northwest Atlantic coast is confined to the period between late June and early September.

Cultural activities follow their own calendar. Formal seasons of opera, concerts and dance usually run from October to May, but there are summer art and music festivals throughout the country. From Holy Week until the harvest festivals of September, only a long streak of bad luck could deny visitors local folkloric fiestas of one kind or another during a 2-week tour.

From mid-June to early September, anywhere south of Madrid can resemble a furnace, with temperatures rising above 95°F (35°C) for weeks on end. You may well find the shops and restaurants of the inland cities closed during July and August. Air conditioning is far from universal in hotels, restaurants and public buildings. Taking all these factors into consideration, the best times for a warm-weather visit to Spain are May-June and September-October.

Where to go

Before any other Spanish cities, it is essential to visit Madrid, Barcelona and Sevilla. They harbor the great museums — the vitality, the creativity, the meaning of the nation, and the perspective on the many cultures that have shaped it. Close behind in importance are the Christian pilgrimage center of Santiago de Compostela, the Moorish enclaves of Granada and Córdoba, and the Roman capitals of Mérida and Tarragona.

Among the many smaller towns and cities that deserve attention are Ronda and Baeza in Andalucía, Cuenca and Toledo in the heartland, Santillana del Mar on the Cantabrian coast, Sigüenza northeast of Madrid, and Albarracín in the province of Teruel.

Sun-seekers who hope to have beaches to themselves should consider the largely undeveloped Atlantic Costa de la Luz, or the island of Formentera in the Islas Baleares. Those who prefer elegance with their sunbathing head for Marbella, on the Costa del Sol. For sunshine but moderate temperatures where Spanish tourists still outnumber foreigners, there are the shoreline resorts of Galicia and Asturias.

Gamblers will find casinos either in or within short drives of Alicante, Barcelona, Madrid, Málaga, Palma de Mallorca, San Sebastián, Santiago de Compostela and Valencia. Golfers will find many greens between Estepona and Torremolinos, as well as in or near every major city and on Mallorca. National reserves are set aside for hunters, primarily in the Pyrenees, the Gredos Mountains and the Sierra Nevada. Saltwater anglers head for Marbella and Estepona, trout fishermen for the Basque territories, and sailors for the Islas Baleares.

Orientation map

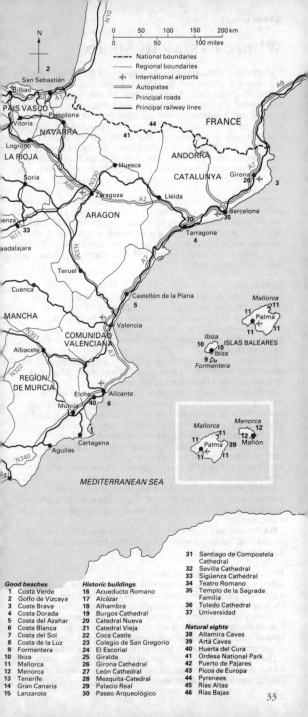

Map legend

```
         0    50    100   150   200 km
         |----|----|----|----|----|
         0        50        100 miles
```

- --- National boundaries
- —— Regional boundaries
- ✈ International airports
- ═══ Autopistas
- —— Principal roads
- ━━ Principal railway lines

Good beaches

1 Costa Verde
2 Golfo de Vizcaya
3 Costa Brava
4 Costa Dorada
5 Costa del Azahar
6 Costa Blanca
7 Costa del Sol
8 Costa de la Luz
9 Formentera
10 Ibiza
11 Mallorca
12 Menorca
13 Tenerife
14 Gran Canaria
15 Lanzarote

Historic buildings

16 Acueducto Romano
17 Alcázar
18 Alhambra
19 Burgos Cathedral
20 Catedral Nueva
21 Catedral Vieja
22 Coca Castle
23 Colegio de San Gregorio
24 El Escorial
25 Giralda
26 Girona Cathedral
27 León Cathedral
28 Mezquita-Catedral
29 Palacio Real
30 Paseo Arqueológico

31 Santiago de Compostela Cathedral
32 Sevilla Cathedral
33 Sigüenza Cathedral
34 Teatro Romano
35 Templo de la Sagrada Familia
36 Toledo Cathedral
37 Universidad

Natural sights

38 Altamira Caves
39 Artá Caves
40 Huerta del Cura
41 Ordesa National Park
42 Puerto de Pajares
43 Picos de Europa
44 Pyrenees
45 Rías Altas
46 Rías Bajas

33

Where to stay in Spain

With advance planning, there is no reason to spend more than an emergency night or two in a hotel or inn that does not meet international standards of comfort. Spanish lodging places can be as memorable as their nearby vistas and monuments. However, it must be conceded that the average Spanish hotel is no better than the average hotel in any other nation of the developed world. The tourist boom that started in the 1950s proved irresistible to speculators in pursuit of easy pesetas. Lacking taste, proper financing and management skills, they were and are responsible for the shabby high-rise blocks that blight both cities and coastal regions. Despite their great number, these are nearly always avoidable.

Once a standard practice, breakfast is now only *sometimes* included in the room rate. Inquire when checking in, for if it is not, a cheaper breakfast can be had at a nearby bar. Value Added Tax (*IVA*) is now imposed at a 6-percent rate for food, goods, services, and at hotels with ratings of three stars or fewer. It jumps to 12 percent for luxury goods and restaurants, car rentals, and four- and five-star hotels.

Standards

Every establishment offering beds and/or food to the public is subject to regular inspection and classification by the government. The standards applied are primarily quantitative, taking into consideration minimum room dimensions and numbers of elevators and rooms with baths. But they do give useful guidance.

Look for signs announcing the following designations, near the entrance to hotels. They are rectangular, with white letters and symbols against a light blue background.

An **H**, underlined by one to five stars (they look more like stylized suns), denotes a hotel with graduated levels of services and facilities. At minimum (one star), hotels have central heating, an elevator in buildings of five floors or more, at least one telephone per floor, shared bathrooms, laundry and ironing service, and a dining room. At the top (five stars), guests are guaranteed air conditioning, elevators, public rooms, a bar, telephones and baths in every bedroom, a hairdresser and, in cities, a garage.

An **HR** designation indicates a residential hotel, often distinguished only by the absence of a formal restaurant. There is usually a Spanish-style cafeteria instead, with limited menus and waiter service.

HA denotes an apartment hotel, usually without bars and restaurants, but frequently offering kitchen facilities with some of the bedrooms.

Reception and personnel

When you check in at the reception desk you will be asked to leave your passport for registration, but it will be returned within an hour or two. Some hotels simply make a copy of the necessary pages while you are signing in. If the hotel offers a foreign exchange service, it will be done by the cashier. While rates of exchange are generally more favorable at a bank, some of the better hotels make a point of observing current bank rates.

The old-fashioned type of *conserje* (concierge or hall porter) is on the decline. That cherished individual was a paragon of fatherly expertise, whether in giving directions, obtaining tickets, arranging transportation or confiding the names of unspoiled clubs and restaurants. All this he conveyed with dazzling multilingual virtuosity. The *conserje* still does these things, in principle, but the position now is too often populated by opportunistic upstarts, who tout dreary "City by Night" bus tours, flashy tourist traps and costly restaurants and shops, presumably to reap some personal commission. Although there are noble exceptions, nowadays the *conserje* is best employed for posting letters and handing out room keys. If he (or, rarely, she), does more than this, a modest tip based on the length of your stay is appropriate.

The paradores

Nothing so enhances Spain's touristic stature as the national *parador* system. Freely translated as a "stopping place," the word *parador* is hardly ever used to describe any other kind of inn or hotel. Over a third of the more than 80 *paradores* are former castles, convents, palaces, mansions or royal hunting lodges, and many of the others are new buildings set within ancient fortifications.

Old or new, most occupy high ground or seaside locations with pleasant, even spectacular, vistas. Whatever their age or origins, rooms are usually spacious and decorated with taste and restraint, often including fine antique furniture, suits of armor, tapestries and splendid ceramic tiles, all kept beautifully clean by the diligent staff. Bathrooms are commodious, with deep, long tubs and towels that wrap two or three times around the waist. Dining rooms serve prodigious portions of regional recipes, with selected local wines to complement them.

The popularity of the *paradores* is ever increasing, and they still represent good value even though they are no longer bargains. Their drawbacks are the occasional whiff of institutional sterility, a shortage of recreational facilities, and the fact that they do not have discos or bars that stay open later than midnight.

Part of the rationale of the *parador* system, which was begun in 1928, is to encourage tourism in less-visited regions of the country by providing lodging in districts not well served by private hoteliers. For that reason, none are located in Barcelona, Madrid or Sevilla. Several are situated in towns near those hubs, however, such as those at Toledo, Segovia and Aranjuez, outside the capital. They should be sampled whenever possible on day trips and longer excursions.

Nonresidents can eat at *paradores*, where there is rarely a wait to be seated. Specialties of the region, written in red ink on the menu, are translated — with sometimes amusing inexpertise — into French, German and English. A particular delight are *entremeses*, a feature at most *paradores*, often available only at lunchtime. The word means "between tables," a reference to the practice of taking snacks between meals. They arrive on dozens of leaf-shaped dishes, each containing a different treat: *chorizo*, fried squid, meatballs, sardines, potato salad, and many other delicacies. Although intended only as a first course, they constitute an ideal full lunch.

Since most *paradores* are small, tour groups are rare. For the same reason, advance reservations are wise; allow three months for high season and at least one for winter. As reserving can be complicated, it is advisable to leave this to a travel agent. In the US, an agency representing all the *paradores* is **Marketing Ahead** (*433 5th Ave., New York, NY 10016* ☎ *(212) 686-9213*).

What to eat and drink

Spanish notions of hospitality have long embraced the conviction that to appear parsimonious is dishonor to the host. So portions of food served were, and often still are, abundant. It was nothing out of the ordinary to watch a family of four coolly dispatching a monstrous repast sufficient to fuel a squad of marathon runners. Five or six courses were the rule, each of them two or three times larger than anyone could realistically need. To a degree, that still holds true — on special occasions, for example, or when friends entertain friends. But fewer and smaller portions have become more normal.

Several influences are at play, including changing fashion, more emphasis on healthy eating, and the need by both patron and restaurateur to keep a close eye on costs. Taste and presentation are therefore becoming as important as simple sustenance. At least, that is the case at finer restaurants, where a form of *nouvelle* cooking called *nueva cocina* has taken hold, with the lightness in saucing and content that the term implies. One result is that in a matter of years, rather than decades, the richly diverse Spanish repertoire has transcended its peasant origins to become one of the three most important cuisines on the continent.

The opinion prevalent in France, that Spanish cooking improves in direct relation to its proximity to the glorious Gallic kitchen, is borne out by the fact that the Basques and Catalans, living within sight of the Pyrenees, are the most accomplished of Spanish cooks. Yet other regions too have developed recipes that have acquired favor throughout the country.

The best-known dish beyond the borders of Spain is *paella*, the only certain ingredients of which are rice flavored with that most costly of spices, saffron. The rest depends on what is available. Usually, this means a combination of clams, mussels, chicken, prawns, lobster, squid, strips of sweet red pepper and peas, all simmered in a colorful mixture. When it is skillfully executed, the ingredients of a *paella* are blended in such a way that each flavor contributes to the others, while uncannily retaining its identity. Valencian in origin, *paella* can be found in every corner of the land.

Next in celebrity is the Andalucían cold soup, *gazpacho*, a blend of uncooked tomatoes, bread chunks, garlic, oil, salt, onions and a splash of vinegar. It is served chilled, sometimes in a bowl nestled in ice, and sprinkled with a variety of garnishes. A close rival, *zarzuela de mariscos*, takes its name from the indigenous form of light opera and might be translated as "operetta of seafood." Again, any marine ingredients that come to hand are used in what is essentially a soup-stew of lobster, prawns, squid, clams, mussels, eel and salt-water fish. The dish is at its best in Catalunya, but is a staple of all districts of the country bordering the sea.

The elaborate concoction *cocido madrileño* combines chicken, pieces of sausage, veal, ham, beef, pork fat, chick-peas, cabbage, potatoes and carrots, traditionally served as three courses. First is the strained broth, with fine noodles added at the last minute; next are the drained vegetables, and finally the meats. Every region of Spain has its variation of *cocido*, but the classic version is that of the central Meseta.

Of the several varieties of the delicious *manchego* cheese from La Mancha, the soft *fresco* is perhaps the most palatable. Other types include one soaked in oil (*en aceite*) and another which is hard, crumbly, mature and pungent.

Andalucíans claim that they eat only to live, which may account for the fact that a platter of seemingly commonplace fried fish — *fritura mixta* — is the characteristic dish. However, *gazpacho* and the red wine punch *sangría* originated in that sultry southern climate, as did the almond-based "white" *gazpacho* and *riñones al Jerez* (kidneys sautéed in sherry).

Aragón is caught between the superior kitchens of the Basques and the Catalans, and its cooking leaves a pale impression. However, pork and rabbit dishes are surprisingly tender and tasty, and *chilindrón* (a savory blend of tomatoes, garlic and peppers, often with pieces of ham) is a delicious sauce applied to almost any meat or poultry.

Gastronomes who note a family resemblance between Asturian cuisine and regional cuisines in France point to the *cassoulet*-type of stew, *fabada*, a hearty concoction of white beans, pork and blood sausage, which may also include ham or pig's feet. Also memorable is the fish stew, *caldereta asturiana*. One of its ingredients is hot pepper, an unusual touch in a country where fiery seasonings are not common. The Asturian *queso de cabrales* is a piquant cheese that blends the milk of goats, cows and sheep.

Castilians make the most of their indigenous ingredients, well beyond *cocido madrileño*, described above. In *sopa de ajo*, garlic cloves and chunks of bread are cooked in oil and broth, with an egg dropped on the top at the last minute. *Cochinillo asado* (roast suckling pig) is almost always delicious, but can be disconcerting to those unaccustomed to eating meat quite so close to its original state. Thin wild *espárragos* and tiny nugget *fresas* (strawberries) must be tried. *Churros* (lengths of fried dough dusted with sugar), with thick, sweet, hot chocolate, make a tasty alternative to the usual breakfast of roll and *café*.

For the uninitiated visitor to Catalunya, the fish stews *zarzuela* and *bullabesa* might exemplify the Catalan spirit, but the Catalans are more complex than that. Hot or pungent spices are more readily used by them than by cooks of other regions, in recipes such as *romescu* (a tangy tomato, pepper and oil sauce) and *ali-oli* (a strong garlic mayonnaise spread over game or pork). *Jabalí* (wild boar) and *conejo* (rabbit) are often astonishingly tender, and salads combining vegetables and fish make delicious light summer meals. By all means, try *botifarra amb mongetes* (sausage with white beans), simple but sublime. That description can also be applied to *migas*, which are little more than breadcrumbs fried with flecks of ham.

From Galicia, in the far NW, comes hearty *caldo gallego*, a meal-in-itself meat broth crowded with beans, potatoes and cabbage. Galician *empanadas* are flat pies with a variety of meat or fish fillings. *Pimientas de Padrón* (small oblong green peppers grilled and salted) make a popular bar snack, their appeal heightened by the suspense of knowing that some of them, about one in five, are fiery hot.

The plains of Valencia, on the E coast, are especially conducive to the growing of rice, the basic ingredient of the best Valencian dishes, *paella* and *arroz con pollo* (rice with chicken and peas). And in the northern Vascongadas and Navarra regions, the sauce is an integral part of most dishes. Ingredients are simmered slowly to help the natural flavors reveal themselves. Cod is a favorite, as in *bacalao al pil-pil* (simmered in garlic, olive oil and possibly hot red peppers). *Trucha a la Navarra* (trout marinated in wines and spices, poached in the liquid, and stuffed with air-cured ham) and *calamares en su tinta* (tender squid in a sauce made from their own ink) are also popular. *Angulas* (baby eels), boiled in oil that is brought to the table popping and snapping, should be twirled around a wooden fork and eaten whole, an experience not unlike eating spaghetti with eyes.

Restaurants, bars and cafeterias

As in most Latin countries, the main meal of the day is lunch, which is not eaten until mid-afternoon. Restaurants are open from 1-4pm, but most customers do not arrive until after 2pm, and then tend to linger over coffee and brandy past closing time. Given that habit, the average Spaniard doesn't even begin to think about dinner until 10pm, and in the cities, people often arrive at restaurants at 11.30pm or midnight. However, as a concession to the curious dining habits of their foreign guests, most restaurants are open by 9pm. Barcelonans tend to eat somewhat earlier than Madrileños, but the peak hour is from 10.30-11.30pm.

In restaurants, service is nearly always attentive and efficient, sometimes to the point of brusqueness. Yet, in the expectation that patrons will linger as long as they wish, waiters tend to bring the bill only after some persuasion. Restaurants are expected to produce a fixed-price menu (*menú del día*) consisting of an appetizer, main course, dessert and drink, at a price that is lower than a comparable selection from the *à la carte* menu. Unfortunately, it invariably includes the least interesting dishes, and owners are understandably reluctant even to mention it.

Nearly every bar serves *meriendas* (snacks) from early morning to late evening. In some cases, these are merely *sandwiches* (slices of meat or cheese between slices of toasted bread) or *bocadillos* (the same fillings in split hard rolls). But in most cases, set out on the bar or available to order is an array of appetizing delicacies. *Tapas* are served in a small dish that holds no more than a few nibbles. When the same items are served on a larger plate they are called *raciónes*. Examples include wedges of the firm potato and egg omelet called a *tortilla; ensaladilla rusa* (potato and vegetable salad); *empanadillas* (half-moon turnover pastries with meat or fish filling); chunks of cheese or *chorizo* sausage; mussels; clams; anchovies in oil; *boquerones fritos* (fried whitebait); several varieties of mushroom, marinated, pickled or fried; *brochetas* (grilled skewers of pork or fish); thin slices of the wonderful *jamón serrano* (air-cured ham), sometimes served on bread rubbed with tomato pulp and drizzled with olive oil; grilled prawns; breaded fried octopus rings; sliced salami; and snails in a sauce, or cold and unadorned.

There are also two types of cafeteria that often stay open until midnight or later. One is an *auto-servicio*, where the customer makes selections from a service counter, pays the cashier, and carries the tray to a table. The other is strictly table-service, but with a shorter menu and longer hours than a restaurant. Fast food is often featured, along with *platos combinados*: dishes that combine meat or fish with potatoes or rice and one or two vegetables.

Drink

Most restaurants and all bars have a cheap house wine, often decanted from cellar kegs and served by the glass or carafe. Local bottlings can be acidic or lifeless, but generally the range is adequate to excellent. The vintages of the Rioja and Penedés districts are superior, often purchased by winemakers of other countries for blending with their own pressings. (For further information, see SPANISH WINES on page 144.)

Coffee is very good, but tea is brewed with bags. Hot chocolate is thick and very rich, and *horchata* is a milky, almond-based cool drink that should be tried. The champagne and sorbet drink known as *sorbeta de limón* is refreshingly cool on a hot day. *Heladerías* (ice cream stores) make lemonade. *Café irlandés* (Irish coffee) is popular, its Spanish counterpart being *carajillo con nata* (coffee with *coñac* topped with whipped cream). *Sangría* is the famous Andalucían iced punch comprising wine, fruit juice, lemonade, soda, brandy and slices of orange and lemon. Among the stiffer drinks, the *sol y sombra*, made of brandy and *anís*, guarantees a good night's sleep. Spanish *coñacs* (brandies) range from thick and sweet to smooth and potent.

Barcelona

Barcelona reveals itself slowly, as do many Iberian cities. In the opinion of many Hispanophiles, however, it surpasses all its rivals in sophistication, culture and vigor. To them, it is second to Madrid only in population, and Sevilla alone deserves to be mentioned in the same company.

Capital of the region of Catalunya and Spain's major seaport and manufacturing center, Barcelona prospers in all aspects of commerce, international trade and the arts. Cars, trucks, locomotives, airplanes and electronics are among the major products of the factories that ring the city. Despite some movement to Madrid, most publishing houses are based here. There are more than 60 art galleries and a munificence of museums and historic monuments. The radical architect Antoni Gaudí left testimony to his genius in a seminary, parks, mansions and apartments, and the unfinished cathedral, TEMPLE DE LA SAGRADA FAMÍLIA, whose towers symbolize this city's creative vitality.

No doubt the Phoenicians and Greeks preceded other seafaring visitors, but the founding of the city is credited to the Carthaginians, and its name is thought to derive from the powerful Barca family. It grew to substantial influence as a Roman port and then as a Visigothic capital, falling to the Arabs in the 8th century. Charlemagne wrested it away soon after and incorporated it into the region known as the Spanish March. In the following centuries, the counts of Barcelona expanded the March to take in parts of France and much of the east coast and Pyrenean fiefdoms. This accounts, in part, for the similarity between Catalan (*català*), spoken today by 5 million people, and the Provençal of southern France.

Barcelona was the center of Catalan separatist activity from the time of the insurrection against Felipe V to the 1936-39 Civil War. Until then, a climate of ideological liberalism nurtured volatile anarchist and socialist movements and their many splinters and appendages. That environment flourished once again after "La Libertad" — the death of Franco and the return of what has proved to be a very resilient democracy.

A measure of autonomy, roughly comparable to that of the American states, has muted separatist fervor. Most Catalans have settled for a regional parliament, the end of censorship and the restoration of Catalan as an official language. This last was made manifest when the names of Catalan heroes replaced those of Falangists on streets and plazas. The Gran Via de les Corts Catalanes (in the prevailing shorthand, "Gran Via C.C.") was the

Avenida José Antonio Primo de Rivera for 35 years, but everybody called it "Gran Via," just as they continued to use the name "Diagonal" for the street that was for the same period called after Generalísimo Franco. The Castilian *calle* is now the Catalan *carrer* on street signs, *paseo* is *passeig*, *plaza* is *plaça*, and *avenida* is *avinguda*.

Catalans joyfully assault each other with torrents of words and opinions. Much discussion is about what they consider to be the innate superiority of the Catalan culture. They never tire of drawing distinctions between themselves and their countrymen, whom they regard as insular and resistant to change. Catalans consider themselves tolerant, energetic and open to new ideas. They alone, they say, are truly European, looking north and east for inspiration, across the water, not across the plains of the interior.

Certainly, the record shows that Catalans are receptive to new movements in the arts. It was Barcelona that gave Picasso, who came from Málaga, his earliest recognition. Among his younger colleagues were Joan Miró and Salvador Dalí, both Catalan. In the 1960s, a new generation, led by Antoni Tàpies, took up the banner. He, Miró and Picasso all have their own museums here, and Dalí bequeathed half his *oeuvre* to the planned museum of contemporary art.

Most people don't know Barcelona before they get there. Those who are about to see it for the first time are to be envied, for this is a city that defies assumptions. No clear image leaps to mind, such as those pictures we effortlessly summon before touching down in London or Paris or Rome. This is curious, for Barcelona, which predates Christ and whose medieval passages and grand boulevards fill the eye at every turn, is far more photogenic than most cities. Apart from a few ill-considered mid-rise office towers that profit commerce but not art, it is a city built to a human scale, the majority of buildings being four to eight stories high.

Timelessness and immediacy coexist in Barcelona, never in greater contrast than when the city is seized by the Spanish compulsion to juxtapose the sacred and the secular, such as when rock concerts are held in front of churches — a not infrequent occurrence. Barcelonans revel in this kind of sensory combat, cherishing every stone and minute of their heritage, yet, as is the case at the moment, routinely transmuting their city into something else. In every quarter, moldering monuments and slumbering repositories of art are being shaken from hibernation, spruced up, rebuilt and redirected to receive the millions of people that the attention focused on the Olympics and the Quincentenary has brought. Arguably, no city in the world in recent years has enjoyed so great a flowering of architectural talent.

The city is within an hour of the beach resorts of the Costa Brava to the north and the Costa Dorada to the south, and 4-5 hours from the ski slopes of the Pyrenees. August is the slowest month, when inhabitants escape to the country. The main events of the year are the feast of Sant Antoni in January, celebrated with parades and fireworks, and the pre-Lenten *Carnaval.* Holy Week, preceding Easter, brings devout processions, as does Corpus Christi. Every Sunday at noon, the citizens of Barcelona dance the *sardana* in front of the cathedral to the wail of oboes, trombones and flutes. The music is by turns spirited and mournful, marked by moments of fierce joy. Anyone can join in, but the uninitiated should be warned: the steps are rather more complicated than they might appear.

Getting around

From the airport to the city

El Prat International Airport was doubled in size during its recent reconstruction, which was begun in 1989 and largely completed by 1992. Only 12km (7 miles) from the city center, the trip takes 25-40mins by bus, train or taxi, depending on traffic and destination.

Both train and bus services are available from the airport to near-downtown locations. The trains run every 30mins from 6am-11pm, depositing passengers at the main **Sants** station. This is situated at some distance from most hotels, but metro trains are available from the same building. Buses are available from 2.30am-11.10pm, dropping passengers at the **Plaça d'Espanya**, where there are stations for two metro lines.

Taxis from the airport cost about 1,500-2,000ptas, including the additional airport supplement. Be certain that the meter has been turned back following the last fare. Especially if you are a first-time visitor, it is unwise to rent a car at the airport to drive to your hotel. Those unfamiliar with the city will find traffic patterns and signposting very confusing, and streets in the older parts are narrow.

Public transportation

The five lines of the city-owned **metro** system are augmented by two more operated by the Generalitat, the regional government. Their layout is similar to that of the Paris system, and some of the entrances even imitate their Art Nouveau model. Clean and reasonably safe, if drab, the metro is also the swiftest and cheapest way to get around the city.

Fares are charged by the ride, not graduated according to distance. At the time of writing, tickets are 60ptas Mon-Fri, 65ptas Sat, Sun and holidays. Ten-trip cards valid on both bus and metro cost 390ptas, and during summer months, there are 1-, 3- and 5-day passes good for unlimited use on all forms of public transportation. Their cost ranges from 275-1,100ptas.

Buses are color-coded, painted red, yellow, green or blue, corresponding to directional signs at bus stops. Tourists are most likely to use the red buses, which pass through or originate in the city center, or the blue ones, which follow similar routes but operate only at night. Buses are very crowded and uncomfortable during rush hours.

An additional service to visitors is the **Barcelona Transports Turístics** ticket, good for one-half or full days from late June to mid-Sept on many different kinds of public transportation. These include the funicular up Tibidabo hill, the cable car and funicular on Montjuïc, and "Bus 100," which follows a circular route through all the principal sightseeing districts. All can be boarded as often as desired throughout the ticket's period of validity. This is essentially a self-guided tour, aided by a booklet that describes the sites and neighborhoods along the way. The bus usually carries a hostess to answer questions. For further information ☎336-0000.

Taxis

Metered taxis are yellow and black. They can be hailed in the street or found parked at stands near hotels and major attractions. During the day, the window sign *Libre* (Spanish) or *Lliure* (Catalan) indicates that a taxi is available for hire; at night, a green roof light is also illuminated. Fares are moderate, unless

Emergency information

Police (Policia) ☎ 092
Fire brigade (Bombers) ☎ 080
Ambulance (Ambulància) ☎ 329-7766 or 300-2020
Traffic accidents ☎ 092

Hospitals
Hospital Clínic Casanova 143 ☎ 323-1414. Map **3**C3.
Hospital Sant Pau Av. Sant Antoni Maria Claret 167
☎ 347-3133.
Red Cross Hospital Dos de Maig 301 ☎ 235-9300.

Medical and dental emergencies
Doctors ☎ 212-8585
Nurses ☎ 417-1994
Contact your consulate for a list of English-speaking doctors
or dentists.

Late-night pharmacies
Pharmacies take turns to stay open past normal business
hours. Each day's *farmacias de guardia* are listed in daily
newspapers; or check the sign on the door of the nearest
pharmacy.

Help lines
Alcoholics Anonymous ☎ 317-7777
Lost property ☎ 301-3923

the taxi becomes stalled in traffic, with an average ride costing
250-350ptas. Supplementary charges apply for extra luggage and
trips to and from the airport and railroad stations. Ensure that the
meter has been turned back following the last fare.

Cars
As might be expected in a city created more than 2,000yrs before
the automobile, traffic in Barcelona is unspeakably bad.
Prosperity has brought cars within the means of most Catalans,
and they have taken advantage of that opportunity. Streets are
poorly marked, and their signs are attached to the sides of
buildings well back from the angled corners. Because of the
afternoon siesta, there are effectively four rush hours, with barely
distinguishable pauses in between.

Parking in the streets is extremely limited, especially in the
older districts, although a number of municipal parking garages
have been built around the city in anticipation of the Olympics,
including one under the plaza in front of the cathedral. It is
unwise to leave your car in many parts of the old town. Visitors
who arrive in their own cars, rather than by plane or train, would
be well advised to park them in hotel garages and confine their
use to excursions out of the city.

Those who intend to rent cars for day trips or extended tours
can have them delivered to the hotel on the day of departure,
thus saving parking fees.

Walking is the best way to get around, although you will need
to use the metro or buses between sightseeing areas.

Useful addresses

☎ The **telephone prefix (area code)** for Barcelona province is **93**.

Tourist information

There are tourist information offices near the international arrivals area at **El Prat airport** (☎ *325-5829*), at the **Sants railroad station** (☎ *410-2594, map 3 D1*) and on the **Gran Via de les Corts Catalanes** near Passeig de Gràcia (*Gran Via 658* ☎ *301-7443, map 4 C4*). They are usually open during customary business hours, and they have extended schedules during the summer.

Pairs of young information officers work the historic heart of the city during July and Aug. They are easily identified by their red-and-white jackets and their *i* badges.

American Express Viajes has its main office at Passeig de Gràcia 101 (☎ *217-0070, map 4 C4*). It is a valuable source of information for travelers in need of help, advice or emergency services.

Main post office

Plaça Antonio López s/n ☎318-3831. Map **6**D4. Open 9am-9pm Mon-Fri, 9am-2pm Sat.

Telephone services

Alarm call ☎096
News ☎095
Road conditions (outside Barcelona) ☎204-2247
Speaking clock ☎093
Weather ☎094

Tour operators

American Express Passeig de Gràcia 101 ☎217-0070. Map 4C4.
Julià Tours Ronda Universitat 5 ☎317-6454 or 318-3895. Map 4D4. Variety of half- and full-day tours, as well as nightlife excursions.
Pullmantour Gran Via 635 ☎317-1297 or 318-0241. Map 3D2. Same variety of tours as above, also with English-speaking guides.

Orientation

Barcelona faces the Mediterranean, along that section of the northeastern coast that bends inland from the French border before straightening to run due s toward Africa. Much that is memorable in the city is found in the ancient quarters near the harbor, especially the two square miles of narrow streets, alleys, palaces and plazas that is the **Barri Gòtic** — the Gothic Quarter. The **cathedral** is there, and most of the **Roman remains** and ramparts.

The *barri* is bordered by the **Rambles**. This colorful pedestrian mall connects the port with the **Plaça de Catalunya**, a large square with trees, flower beds, and two large illuminated fountains that work according to an unpredictable schedule.

To the s of the old city, forming one pillar of the harbor, is the hill called **Montjuïc** — the "Mountain of the Jews." It has a fortress at the summit, and its slopes are host to gardens, several museums and the principal Olympic stadium.

In the other direction, NE of the Barri Gòtic and the **Via Laietana**, is a district nearly as old as the Barri Gòtic, called **Ribera**, with a number of 15th and 16thC mansions, two of which contain the **Museu Picasso**. Recent gentrification has transformed tha appearance of some of these dark streets, with restaurants, quirky shops and small clubs.

To the SE is **Barceloneta**, a fisherman's quarter on a tongue of land that encloses that end of the harbor. The area contains many medium-cost seafood restaurants. Long shut off by warehouses, railroad yards and deteriorating housing, access to the beach has now been provided through demolition and renewal. Farther N, beyond Ribera, a dilapidated waterfront district of railroad yards and factories was cleared to make room for a new Ritz-Carlton hotel, an office building and an Olympic Village, which is to be transformed into blocks of public flats. The area is now known as **Poblenou**.

Immediately above this district is the **Parc de la Ciutadella**, the city's major park, created for an 1888 exposition and containing a **zoo**, **aquarium**, the **Museu d'Arte Modern** and the **Catalunya Parliament**.

To the N of these quarters, the streets adhere (for a while, at least) to a grid plan imposed in a grand scheme promulgated in the mid-19thC. It is called the **Eixample** — the Extension — an ambitious act of city planning that connected the old city to the growing suburbs in the NW. The district bears a marked resemblance to parts of Paris, with every street corner sliced off at a 45° angle, creating diamond-shaped plazas, and plane trees lining the streets. Scores of buildings are designed in the uniquely Catalan version of Art Nouveau called *modernisme*. Behind their sinuous facades are many of the city's most classy bars, restaurants and clubs.

Cutting through the Eixample is the **Passeig de Gràcia**, a Champs-Élysées of banks, hotels and exclusive shops. The **Gràcia** quarter, N of the upper end of the Passeig de Gràcia, climbs the increasingly steep slope toward **Tibidabo**. Its plazas, shops, music bars and cafés with outdoor tables are especially popular with young Barcelonans.

A walk in Barcelona

No city in Spain more amply rewards exploration on foot. A meander through the Barri Gòtic is time travel, through half of written history. Here, a cathedral begun at the end of the 13thC rests upon the ruins of a Visigothic church that are in turn atop a pagan temple, all of it flanked by walls the Romans set in place 1,000yrs before.

It is a place of hidden and flamboyant delights: the ruins of an entire Roman village in the basement of a Renaissance mansion, geese swimming in the cathedral cloister, a patio shaded by orange trees heavy with fruit, shafts of light picking out the chiseled features of gargoyles and saints. The quarter is bordered on the S by the RAMBLES, an apt name for a boulevard where people, not vehicles, prevail, and there is something to do or to witness at every hour on the clock.

This walk is an introduction to both districts.

1. BAIXADA DE LA CANONJA
2. PLAÇA DEL REI
3. BAIXADA DE SANTA CLARA
4. PLAÇA DE SANT IU
5. MONTJUIC DEL BISBE
6. CARRER DE PARADIS

LA CIUTAT ANTIC

See maps 5C3-6D4 and above. Metro: Jaume I.

To begin, stand in the plaza in front of the main (w) facade of the cathedral, facing the entrance. Look left. Over there is a narrow lane called the Baixada de la Canonja. Walk down that way, turning right at the bottom onto **Carrer Tapineria**, once a street of cobblers. The walls on the right date, in part, from the Roman era, but with much rebuilding and modification over the centuries and surmounted by medieval and later improvements. An equestrian statue of Ramon Berenguer III (a monarch of no great distinction) is soon encountered, and beyond there is a fragment of Roman statuary. Keep to the right around the small plaza, following Carrer Tapineria to the Plaça de Angel. There is a break in the wall, so turn right on Baixada de la Llibreteria, back into the Barri, then right again at the next corner, following the sign toward the Plaça del Rei.

The second building on the right is the 16thC **Casa Clariana-Padellàs**, moved here in 1931. It contains the MUSEU D'HISTÒRIA DE LA CIUTAT, well worth visiting, especially for the Roman village unearthed in the basement. Continue into the **Plaça del Rei**, where a modern iron sculpture graces the near corner, in sharp contrast to its surroundings. The 14thC Gothic church of **Santa Àgata** forms the right (N) wall of the square. At the far corner, a staircase leads up into what was once the 14thC **Palau Reial Major**. Queen Isabel and King Fernando are said to have greeted Columbus here on his return from his first voyage of discovery. The great hall inside on the left — the **Saló del Tinell** — is now used for exhibitions of various kinds. Right of the main door is the entrance to the church. Leave the plaza by the passage called the Baixada de Santa Clara. This emerges at the back of the CATEDRAL (on the left is the restaurant **La Cuineta**). Turn right (W) on Carrer dels Comtes, the side of the cathedral on the left.

Shortly, off the small Plaça de Sant Iu, is the entrance to the MUSEU FREDERIC MARÈS. After a visit, continue in the same direction, out into the Avinguda de Catedral. Bear left, observing the continuation of the Roman wall, surmounted by the upper floors of the 15thC **Casa de l'Ardiaca** (Archdeacon's House).

The two semicircular towers at the end are Roman, guarding one of the gates to the old city. Go up the ramp between them, a pedestrian street called the Carrer del Bisbe. Note the pure Romanesque portal of the 13thC chapel, the **Capilla de Santa Lucia**, on the left, much older than the cathedral to which it is attached.

Turn right at the next corner, down an alley called Montjuïc del Bisbe. After a couple of turns and under an arch is the tranquil little **Plaça de Sant Felip Neri**, with its two spreading trees and pattering fountain. (Quiet, that is, until youngsters pour out of the school next to the church to kick a ball around.) There is also a museum, arguably the city's most obscure, devoted to antique footwear.

Return to Carrer del Bisbe and turn right. The large doorway immediately on the left leads into the cloister of the cathedral. Sunlight filters through the leaves of the magnolias and palm trees growing there. Several fat geese glide in a pool that is fed by a water jet from the mouth of a stone frog. Circle the fenced garden in a clockwise direction, past gilded chapels and racks of votive candles flickering in the gloom. This passes another fountain, this one with St George as its centerpiece. Saving the cathedral proper for another time, leave the cloister by the door straight ahead. (If the cloister doors are locked, continue along Bisbe to the next corner, turn left and pick up the walk at the next corner, turning right.)

Follow the wide passage around the back of the cathedral, turning right into the lane called Carrer de Paradis. Dim and grimy, it is hardly paradisaical, but not far along, at #10, is a building owned by the municipal government. Inside are four fluted columns of the Roman temple of Emperor Augustus. If the door is open, you are free to step inside for a look. Continue along Paradis, passing, at #4, another branch of the restaurant **La Cuineta**, housed in a former 17thC *bodega.*

Soon, the alley opens into the light and bustle of Plaça de Sant Jaume. This was the heart of the Roman city, the market and forum and intersection of the two main streets, Cardus and Decumanus. Turn right. At the corner, look right up Carrer del Bisbe to see the enclosed **Gothic-style footbridge** connecting the facing buildings. On the right is the **Casa dels Canonges**, on the left the **Palau de la Generalitat**, part of which dates back to the 15thC.

The *palau* houses the government of the semi-autonomous region of Catalunya. The main entrance faces the plaza, a sculpture of Sant Jordi (St George) slaying his dragon in a niche above the door. Inside is a fine Gothic courtyard with an open staircase that used to be one of the most photographed sites in Barcelona. Unfortunately, this very active building can now be visited only after a written request submitted at least 15 days in advance, and then only on Sat and Sun. The only exception is the feast of Sant Jordi on Apr 23, when the palace is open to the public.

On the opposite side of the square is the **Ajuntament** (city hall). Cross over, being cautious about the traffic that zips through what looks like a pedestrian plaza. Turn right (s), exiting the *plaça* along the busy shopping street, Carrer de Ferran. Two streets down, a few steps left on Carrer d'Avinyó, is a white-fronted store, **La Manual Alpargatera**, which sells hand-made *espadrilles* in many styles. These are the rope and canvas shoes seen on many of the *sardana* dancers in front of the cathedral every Sun noon. Farther along Ferran, at #26, is **Itaca**, selling a substantial selection of ceramics from various regions of the country.

After that, keep an eye open for a triple-arch opening on the left, opposite the fanciful Art Nouveau facade of the store called **Wolf's**. Turn in, going through a second set of arches into the **Plaça Reial**. After long decline, the facades of the enclosed square were scrubbed clean some years ago, and new stone paving was laid on the ground and around the several sentinel palms. The street lamps and the iron fountain in the center were designed by the young Gaudí, and there is a lively stamp-and-coin market here on Sun when the weather is good. Soon after the renovation, unfortunately, the *plaça* became a gathering place for drifters and addicts, all of whom were scruffy at best and some of whom begged from passers-by in a threatening manner. That trend appears to have been contained by a pronounced police presence, especially evident at night. Presumably it will remain so. Several cafés around the square provide an opportunity for wine and *tapas* or coffee and *churros*.

Leave the *plaça* through the exit over to the right. This corridor intersects with LES RAMBLES, a street like no other in Spain. It runs from the port (to the left) for about 2km (a little over a mile) up to the Plaça de Catalunya. Down the center is a broad pedestrian concourse bordered by one-way N-S streets. Trees form a leafy corridor over newsstands, cafés, flower stalls, and the throngs of visitors and citizens that flood the sidewalk 20hrs a day.

From here, there are several options. Along the way to the water are the new CENTRE D'ART SANTA MÒNICA, the MUSEU DE CERA (wax museum), the MUSEU MARÍTIM (maritime museum), the MONUMENT A COLOM (Columbus monument) and the replica of his *Santa María*. Almost directly across the Rambles is Carrer Nou de Rambla, with Gaudí's PALAU GÜELL a few doors down, and farther on, the terminus of the **Montjuïc funicular** (but make that walk only in bright daylight). Or, turn right, perhaps pausing for a coffee to watch the passing crowds. Two streets up, on the left, is the GRAN TEATRE DEL LICEU, the opera house. Just beyond, on the right, detour along the narrow Carrer Cardenal Casañas for a glimpse of the 15thC **Església Mare de Déu del Pi** and its vivid rose window. The church dominates two quiet squares: one has an intriguing shop of ceramics and crafts and a pleasant corner bar, and the other has a market selling bric-a-brac.

Return to the Rambles and turn right (N). Shortly, on the left, is the **Mercat de Sant Josep** (or **de la Boqueria**) (*open 8am-1.30pm, 4.30-8pm*), a splendid market that opened in 1836 and is certainly worth a detour. Beneath its high, leaded glass roof are dozens of stalls with luxuriant heaps of sea creatures, loaves of bread, wheels of cheese, marzipan, dried fruits and dewy piles of grapes and melons. Above hang rows of *serrano* hams and sausages and garlands of garlic and peppers.

Near the top of the Rambles, on the left, is a 4-spigot iron fountain. It is said that after a sip of its waters you will never leave Barcelona, but most people won't be tempted to test the legend. Nearby, old men gather in voluble groups, discussing politics and soccer, and activists often put up their banners and pass out literature. One of the most popular cafés is the **Zurich**, directly across the way.

For a quieter stroll, there is a continuation of the Rambles, running from the NW corner of the **Plaça de Catalunya** to El Diagonal. Its shops are more stylish, and it is lined with first-class hotels.

Sights and places of interest

With no less than 36 museums, celebrating such minutiae as antique shoes and perfume and such profundities as the accomplishments of Pablo Picasso and Joan Miró, Barcelona provides prodigious nourishment for eye and intellect. Without setting foot inside a museum, however, you can hardly avoid the lessons in history, art and architecture provided by the BARRI GÒTIC and the grand avenues and districts spreading inland from the sea. The hill called MONTJUÏC has, all by itself, seven museums, a Greek theater, a fort, a fairground, and an entire village of examples of Spanish domestic and municipal architecture. Given the furious activity attending the approach of 1992 and beyond, expect to encounter construction and renovations at every turn. Fortunately, up until the time of writing, this has denied visitors little, for with one or two exceptions, most museums and other places of interest have remained open to the public.

Following each street address in the listings below, in parentheses, is the cross street or prominent landmark nearest to the described site. Look for the ★ symbol against the most important sights and ▥ for buildings of great architectural interest. Places of special interest for children (✽) are also indicated. If you only know the name of a museum, say, in English, and cannot find it in the following A-Z, try looking it up in the INDEX. Some lesser sights do not have their own entries but are included within other entries: look these up in the INDEX too.

ARC D'TRIOMF
Map 6B5. Metro: Arc d'Triomf.
Erected for the 1888 international exposition, the arch has the classic profile of such monuments, but is executed in intricate Mudejar brick patterns with Neoclassical embellishments. At the head of a fittingly majestic boulevard called the Passeig Lluis Companys, it and the bordering blocks were long neglected. But the arch has been spruced up and double files of new palms have been planted along the promenade, in time to do duty at the 1992 Olympics.

BARRI GÒTIC *(Barrio Gótico)* ▥
Maps 5 and 6.
Much that is memorable in Barcelona is in the old town district known as the Gothic Quarter, or, sometimes, as the Roman Quarter, for its walls and excavations of dwellings from the Roman period. Most of it was built between the 12th and 15thC, and it has successfully preserved its medieval character. Constricted lanes pass beneath overhanging balconies and guild signs, and lead to enclosed *plaças* of palaces and mansions. Behind small-paned windows are antique- and book-emporia, *tapas* bars, and several of the city's celebrated traditional restaurants. There are also a number of small, inexpensive hotels. (See A WALK IN BARCELONA, page 44.)

CASA BATLLÓ AND CASA MILÁ   See LA PEDRERA and
EL QUADRAT D'OR.

CASA-MUSEU GAUDÍ   See PARC GÜELL.

CATEDRAL ★
Av. de Catedral s/n (Via Laietana). Map 5C3. Open 7am-1.30pm, 2-7pm. Metro: Jaume I.

Most of the existing structure dates from the 13th and 14thC, a replacement for an 11thC Romanesque cathedral that was itself preceded by an earlier church on the same site. Despite some modified Romanesque elements, including the s transept portal that survives from the 11thC, the exterior is Gothic. The main w facade was built only in the late 19thC, but to plans drawn up 400yrs earlier. The filigreed, pointed central tower is echoed by smaller, older versions at the corners, which date from the 14thC. At the rear are two 14thC octagonal towers, marking the ends of the transept. A 14th-15thC **cloister** is appended to the s wall. It has a shallow pool, where live geese are kept as reminders of the Roman occupation.

The interior of the cathedral is divided into three apses. In the middle are a series of adjoining stalls, carved and assembled during the 14th and 15thC. The other aisles are lined with chapels of the 16th-18thC, with interesting decorated grilles (*rejas*). Energetic visitors may choose to mount over 200 steps in the sw tower for a spectacular view from the top. The **sacristy** and **treasury** (🖾 *open 9am-1pm, closed Mon*) contain a reliquary, illuminated manuscripts, carved altar panels, and crucifixes of precious metals and gems.

CENTRE D'ART SANTA MONICA
Rambla Santa Monica 7 (Portal de Santa Madrona). Map 5E2 🖾 *Open usually 11am-2pm, 5-8pm, but hrs change with exhibitions. Metro: Drassanes.*
This persistently recycled 17thC structure was once a church, then a museum. Now an exhibition hall, its spacious vaulted rooms can easily contain works of considerable size. The emphasis is on contemporary Catalan artists, exploring many styles and approaches in painting, sculpture, mixed media, and photography.

COLUMBUS MONUMENT   See MONUMENT A COLOM.

EIXAMPLE   See EL QUADRAT D'OR.

FUNDACIÓ ANTONI TÀPIES (*Tàpies Museum*)
Aragó 255 (Rambla de Catalunya) ☎ *487-0315. Map 4C4* 🖾 *Open Tues-Sun 11am-8pm. Closed Mon. Metro: Passeig de Gràcia.*
There is no difficulty in finding this *modernista* building. Its distinctive iron-and-brick facade was designed by Lluís Domènech i Montaner in 1881 and restored by his great-grandson in 1989. Yet the building itself is all but overwhelmed by the huge silvery coils of metal wire and tubing that stand two stories high above the roof, the largest sculpture of the artist honored inside.

The spectacularly redesigned interior rivals, in quite different ways, the very engaging local MUSEU PICASSO and FUNDACIÓ JOAN MIRÓ. Leader of the generation of Spanish abstractionists who first made themselves known to the art world in the 1960s, Tàpies is still alive and active. His work has always avoided predictability, and he continues to probe the outer boundaries of his chosen esthetic. In addition to frequently rotated examples of his work, space is given in the museum to temporary exhibitions by like-minded artists.

FUNDACIÓ JOAN MIRÓ (*Miró Museum*)
Plaça Neptú s/n (Montjuïc) ☎ *329-8609. Map 3F2* 🖾 ◻

Open Tues-Sat 11am-7pm (Thurs until 9.30pm); Sun and holidays 10.30am-2.30pm. Closèd Mon. Access: Funicular de Montjuïc.

Devoted to one of Catalunya's most influential artists — his contemporaries were Pablo Picasso and Salvador Dalí — this minimalist Bauhaus-like structure is an effective setting for the prolific lyrical Surrealist. His long creative life is manifest in his thousands of paintings, lithographs, posters, sculpture and weavings. Most people don't think of him as a sculptor, but the playful objects on display here — on the roof as well as in the galleries — give a new perspective on his more familiar paintings. Frequent special exhibitions often squeeze the master's works down to a room or two, but even those few overwhelm most visiting artists. The cafeteria is uncommonly good.

FUNICULAR AEREO

Map 4F4-5. Open Oct-June Mon-Fri 11.30am-6pm, Sat, Sun, holidays 11am-6.45pm; July-Sept Mon-Fri 11am-9pm, Sat, Sun, holidays 11am-6.45pm .

Of the several offbeat forms of public transportation available in the city — the funiculars, elevators and trams negotiating MONTJUÏC and TIBIDABO — none is more breathtaking than this high-riding cable car gliding over the harbor from Montjuïc to Barceloneta. It can be boarded from either end or via the tower on the jetty in the middle of the bay. Actually, many people will be satisfied with just the elevator ascent to the top of that hulking steel structure. From the 4th-floor platform are unsurpassed views of the city and harbor and surrounding hills. But those who board the cable car will move slowly over the water above ferries, sailboats, the fishing fleet, warships, cruise liners and pleasure craft. It is a thrilling sight, *too* thrilling for acrophobics. Save the experience for a clear day, and dusk may be the best time of all. The elevator ride alone is 200ptas, the one-way cable-car trip in either direction, 500ptas.

GRAN TEATRE DEL LICEU *(Opera House)*

Sant Pau 1 (Rambla Caputxins) ☎ 318-9122 or 318-9277. Map 5D2 ▨ ✗ Mon-Fri 11.30am and 12.15pm for 1-5 persons, Tues, Thurs 10am-1pm for larger groups. Metro: Liceu.

Opened in 1847, the Liceu has remained one of the great showcases of Europe for opera, ballet, classical music and, on occasion, plays. The restrained Neoclassical exterior only hints at the palatial interior, decidedly Baroque in inspiration.

GOTHIC QUARTER   See BARRI GÒTIC.

MOLL DE LA FUSTA *(La Fusta Wharf)*

Map 5F3-6E4.

Part of the ambitious master plan for the Barcelona of the third millennium was the reclamation of the waterfront. Dark, deserted and dangerous after nightfall, it had been all but abandoned by law-abiding Barcelonans. One of the worst sections was along the Passeig de Colom, NE of the Columbus monument, a stretch of deteriorating wharves and not much else. This recent project (a.k.a. **Moll Bosch i Alsina**) markedly altered that situation, and helped solve a couple of other problems, as well. An underground roadway was built, which helps carry heavy traffic past the city center. Also, large parking garages were installed below the surface, and roofed over to create a long promenade, with a row of restaurants and sidewalk cafés. That wasn't all, for a wide terrace was extended out into the harbor, with space for a grove of mature palms, two yacht clubs, and mooring for tall-masted ships making courtesy calls.

MONTJUÏC ★
Map 3F3. Overlooking harbor S of city center ◁€
Access: Funicular de Montjuïc and Telesferic (cable car).
The hill seen in gray silhouette to the SW of the harbor is Montjuïc. At its summit is a **castle**, which contains the MUSEU MILITAR and affords good views of sea, port and mountains. The fortress dates from 1640, when Catalunya allied itself with France against Felipe IV. It was captured by the British 65yrs later during the War of the Spanish Succession, and served as a prison during and after the Civil War of 1936-39. Broad streets lead down to a **public garden** (*open 10am-9pm*) and an **amusement park** (⛁ *variable opening hours, but usually July-Aug noon-9.30pm, closed late Sept-June*), which has a modest number of rides and snack booths. Slightly lower on the hill is the stadium originally built for an Olympics the Spanish hoped to be awarded in the 1930s, now refurbished and expanded for the 1992 Olympics. While the stadium dominates the Olympics complex, the nearby **Palau d'Esports Sant Jordi** is arresting, an apparent homage to Gaudí by the Japanese architect Isozaki.

There is also a wealth of museums, which occupy the middle district of the northerly slope, including the FUNDACIÓ JOAN MIRÓ, the MUSEU D'ARTE DE CATALUNYA, the MUSEU ARQUEOLÒGIC and the MUSEU ETNOLÒGIC, which displays objects from the colonies of the Spanish Empire. Nearby is the POBLE ESPANYOL and a **Greek theater**, built in 1929 and the scene of summer productions.

MONUMENT A COLOM *(Columbus Monument)*
Passeig de Colom s/n (foot of Les Rambles)
☎ *302-5224. Map 5F2* ⛁ ◁€ *Open June 24-Sept 24 Tues-Sat 9am-9pm; Sept 25-June 23 Tues-Sat 10am-2pm, 3.30-5.30pm. Closed Sun; Mon from Sept 25-June 23.*
One of the most recognizable Barcelona landmarks is this 1890 monument to Christopher Columbus. Atop the 52m (171ft) column is a statue of the explorer, his arm pointing off somewhat vaguely to the S. The design is late Victorian Neoclassical, hardly a shining moment in the history of the arts, but there is an elevator to the observation deck near the top for views of the port area. Moored in the water nearby (when it is not off on promotional cruises) is a replica of the ***Santa María***, and the MUSEU MARITÍM on the western side of the traffic circle in which the monument stands.

MUSEU ARQUEOLÒGIC
Plaça Santa Madrona s/n (Montjuïc) ☎ *423-2149. Map 3E2* ⛁ *(☒ on Sun). Open Tues-Sat 9.30am-1pm, 4-7pm; Sun 9.30am-2pm. Closed Mon; holiday afternoons. Access: Funicular de Montjuïc.*
Prehistoric cultures encountered in the Islas Baleares and on the mainland are represented by fragments of the Stone and Bronze Ages. Recently renovated, the museum takes its mission seriously, starting with animal fossils and skulls of Paleolithic man, then narrowing to bones and artifacts of prehistoric Catalunya — arrowheads, pottery and jewelry as fascinating for the obscurity of their origins as for their intrinsic artistic value.

Continuing through the Neolithic and Megalithic ages, there are displays of interment methods, in which skeletons are shown crouching, prone, and curled in urns, with pots of food beside them. They are supplemented by mosaics, bronzes, sculptures and other stone carvings of the Greek, Iberian, Carthaginian and Roman epochs. It would help if there were brochures available in several languages, as there are in other museums, or even if the sketchy labeling were at least in Spanish, not just Catalan.

MUSEU D'ARTE DE CATALUNYA
Palau Nacional (Montjuïc) ☎ *423-1824. Map 3E2. Metro: Espanya.*

Little is understated about the so-called **Palau Nacional de Montjuïc**, built in ponderous imitation Renaissance-Baroque for the 1929 Exposition, which announces itself from the plaza below by the spectacle of its great dome, ornate flanking towers and pillared and arched facade, as well as the sound of tiered fountains and waterfalls. Intended as a temporary building to be dismantled after the Exposition, it was saved to house a collection of medieval paintings, frescoes, sculpture and woodcarvings, as well as canvases by Murillo, Velázquez, Zurbarán, Tintoretto and El Greco. For some time, it has been subject to a costly, controversial and much-delayed overhaul. Originally scheduled for reopening before the lighting of the Olympic torch, it will miss that event by at least a year. Even in 1993, call ahead to find out if it is accepting visitors.

MUSEU D'ARTE MODERN
Parc de la Ciutadella ☎ *319-5728 or 310-6308. Map 6C6* ▨ ✗ *(to reserve* ☎ *487-1861, 10-11am). Open Tues-Sat 9am-7.30pm; Sun, holidays 10am-3pm. Closed Mon. Metro: Arc d'Triomf.*

The name is misleading, for this "modern" art is largely 19thC and in the Romantic or Neoclassical style, although there are a Picasso or two and some more recent works, including paintings and sculptures by Catalan artists little known outside the region. On occasion, the entire facility is given over to special exhibitions, such as the important show that recently illustrated the *modernisme* movement and its effect on painting, sculpture, clothing, jewelry, furniture and interior design, as well as architecture. The permanent collection is marked for eventual transfer to the MUSEU D'ARTE DE CATALUNYA in the Palau Nacional on Montjuïc.

MUSEU DE CERA *(Wax Museum)*
Ptge. de la Banca 7 (Rambla Santa Monica) ☎ *317-2649. Map 5E2* ▨ *Open 11am-1.30pm, 4.30-7.30pm (Sat, Sun, holidays until 8pm). Metro: Drassanes.*

The wax museum, up an alley near the foot of the Rambles, is a strictly commercial enterprise with no pretense to scholarship. Still, it is one of the few museums of any sort open on Mon, and makes for a mildly entertaining stop on a tour of the port area. The tableaux within are as varied as a scene showing Picasso at work, Henry VIII condemning another wife, and Richard Burton and Elizabeth Taylor costumed for their roles as Anthony and Cleopatra.

MUSEU DE CERÀMICA
Diagonal 686 (Fernando Primo de Rivera) ☎ *205-1967*

🚾 *Open Tues-Sun 9am-2pm. Closed Mon. Metro: Palau Reial.*

Moved from its former home in the Palau Nacional de Montjuïc to this, the PALAU DE PEDRALBES, the fascinating and comprehensive collection is here shown to far better advantage. The several abundantly stocked galleries include Spanish ceramics from the 13thC onward, illustrating colors and decorative patterns that are still in use in the many Spanish regions that produce ceramics. They are instructive for both serious collectors and those visitors who might like to purchase a pitcher or vase executed in authentic styles. A few pieces on display are even older, reaching back to the 10thC and including a few Moorish pieces. The contemporary section presents 15 instantly recognizable plates and other pieces by Picasso and Joan Miró. Still newer objects are the kind of free-form wall reliefs and free-standing sculptures that differ from other nonobjective art only in the fact that they are made of fired clay.

At the least, a visit is an excuse to stroll around the lovely grounds of the former palace, which constitute the city's very attractive **Parc Palau Reial**. Plantings are carefully groomed, the reflecting pools cleared of debris, and luminous green birds swoop in and out of the palm trees. The palace is in the University district.

MUSEU DE LA CIÈNCIA
Teodor Roviralta 55 (W of Av. del Tibidabo) ☎ *212-6050* 🚾 *✗ ⬤ Open Tues-Sun 10am-8pm. Closed Mon. Metro: Tibidabo.*

A half-new, half-old building with a submarine in front, this science museum and its attached planetarium are apt to be of limited interest to visitors who speak neither Spanish nor Catalan. Those are the languages of the explanatory notes attached to the many "hands-on" exhibits, which include TV cameras, computers and microscopes. And unlike a zoo or art gallery, a knowledge of the explanatory language is all but essential to appreciation of this sort of museum. It also has a rather inconvenient location on Tibidabo, the hill that overlooks the city from the NW.

MUSEU ETNOLÒGIC
Plaça Santa Madrona s/n (Montjuïc) ☎ *424-6402. Map 3E2* 🚾 *✗ by appointment. Open Mon-Sat 9am-8.30pm; Sun, holidays 9am-2pm. Access: Funicular de Montjuïc.*

While hardly comprehensive in coverage, with collections relating primarily to Japan, the Philippines and New Guinea, what is on view is certainly worth seeing. Most impressive are the 1st-floor exhibits of Japanese ceramics, basketry, tools, kimonos, dolls, masks, fans, prints and musical instruments. Galleries are available on the same floor for temporary exhibitions, such as the recent showing of textiles and ceremonial implements from Guatemala. The 2nd floor is given to a wealth of objects and materials from New Guinea, among them ceramic vessels, body ornaments, weaponry and wooden masks.

MUSEU FREDERIC MARÈS
Carrer dels Comtes de Barcelona 10 (Comtes Frenerta Dagueria) ☎ *310-5800. Map 5C3* 🚾 *Open Tues-Sat 9am-2pm, 4-7pm; Sun, holidays 9am-2pm. Closed Mon. Metro: Jaume I.*

Sculptor and collector Marès gave his extensive collection of medieval sculpture to the city, which housed it in this ancient palace. On display are bronzes depicting warriors and mythical creatures, and cases of terra cotta sculptures of the era, along with Iberian coins, Arab oil lamps and Greek ceramics. In the basement are tombs and architectural fragments, dominated by complete Romanesque portals. There is a numbing profusion of religious sculptures and woodcarvings from the Middle Ages, lightened by a charming jumble of ordinary objects from the past: dressing gowns, toiletries, jewelry, dolls, matchboxes, women's clothes and accessories. Inside the outer door is a courtyard (🖼) with a semicircle of orange trees around a small fountain.

MUSEU D'HISTÒRIA DE LA CIUTAT

Plaça del Rei s/n (Comtes Frenerta Dagueria)
☎ *315-1111. Map 5C3* 🖼 *𝑋 by appointment (☎ 315-3053).*
Open Tues-Sat 9am-8pm; Sun, holidays 9am-1.30pm.
Closed Mon. Metro: Jaume I.

An unexpectedly extensive repository of art and artifacts concerned with the abundant heritage of Barcelona is found in the 16thC **Clariana-Pedellás mansion** in the Barri Gòtic. In the basement are chambers enclosing the excavated remains of a **Roman settlement**, complete with amphorae and a necropolis. The ruins were discovered when the foundation was being dug to accept the mansion above, which was moved here from the Carrer de Mercaders.

The upper three floors are crowded with fragments of monumental sculpture, household utensils, weaponry, ceramics, mosaics and paintings. Much of the array is religious in inspiration, but of many creeds: Iberian, Phoenician, Greek, pagan and Christian Roman, Islam and Judaism. Charts and drawings show the evolution of the city, and there is access to the adjacent 14thC chapel of **Santa Àgata** from the 1st floor.

MUSEU MARÍTIM

Portal de la Pau 1 (Av. de les Drassanes) ☎ *318-3245 or 301-6425. Map 5F2* 🖼 *𝑋 by appointment. Open Tues-Sat 10am-2pm, 4-7pm; Sun, holidays 10am-2pm. Closed Mon. Metro: Drassanes.*

What an enchanting surprise is this under-visited repository of the nautical past, even for devout landlubbers. Situated at the harbor's edge near the MONUMENT A COLOM, the 14thC royal boatyard has been converted to serve as a maritime museum. Beneath its Gothic stone-vaulted ceilings are both intricate models and actual examples of sailing and steam vessels of the seven centuries since the enclosed dockyard was erected.

Models range from those so small that they could fit in a whiskey bottle to meticulously rendered Spanish galleons 8ft high, complete with anchors, scores of cannon, and hanks of rope looped over rows of belaying pins. Of the several real boats, the most impressive is the sumptuously decorated **royal galley**, which is 60m (197ft) long and displaced 237 tonnes. There is much more too: navigation instruments, drawings, figureheads and maps, including one by Amerigo Vespucci, the explorer credited with discovering the North American continent.

MUSEU MILITAR

Parc de Montjuïc s/n ☎ *329-8613. Map 3F3* 🖼 *Open Tues-Sat 10am-2pm, 4-7pm; Sun, holidays 10am-7pm (Apr-Sept until 8pm). Closed Mon.*

Part of the fun is getting there, for the military museum is, logically, in the fortress at the summit of MONTJUÏC. Take the funicular at the w end of Nou de la Rambla halfway up the hill to the terminal, then transfer to the cable car, which swings over the fairground and stops next to the restaurant at the top. The entrance to the fortress is a few steps away. Deep within are models of Catalunyan castles, military uniforms, battlefield banners, and racks and cases of weapons.

MUSEU-MONESTIR DE PEDRALBES
Baixada del Monestir 9 (Av. de Pedralbes) ☎ *203-9282*
▨ *Museum open Tues-Sun 9.30am-2pm. Church open 10am-1pm, 5-7pm. Both closed Mon. Metro: Reina Elisenda.*
A pause from the always brisk pace of the city is often welcome, and there is no better place to take it than this large 14thC monastery. It dominates a cluster of equally aged buildings in a residential district at the western corner of the city, in an enclave representative of similar settlements all over northern Spain. Stop first in the plain, stolid, early Gothic church, with its jewel-like stained-glass windows. The organ is often played at noon. Entrance to the monastery proper is up the flight of stairs passed on the way to the church. It has an especially impressive 3-tiered cloister with a garden shaded by palms, hemlocks and small orange trees. Architectural details show that the building straddled the Romanesque and Gothic eras. Doors in the outer walls provide glimpses of rooms devoted to various enterprises: the cell of a monk herbalist, a wine cellar, storage areas with large, half-buried amphorae, an infirmary, a room filled with antique pottery, an old kitchen, and another, newer one, which seems to have been in recent use, in view of the gas stove and refrigerator next to the worn stone sinks.

MUSEU DE LA MÚSICA
Diagonal 373 (Passeig de Gràcia) ☎ *217-1157. Map 4B4*
▨ 𝒳 *by appointment. Open Tues-Sun 9am-2pm. Closed Mon. Metro: Diagonal.*
Another fine *modernista* building, with an enormous amount of sculptural detail on the outside, which overshadows the collections inside. Visitors are directed to the top floor, to descend through the small galleries, always a sensible method of museum-going. Up there on the 3rd floor begin the cases of stringed instruments, some of unusual configuration, including a guitar with double fretted necks and another as big as a bass fiddle. On the 2nd floor, zithers and harps are followed by percussion and wind instruments. Spinets, pianos, organs, harpsichords and harps fill the rooms of the 1st floor, among the visual distractions of the architectural details, faintly Moorish here, vaguely Grecian there.

MUSEU PICASSO ▥
Montcada 15-19 (Princesa) ☎ *319-6310 or 315-4761. Map 6C4* ▨ 𝒳 *by appointment. Open Tues-Sun 10am-7.30pm. Closed Mon. Metro: Jaume I.*
Most of Barcelona's museums are in buildings of historical or architectural interest, none more appealing on either count than this. Housed in adjoining 15thC Gothic-Renaissance palaces, entry is through a courtyard open all the way to the roof, past an arcaded 1st floor with pointed arches surmounting slender columns. The present use is relatively recent, concentrating on Picasso's early years in Málaga and Barcelona (c.1889-1904). Most of the works on display are sketches, prints, drawings and rather

tentative paintings. There are none from his later career, but they are intriguing to scholars and to those persons unaware that the creator of three-eyed, two-headed women had a solid, traditional apprenticeship.

Across the street (*#12-14* 🕿 *open Tues-Sat 9am-2pm, 4.30-7pm, Sun 9am-2pm, closed Mon*), and also housed in a Renaissance mansion, is the **Museu Tèxtil i d'Indumentària** (textile museum).

PALAU DE LA MÚSICA CATALANA 🏛

Amadeu Vives 1 (Sant Pere Més Alt) 🕿 *268-1000. Map 5B3* 🕿 𝕏 *Open according to scheduled musical events. Tickets at Sant Francesc de Paula 2. Metro: Urquinaona.*

Lluís Domènech i Montaner was a leader of the *modernisme* movement, as daring and nearly as prolific as Gaudí. This is one of his most notable contributions, a concert hall for classical music and jazz, with acoustics as superb as its design is bizarre. The stepped stage is backed by a massive organ and flanked by giant granite sculptures. Throughout the hall and corridors are eye-popping combinations of glossy relief tiles, mirrors and stained glass, less gracefully married than in Gaudí's designs, but no less arresting. Guided tours are at 11.30am. Failing that, there is a bar just beyond the ticket booths, with access to the theater proper. Visitors who stray in that direction are unlikely to be challenged.

PALAU GÜELL 🏛

Nou de la Rambla 3-5 (Rambla Caputxins) 🕿 *317-3974. Map 5E2* 🕿 *Open Mon-Sat 11am-2pm, 5-8pm. Closed Sun; holidays. Metro: Liceu.*

A few steps w of the Rambles is yet another Gaudí commission, this one a mansion for his Parc Güell patron. The exterior is, by his standards, calmer and more orderly than his better-known projects. There is heavy use of decorative wrought iron on the facade above the uninvitingly gloomy entrance hall. Proceed immediately to the 2nd floor to see to best advantage his use of stained glass and carved wood. There is a splendid fireplace in the farthest room, and along the way a curious combination settee-mirror-sidetable-cabinet, said to be Gaudí's design.

The building houses, quite incidentally, the **Museu de les Arts de l'Espectacle**, a museum of show business. Photos and paintings of show folk of the late 19th and early 20thC Spanish theater hold slight interest, it can be assumed, even for most Spaniards.

PALAU REIAL DE PEDRALBES

Diagonal 686 (Fernando Primo de Rivera) 🕿 *203-7500* 🕿 *(but* 🔲 *for minors). Open Tues-Fri 10am-1pm, 4-6pm; Sat, Sun, holidays 10am-1.30pm. Closed Mon. Metro: Palau Reial.*

This royal residence was built between 1919 and 1929 especially for Alfonso XIII, grandfather of the present king. Italianate Neoclassicism might best describe its architecture. It now contains the MUSEU DE CERÀMICA, as well as a museum of decorative arts.

PALAU DE LA VIRREINA

Rambla de Sant Josep 99 (Carme) 🕿 *302-1430. Map 5C2. Open Mon-Sat 9.30am-2pm, 6-9pm. Closed Sun; holidays. Metro: Liceu.*

The 18thC palace of a Peruvian vice-reine is now, after recent renovations, a center for exhibitions of a diverse nature.

PARC DE LA CIUTADELLA
Map 6C5-D6. Open Oct-Mar 8am-8pm; Apr-Sept 8am-9pm. Metro: Barceloneta, Arc d'Triomf or Jaume I.

Barcelona's major park was once the site of a fortress erected during the reign of Felipe V. It was dismantled in the 19thC, but a few buildings remain. Later, the 1888 Universal Exposition was set on the same grounds, which prompted some of the improvements that remain today.

A former palace now houses the MUSEU D'ARTE MODERN. At the western corner of the park is the **Museu de Zoologia** (🔉 *open Tues-Sun 9am-2pm, closed Mon*), and nearby is the **Museu de Geologia** (*closed in late 1990 for remodeling*). At the N corner is an extravagantly Neoclassical fountain called **La Cascada**, an early municipal commission completed by Antoni Gaudí in 1882. Angry griffins guard its moat and pool, which are backed by monumental staircases leading to a pavilion, at intervals providing pedestals for sculptures of mermaids and winged and rearing horses. Toward the SE end of the park is a **zoo** and adjoining **aquarium**. The park has a large population of cats, and, it must be said, some nodding drug addicts, sometimes seen openly injecting their poisons of choice.

PARC GÜELL ▥
Larrad s/n 🔲 Open May-Sept 8am-9pm; Oct-Nov 9am-7pm; Dec-Apr 9am-6pm. Metro: Lesseps.

Antoni Gaudí's sudden death beneath the wheels of a tram ended construction of this project, as well as the TEMPLE DE LA SAGRADA FAMILIA. It was to be not simply a park, but a housing complex that would inspire a fresh direction in urban planning. The entrance is guarded by roughly circular houses with free-form roof protuberances, and a faceted tower surmounted by a 4-sided star-cross. Beyond the gate, a double staircase rises to a covered pavilion. Fluted columns in front and angled pillars along side corridors suggest troglodyte influences. The scalloped roof is edged with an undulating bench coated with a crazy-quilt mosaic of broken tiles and glass.

One of the two houses on the property is the **Casa-Museu Gaudí** (🔉 *open Mar-Nov 10am-2pm, 4-7pm*), owned by the architect from 1905-26. It contains drawings, models of some of his projects, furniture and other memorabilia.

LA PEDRERA ▥
Passeig de Gràcia 92 ☎ 215-3398. Map 4C4 🔲 𝒦 Mon-Fri at 10am, 11am, noon, 1pm, 4pm, 5pm, 6pm; Sat at 10am, 11am, noon, 1pm; Sun at 11am, noon, 1pm. Metro: Diagonal.

Known also as **Casa Milá**, the apartment house created by Antoni Gaudí curls around the NE intersection of Passeig de Gràcia and Carrer Mallorca. A biomorphic skin of sculpted limestone undulates over the 3-sided facade, with soft-edged rectangular openings for windows and balconies.

You can enter the building and wander through, but the guided tours provide access to off-limits areas. Individuals need only show up at the hours listed above; groups of ten or more must make advance reservations. Down three streets on the other side of the *passeig* is the similar but somewhat less flamboyant **Casa Battló**, by the same architect (see illustration on page 16).

57

POBLE ESPANYOL *(Pueblo Español)*
Marquès de Comillas s/n ☎ 325-7866. Map *3E1* 🔳 🅿 ✳
Open 9am-1am. Metro: Paral-lel or Espanya, then a funicular ride or uphill walk.

This "Spanish Village," left behind from the 1929 Exposition, is an amalgamation of native architectural styles, full-size replicas of domestic and municipal buildings from every region of the country. Most are modeled on actual structures. A stroll through the simulated streets and *plaças* of the complex emphasizes the remarkable diversity of Spanish architecture. Noticeable deterioration had set in some years ago, but recent renovations have upgraded the complex substantially. Craftspeople, including glassblowers and woodcarvers, are still seen at work, and most of the gift- and craft-stores are reasonably tasteful. (Expect no bargains, but there are goods of decent-to-high quality.) Shops observe conventional hours, as do the increased number of eating places (14) and snack bars/taverns (15), the reasons the Village remains open past midnight. One restaurant, **Los Corales** (☎ 325-6895 ▦), even offers flamenco shows with dinner.

EL QUADRAT D'OR *(The Golden Square)*
Map *3C4-4C5.*

This "Square of Gold" refers to the wealth of *modernisme* buildings found in the central **Eixample** district. Well over 100 structures designed by Gaudí and his fellows are found within the area bounded by Carrer Aribau, Avinguda Diagonal, Passeig de Sant Joan and Gran Via de les Corts Catalanes. Silver and purple banners are hung in front of buildings designated as good examples of the *modernista* impulse, in considerable number along Rambla de Catalunya, one of the city's most agreeable promenades. For a cluster of structures by the leading architects of the movement, seek out the block of Passeig de Gràcia between Carrer del Consell de Cent and Carrer Aragó. At the corner of Consell de Cent and Gràcia (*#35*) is the refurbished **Casa Lleó Morera**, the work of Lluís Domènech i Montaner, completed in 1906. Its fanciful tiled cupola and corner spires catch the eye, as do the richly detailed balconies rising above the trees of the Passeig. On the 1st floor are the offices of the **Patronat de Turisme**, or Barcelona Tourist Board, who can be visited by prior arrangement (*i* ☎ 215-4477). It's worth the effort to view the abundance of stained glass, mosaic panels and sculptural door frames he had installed.

A few steps up the Passeig is the **Casa Amatller**, by another *moderniste* luminary, Josep Puig i Cadafalch. As fetching as it certainly is, it must languish in the shadow of the blazing light of its neighbor, **Casa Battló**. That sparkling edifice, its facade encrusted with multicolored bits of glass and mosaic beneath a molten stone roofline, is one of Antoni Gaudí's commissions.

LES RAMBLES *(Las Ramblas)*
Map *5B2-E2.*

Tawdry, charming, clangorous, venal, colorful, Les Rambles is at the thumping heart of Barcelona. A broad, tree-canopied promenade with a one-way street on either side lined with 5- to 9-story 19thC buildings, it runs NW from the MONUMENT A COLOM by the port to the SE corner of the **Plaça de Catalunya**, a distance of approximately 2km (just over one mile). It is in fact a single street, although each of its several sections has a different name: "Rambla Santa Monica," "Rambla Caputxins," "Rambla de San Josep," "Rambla dels Estudis," and, at the top end, "Rambla

Canaletes." It separates the BARRI GÒTIC and its medieval monuments on the E from the **Barri Xinés** (Chinese Quarter) on the W. The latter is an impoverished neighborhood of fly-specked bars and no-star doss houses, notable primarily for its utter absence of persons and things Chinese. (It isn't advisable to wander in this area alone after nightfall, especially more than two or three streets W of the Rambles.)

Along the entire route are all-night book- and magazine-stands, sidewalk cafés, pet- and flower-stalls, and several hotels. It teems with people at all hours: four-generation families, carousing sailors on leave, leather punks in dated cockatoo hairdos, beggars, hustlers, transvestites, soapbox orators, street musicians, pimps, and watchful policemen — an unending pageant of the outrageous and the outraged. Many Barcelonans insist they never go to the Rambles, which leaves unanswered the question of why there are always so many Spaniards there. The best time to see it all is early evening, although on warm nights the street is still lively at 4am.

SANTA MARÍA   See MONUMENT A COLOM.

TEMPLE DE LA SAGRADA FAMÍLIA 🏛 ★
Plaça de la Sagrada Família (Marina). Map 4B5 🔤
Open July-Aug 9am-9pm; Apr-June 9am-8pm; Sept-Mar 9am-7pm. Metro: Sagrada Família.
Although the unfinished church is widely regarded as Antoni Gaudí's masterpiece, or, conversely, as a travesty in stone, it was originally another architect's commission. Francisco del Villar started it in 1882, when Gaudí was still working in a relatively sedate Neoclassical style. He assisted Villar at first and then took control in 1891. The crypt was partially finished, but little else.

Gaudí's evolving style was extraordinary for the time, and is hardly less startling now. His scheme was to erect three main facades, each with four towers, the total representing the Apostles. A dome above the transept crossing was to have four more spires, larger still, a bristling profile piercing the sky. Only the E face was completed, but it is enough to create a picture of what the whole might have been. Peaked canopies above the three doors are carved to suggest molten stone or stalactites, until the eye picks out the groups of sculpted figures illustrating scenes celebrating the Nativity. At the same level, open piers support the perforated towers narrowing at their tips into colorful tile pinnacles ending in vivid starbursts.

Work continues on its completion. The current controversy lies not with Gaudí's scheme, but whether or not it should be left as it was at his death, since he carried the details of his concept with him. At the present pace, the cathedral is unlikely to be finished before the middle of the 21stC.

TIBIDABO
🔤 《 ☰ 🍴 *Open 7.30am-9.30pm. Metro: Av. Tibidabo.*
On evening walks around the city, you will notice the illuminated church on top of the precipitous hills that rear up to the N and W. To get up there, which is half the fun, take the metro to the end of the line at Avinguda Tibidabo. At the exit, the bedraggled but exuberant *modernista* building called **La Rotunda** rivets the eye. Next to it, a relic as charming as San Francisco's cable cars, the *tramvía blau* (blue tram) makes the first half of the ascent of Tibidabo (🔤 *7am-9.30pm*). (Road construction disrupted service in the years preceding the Olympics, but the tram was

expected to return by then. If not, a bus is substituted.) It creaks up the steep hill past ranks of curious mansions that belonged to the turn-of-the-century rich. Many are now schools and institutes of one kind or another, but they remain bizarre compilations of every architectural style from the Moors to Gaudí, each higher one surpassing the ones below. This trip connects with the **funicular (🔲 open 7.45am-9.45pm)** for the final leg.

It is alleged that the island of Mallorca can be seen from the top, but if true, this can only be verified on exceptionally clear days, rare in Barcelona. Nevertheless, the city sprawls to the sea in a panorama best viewed at dusk. The belvederes are surrounded by a clean, compact, 3-tiered and amusingly dated **fairground (🔲 ✳ usually open Sat-Sun 11am-8pm Jan-Mar and Oct-Dec, daily 11am-8pm Apr-Sept, but with seasonal variations, so 🕿 211-2111 before making the trip).** On the premises is the **Museu d'Autòmats (🕿 211-7942, same hrs as the amusement park)**, containing briefly diverting displays of robots and other miscellany. Behind the fairground is a crudely realized church, where a boy's choir sings daily (6pm). Above the small church is the granite basilica, which can be seen, illuminated, from the city center.

ZOO DE BARCELONA
Parc de la Ciutadella 🕿 309-2500. Map 6D6 🔲 ▣ ✳
Open winter 10am-5pm; summer 9.30am-7.30pm. Metro: Barceloneta.

This zoo hardly compares with the far superior zoos of Berlin, New York or San Diego. Still, it isn't without appeal, especially to parents with children to distract and inform. Near the main gate, in fact, is the **zoo infantil**, with snack bar, toilets, playground and children's mini-zoo, all in one place. It has animals for petting, a cage of birds to enter, rope swings and slides, and a row of 14 different kinds of decidedly cuddly rabbits. Moats are used instead of bars whenever possible. Star of the collection is **Snowflake**, a rare, and possibly unique, albino gorilla. Reptiles have their own temperature-ontrolled home, and there is a large **aviary** and an **aquarium**, with a central pool in which dolphins and a killer whale cavort for appreciative audiences.

Where to stay in Barcelona

Barcelona has always had fewer hotels than diversions. When the **Ritz** opened in 1919, it was the first and only true luxury hotel in the city — and still is. There are only seven other hotels that boast the government's highest rating of five stars, and while two or three of them equal or surpass the Ritz in number of facilities, none of them can match the master for grace, panache and seamless operation. That said, there are 30 hotels in the 4-star category, most of them entirely adequate for all but the most demanding travelers: there are representative examples in our selection. The difficulty is in finding satisfactory but economical accommodations, for there are huge differences in quality at the 3-star level and below. We include a few happy exceptions in this category.

Plans for at least a dozen new hotels were announced in the wake of the award of the 1992 Olympics to Barcelona. Most are now in operation, while two or three are delayed or under construction. Unfortunately, they make barely a dent in the still attenuated housing picture. The largest of them, the **Hilton**, has only 290 rooms, and most of the rest are targeted at that segment of the market which is willing to pay dearly for quiet elegance. If every last bed in every last hotel is counted, Barcelona can provide for a total of slightly more than 29,000 visitors at a time. Yet the city welcomes millions every year, and expected *more than 600,000* for the Olympics alone.

Take seriously, then, the admonition to make reservations far in advance, or steel yourself for the likelihood that the only available beds will be in no-star horrors out of a Bogart *film noir*. Most of the hotels described here have telex and fax numbers, which are the best ways to arrange reservations and obtain written confirmations. (The postal service is tortuously slow.) While it is possible to blunder into a decent hotel at the last minute, persons who have matured past the backpacking stage are unlikely to regard the quest as merely another adventure. The tourist offices at the airport and railroad station might be of assistance to last-minute arrivals without reservations.

Most of the larger contemporary hotels, including the new **Hilton**, the **Princess Sofía**, the **Sarrià** and the **Presidente**, are strung along the middle and upper reaches of the Diagonal. They are most attractive to people in town on business, for many office buildings and corporate headquarters are located in the same neighborhood, and some of the top restaurants and clubs are in the vicinity, too. Smaller quality hotels are found primarily in the midtown Eixample district, several of them, such as the **Regente** and **Condes de Barcelona**, in captivating *modernista* mansions. Most of the hotels in the Barri Gòtic and along the Rambles are recommendable only to strict budgeteers, as they are often seedy and on streets that can be unsafe at night. Exceptions to this rule are the revamped **Colón**, opposite the cathedral, and the luxury-class **Ramada Renaissance**.

In the following selection, addresses, telephone, telex and fax numbers and nearest metro stations are given, and symbols showing which hotels are particularly luxurious (🏨) and which represent good value (♣). Other symbols show price categories and charge/credit cards, and give a résumé of the available facilities. See the KEY TO SYMBOLS on page 5 for the full list of symbols. Following each street address, in parentheses, is the nearest cross street or prominent landmark to the described site.

☎ The **telephone prefix (area code)** for Barcelona is **93**.

Hotels classified by price

Very expensive (▦▦▦▦): Avenida Palace, Barcelona Hilton, Gran Derby, Havana Palace, Meliá Barcelona Sarrià, Presidente, Ramada Renaissance, Ritz 🏨
Expensive to very expensive (▦▦▦ to ▦▦▦▦): Alexandra, Colón, Derby, Diplomatic, Grand Passage Suites Majestic 🏨
Expensive (▦▦▦): Calderón, Condes de Barcelona, Duques de Bergara, Princesa Sofía 🏨
Moderately priced to expensive (▦▦ to ▦▦▦): Regente, St Moritz
Moderately priced (▦▦): Gravina, Reding
Inexpensive to moderately priced (▦ to ▦▦): Regencia Colón
Inexpensive (▦): Mesón Castilla

ALEXANDRA
Mallorca 251 (Rambla de Catalunya), 08008 Barcelona
☎ 487-0505 ● 81107 ℻ 216-0606.
Map 3C3 ▦▦▦ to ▦▦▦ 75 rms 🔲 75
▦ ⚏ AE ⊙ ◯ ▦ Metro:
Diagonal.

Location: In Eixample, one street w of Passeig de Gràcia. A large glass front provides a wide-angle look at the carefully designed interior of this starkly contemporary entry, opened in 1987. The rooms in front have double-glazed windows, while

61

those in back are even quieter. Among the amenities are bedside controls of lights and TV and closed-circuit movies in English, French and German. Over 25 units have extra-large beds, no irrelevancy in a country where 6-footers are too often expected to sleep on little beds reminiscent of kiddie camp.

🖼️ ✳ □ 🖼️ 🐾 ➡

AVENIDA PALACE
Gran Via 605 (Passeig de Gràcia), 08007 Barcelona
☎ 301-9600 ⓢ 54734 ⓕ 318-1234.
Map 4C4 ⦀⦀⦀ 229 rms 🖂 229 🍽
�︎ AE ⦁ ⦁ VISA Metro: Gran Via.
Location: Just w of the Passeig de Gràcia. The Avenida Palace doesn't qualify for *grande dame* status on the basis of age (it opened only in 1952), but it is nearly as dignified as the **Ritz**, if not as luxurious. Beneath its mock towers, from which pennants fly, is a crisply run yet gracious hotel with carefully trained and attentive staff. Bedrooms are adequate in size and comfort. The location is ideal, equidistant from nearly everything the city offers. That includes restaurants, which is fortunate, since the dining room does little to elevate the image of hotel food.

✳ □ 🖼️ Y ➡

BARCELONA HILTON
Av. Diagonal 589-595 (Numància), 08014 Barcelona
☎ 419-2233 ⓢ 99623 ⓕ 322-5291
⦀⦀⦀ 290 rms 🖂 290 🍽 🚭 🖃 AE
⦁ ⦁ VISA Metro: Maria Cristina.
Location: Near the NW business and university district. One of a dozen hotels initiated under the stimulus of the approaching Olympics, the Hilton challenges the nearby **Princesa Sofía** for the international business trade. While not exactly a contribution to the art of architecture, the skin of the minimalist high-rise is restrained gray marble and no disgrace to the breed. The sleek, functional interior lacks personality but not comforts. One special feature, in this nation of tobacco addicts, is the availability of nonsmoking rooms. Otherwise, expect the expectable of this representative of the famous chain (which is not the same organization, by the way, that runs the hotels of the same name in the US).

✳ □ 🖼️ 🐾 Y ➡

CALDERÓN
Rambla de Catalunya 26 (Diputació), 08007 Barcelona
62

☎ 301-0000 ⓢ 99529 or 51549 ⓕ 317-3157. Map 4C4 ⦀⦀⦀ 263 rms 🖂 263 🍽 🖃 AE ⦁ VISA Metro: Passeig de Gràcia.
Location: On one of the city's prettiest streets, one street N of Gran Via. The ill-conceived "modern" facade is disconcerting, as are the often glum gents behind the service desks, but there are ample compensations. Among these are the rooftop outdoor pool and solarium, which tender splendid vistas of the city. Recent renewal incorporated a small but well-equipped fitness center to complement the *indoor* pool, two squash courts and sauna. Most guest rooms are generously proportioned and equipped with the gadgets frequent travelers have come to expect: remote control TV with satellite reception, direct-dial telephones and hairdryers.

🌊 ⛵ ♥ ✳ □ 🖼️ 🐾 Y ➡

COLÓN ♣
Av. de la Catedral 7 (Via Laietana), 08002 Barcelona
☎ 301-1404 ⓢ 52654 ⓕ 317-2915.
Map 5C3 ⦀⦀⦀ to ⦀⦀⦀ 162 rms
🖂 161 🍽 🚭 🖃 ⦁ ⦁
VISA Metro: Jaume I.
Location: In the heart of the Gothic Quarter. For those who expect to spend most of their time in the Rambles-Barri Gòtic district, there isn't a better choice. The balconied front rooms (the ones on the 6th floor have large terraces) face the 13thC CATEDRAL and overlook the endless activity that eddies around it. Public rooms, including the woody bar, are generously appointed, and the bedrooms are comfortable. During long-term top-to-bottom renovations, several rooms on each floor were reconfigured into suites. Recent painting has brightened the once gloomy single rooms at the back, but they are still cramped and viewless.

Behind the Colón is the more modest **Regencia Colón** (*Sagristans 13-17* ☎ 318-9858 ⦀ to ⦀⦀⦀), separately managed, but under the same ownership. It represents relatively minor sacrifices for substantially lower tariffs.

《 ✳ □ 🖼️ Y ➡

CONDES DE BARCELONA
Passeig de Gràcia 75 (Mallorca), 08008 Barcelona ☎ 487-3737
ⓢ 51531 ⓕ 216-0835. Map 4C4 ⦀⦀⦀
100 rms 🖂 100 🍽 🚭 🖃 AE ⦁
⦁ VISA Metro: Passeig de Gràcia.
Location: In Eixample, on the city's

grandest boulevard. This welcome
addition to a hotel-poor city
retained its handsome old exterior
but swept the inside into the rabidly
Post-Modernist 1990s. Some details
of the building that was have been
retained — carved granite and
wrought-iron balustrades, faintly
Moorish archways — enhanced by
massive marble pillars and an
onyx-topped cocktail bar. Most of
the people at the front desk are
helpful young multilingual women,
a pleasant change from the dour
males who more often deal with
guests. Rooms are commodious,
spare, with tiny balconies hanging
above the boulevard, which, for
some, means a view of Gaudí's LA
PEDRERA. There is no better option in
this price band.

♦ ☐ ⌂ 🎾 ❤ ➡

DERBY

*Loreto 21-25 (Av. de Sarrià),
08029 Barcelona* ☎ 322-3215
⊙ 97429 ⊛ 410-0862. Map **3C2** ▮▮▮▮
to ▮▮▮▮ 116 rms ▭ 116 ▦ ➡ ➡
➡ ⏤ ⏷ ⏻ ⏸ *Metro: Hospital
Clinic.*
*Location: Near Plaça Francesc
Macià, in the NW.* Pronounce the
name with either inflection — horse
race or hat — the intent remains
clear. The Anglophilic Derby strives
to emulate a Mayfair club, and the
result is a surprisingly successful
evocation of that ambience. Wood
trim and ornamentation are polished
to a satin finish, fingerprints wiped
off as they appear. Lighting is
diffused, colors are hushed. They
call their coffee shop **The Times**
and, in the **Scotch Bar**, a capable
duo whisks up any cocktail one
might care to drink. Guinness is on
tap in the simulated pub. Two
rooms on each floor have large
beds, by no means the Spanish
norm, and those on the top floor
have terraces. Across the street is the
newer and more expensive **Gran
Derby** (*Loreto 28* ☎ 322-2062 ▮▮▮▮).
All of its accommodations are suites,
many of them duplexes. Note that
the nearest metro station is a long
six blocks away.

▣ ♦ ☐ ⌂ ❤ ➡

DIPLOMATIC

*Pau Claris 122 (Consell de Cent),
08009 Barcelona* ☎ 317-3100
⊙ 54701 ⊛ 318-6531. Map **4C4** ▮▮▮▮
to ▮▮▮▮ 217 rms ▭ 217 ▦ ➡ ➡
⏤ ⏷ ⏻ ⏸ *Metro: Passeig de
Gràcia.*
*Location: One street E of Passeig de
Gràcia.* Glassy, brassy, mirrored and
marbled, the Diplomatic's lobby

obviously sees no virtue in
understatement. It contains a bar
(one of four) and the **La Salsa**
restaurant, and, on the periphery, a
car rental office and snack bar-
pizzeria. Up on the flag-lined roof is
a fair-sized pool; down below is a
spangled disco. Streetside rooms
have double-glazed windows to
muffle traffic noise.

≈ ♦ ☐ ⌂ 🎾 ❤ ➡ ⦿

DUQUES DE BERGARA

*Bergara 11 (Plaça de Catalunya),
08002 Barcelona* ☎ 301-5151
⊙ 97429 ⊛ 317-3442. Map **5B2** ▮▮▮▮
68 rms ▭ 68 ▦ ➡ ➡ ⏤ ⏷ ⏸
Metro: Catalunya.
*Location: A few steps from Plaça de
Catalunya.* An island of calm on a
noisy street with a movie theater, a
video club, a restaurant and a bingo
parlor, the designers made the most
of this late 19thC *modernista*
mansion. The lobby is most
impressive, with its white marble
staircase and coffered brass ceiling
with stained-glass skylight.
Furnishings are a careful blending of
traditional and contemporary styles.

♦ ☐ ⌂ 🎾 ❤

GRAN DERBY See **DERBY**.

GRAND PASSAGE SUITES

*Muntaner 212 (Paris), 08036
Barcelona* ☎ 201-0306
⊛ 201-0004. Map **3C3** ▮▮▮▮ ➡ ➡
⏤ ⏷ ⏻ ⏸ *Metro: Hospital
Clinic.*
*Location: In the heart of the
Eixample.* For the price of a
standard double room in other 4-star
hotels, you can have a suite here
with bedroom, living room and
bath. That might be reason enough
to choose a place too new for
extended evaluation of service and
other intangibles, especially since
appearances suggest that it
measures up to its older rivals on
those counts.

➡ ♦ ☐ ⌂ ❤

GRAVINA ✿

*Gravina 12 (Pelai), 08001
Barcelona* ☎ 301-6868 ⊙ 99370
⊛ 317-2838. Map **4D4** ▮▮▮ 60 rms
▭ 60 ➡ ⏤ ⏷ ⏸ *Metro:
Universitat.*
*Location: Between Plaça de
Catalunya and the downtown
University.* While officially awarded
three stars, this hotel equals many
with four stars and significantly
higher prices. The aging structure
was cleared to the walls and redone
in crisp, uncluttered modernity.
Rooms are compact, not

63

claustrophobic, and outfitted with
the usual gadgets. There isn't a
better deal for the money. Directly
across the street is the very similar,
and even newer, **Reding** (☎ 412-
1097 ▮▮).

☷ ❏ ❐ ✿ ☂ ▤

HAVANA PALACE

*Gran Via C.C. (Bruc), 08008
Barcelona* ☎ 215-7931 ☻ 51531
☻ 216-0835. *Map 4C4* ▮▮▮▮ *149 rms*
▭ 60 ☰ ➾ ☲ ▣ ⓪ ⓪ VISA
Metro: Urquinaona.

*Location: Three streets N of Passeig
de Gràcia.* With a grander design
and more costly materials, the
owners of the **Condes de
Barcelona** have here made
themselves a hostelry to match just
about any in the city. The 19thC
corner facade was retained, the
interior scooped out and totally
rebuilt. A roof-high, kidney-shaped
atrium is the lobby, which focuses
on the cocktail lounge, transformed
into a piano bar at night. Baths are
of green marble, with stainless-steel
sinks, and all gadgets and comforts,
including terry robes, are at hand.
Many of the young people at the
front desk and in the bar and
restaurant earned their stripes at the
other hotel.

▣ ☷ ❏ ❐ ✿ ☂ ▤

MAJESTIC ☖

*Passeig de Gràcia 70 (Valencia),
08008 Barcelona* ☎ 215-4512
☻ 52211 ☻ 215-7773. *Map 4C4* ▮▮▮▮
to ▮▮▮▮ *336 rms* ▭ 336 ☰ ➾ ▣
☲ ☲ ▣ ⓪ ⓪ VISA *Metro: Passeig
de Gràcia.*

*Location: In the city center, N of
Plaça de Catalunya.* Despite an air
of chilly formality, the Majestic is
nearly the ideal Barcelona hotel, a
fact reflected in its prices. It fronts
on the grand Passeig de Gràcia,
Barcelona's Champs-Élysées, and is
within walking distance of most
major sightseeing attractions and
many of the best shops. For those
afflicted with the international
fitness mania, there is a gymnasium,
sauna and rooftop pool. Bedrooms
have TV, radio, alarm clock, smoke
detectors, hair dryers and stocked
minibars.

▣ ☷ ✿ ☂ ☷ ❏ ❐ ☂

MELIÁ BARCELONA SARRIÀ

*Av. Sarrià 50 (Diagonal), 08029
Barcelona* ☎ 410-6060 ☻ 51033
or 51638 ☻ 321-5179. *Map 3B2*
▮▮▮▮ *311 rms* ▭ 311 ☰ ➾ ☲ ☲
⓪ ⓪ VISA *Metro: Hospital Clínic.*

*Location: Within walking distance
of the restaurants and clubs of the*

uptown Francesc Macià district.
This modern tower, less than two
decades old, recently received a
comprehensive overhaul of both
facilities and services. One widely
appreciated innovation is the lavish
weekend brunch, an American
invention given glorious realization
here. With several tables laden with
fruit, cheeses, smoked fishes, hot
dishes and candies, it would take a
family of four a month of Sundays to
sample it all. Guest rooms are large,
with furnishings and conveniences
that meet international standards.
The two premium floors, called the
Elite Club, offer fax and
photocopying machines, secretaries
and messengers, meeting rooms,
library, and free beverages and
canapés throughout the day. Even
regular room have the morning
newspaper slipped under the door,
the outside temperature written on
an attached tag. The new health
club may be the most fully
equipped in town, with many
exercise machines, racks of free
weights, and aerobics classes. It
stays open until midnight.

✿ ☞ ☷ ❏ ❐ ✿ ☂ ▤

MESÓN CASTILLA

*Valldonzella 5 (Plaça de
Castella), 08001 Barcelona*
☎ 318-2182 ☻ 412-4020. *Map 4E4*
▮▯ *60 rms* ▭ 56 ☰ ➾ ☲ ➾
VISA *Metro: Universitat.*

*Location: On a busy square near
the Rambles and Plaça de
Catalunya.* Finding satisfactory
lodgings in this economical price
range is a discomfiting experience.
Here's a safe, folksy choice that
gives fair value. Public rooms are
fairly large, decidedly old-fashioned,
and elaborately, if awkwardly,
decorated, with much knotty wood-
paneling and paintings of folk
scenes. Guest rooms have painted
bedsteads, firm mattresses, bare
floors, snug baths. TV sets are
available on request.

☷ ❐ ☂

PRESIDENTE

*Av. Diagonal 570 (Muntaner),
08021 Barcelona* ☎ 200-2111
☻ 52180 ☻ 209-5106. *Map 3C3* ▮▮▮▮
160 rms ▭ 160 ☰ ➾ ☲ ☲ ☲
VISA *Metro: Hospital Clínic.*

*Location: At the edge of the
fashionable Sarrià district.* A 4-story
slab of glass and steel sweeps
around this corner of the Diagonal
and over the wide entrance
staircase. Atop this section is a patio
with a pool, backed by two towers
of unequal height. All this was

thought quite stylishly contemporary a decade or so ago. Now it's starting to show its age, despite the presence of such symbols of luxe as the **Loewe** shop on the lobby floor and the pricey German cars purring at the front door. Rooms are fairly spacious, but somewhat uninspired in decor; those on upper floors have good views toward the harbor. Discount weekend rates are available.

≈ ‡ □ ⌂ % ⋎ ▭

PRINCESA SOFÍA 🏨

Plaça de Pius XII (Diagonal), 08028 Barcelona ☎ *330-7111* ⓣ *51683* ⓕ *330-7621* ⅢⅡ *to* ⅢⅡ *505 rms* ▭ *505* ▦ ⌂ ⇌ AE ◉ ◉ VISA *Metro: Palau Reial or María Cristina.*
Location: Near University City. Apart from its distance from the city center, the picture here is overwhelmingly positive, assuming gentility and charm are not on your list of requirements. This hotel is a veritable hospitality machine, scrupulously engineered to gratify the needs and whims of knowledgeable travelers. That's the reason it was selected as headquarters for the 1992 Olympics. Rooms are equipped with the usual electronic devices and, after recent renovations, with computer jacks and remote control satellite TV with 19 channels. The spare, Scandinavian furniture has been replaced by more traditional, British-style ensembles. Enlargement of the fitness center has made room for a well-equipped weights room, massage cubicles, whirlpool, sauna and an indoor/outdoor pool. Instructors are on duty from 7am-10pm and hold aerobics classes according to demand. Jet lag can also be smoothed out in the two bars, one of which has live music for dancing. The food issuing from the central kitchen has markedly improved, whether served in **El Snack 2002** or **Le Gourmet**. About 100 rooms were not included in the renovations, so ask for one of the 400 that have been upgraded.

🛥 《 ≈ ♈ ‡ □ ⌂ % ⋎ ♫ ⚓ ▭

RAMADA RENAISSANCE

Rambles 111 (Pintor Fortuny), 08002 Barcelona ☎ *318-6200* ⓣ *54634* ⓕ *301-7776. Map 5C2* ⅢⅡ *210 rms* ▭ *210* ▦ ⌂ ⇌ AE ◉ ◉ VISA *Metro: Catalunya.*
Location: Facing the Rambles, three streets from Plaça de Catalunya.

Graying former flower children might remember this as the sagging budget Hotel Manila, but those salad days are gone forever, with current prices second only to those of the **Ritz**. They are justified by the damn-the-expense renovation, which included such touches as heated bathroom floors, multichannel TV and radio, and extra-large beds. With advance notice, rooms can be equipped with a personal computer, a printer, a fax machine and/or a telephone with private number. Conceding that all is done with taste and thoughtfulness, the question remains of whether this funky location is appropriate for the high-powered executives the hotel is designed to attract.

‡ □ ⌂ ⋎ ▭

REGENCIA COLÓN   See
COLÓN.

REGENTE ♣

Rambla de Catalunya 76 (València), 08008 Barcelona ☎ *215-2570* ⓣ *51939* ⓕ *487-3227. Map 4C4* ⅢⅡ *to* ⅢⅡ *80 rms* ▭ *80* ▦ ⌂ ⇌ AE ◉ ◉ *Metro: Passeig de Gràcia.*
Location: Six streets n of the Plaça de Catalunya. The Regente has so much going for it, from its tiny rooftop pool and its quiet and convenient location, to its understated Art Nouveau fittings, that it is surprising how little attention it receives. The hotel began life, before the turn of the century, as an elegant private home, and was converted to its present use in 1964. Rooms are of at least adequate dimension, decorated in soft hues. There are thoughtful extra touches, such as trouser presses and radios. The street outside is a tree-lined, mostly calm, extension of the Rambles.

‡ □ ≈ ⋎

RITZ 🏨

Gran Vía 668 (Roger de Llúria), 08010 Barcelona ☎ *318-5200* ⓣ *52739* ⓕ *318-0148. Map 4C4* ⅢⅡ *161 rms* ▭ *161* ▦ ⌂ ⇌ AE ◉ ◉ VISA *Metro: Urquinaona.*
Location: Two streets n of Passeig de Gràcia. The Ritz was built (in 1919) to accommodate the well-born and well-heeled who toured Europe with steamer trunks and servants, and settled into a hotel for three months at a time. They demanded room to entertain and impress, and the Ritz provided it. Ceilings in both private and public rooms are

unusually high. Gold-leaf, damask, brocade and crystal have been used with a lavish hand. Even the skirting boards are marble. After some years of decline, ambitious renovation work was begun. Now, the Ritz is back, challenging its Madrid sibling in every adroitly realized detail. It gently lectures the chrome-and-glass upstarts on what a grand hotel should be. Service is unexcelled, with a waiter and two maids assigned to each floor every hour of the day. A button can be sewn on, or an iced magnum of *cava* uncorked, within minutes of a touch of a switch at the bedside. The restaurant **Diana** is among the best in Barcelona.

Despite all this, it is wise to check your room before accepting it, as some were designed for the family retainers of several decades ago, and are rather less grand than you might expect.

✥ ☐ ⬚ ⚓ ☒ ▣

ST MORITZ
Diputació 262 (Pau Claris), 08007 Barcelona ☎ *412-1500*
Ⓕ *412-1236. Map 4C4* ▯▯ *to* ▯▯▯▯ *92 rms* ▭*92* ▦ ▦ ⬚ *AE* Ⓜ *VISA*
Metro: Passeig de Gràcia.
Location: Only steps away from Passeig de Gràcia. One of Barcelona's youngest hotels — opened in Feb 1990 — the St Moritz bears the patina of graceful age. That's because the owners retained the Neoclassical facade and part of the lobby, while gutting and rebuilding the rest of the structure. The results are impressive, from the dignified, efficient reception to the coded plastic cards that are used to open doors and turn on electricity. Rooms are of average size, decorated in soothing tones. Some have beds for extra tall guests. There is no full-service restaurant, but breakfast is served next to the lounge at the back.

✥ ☐ ⚓ ☒ ▣

Where to eat in Barcelona

Cosmopolitan and sophisticated the Catalans undeniably are — a result of more than two millennia of trade and conquest. It is perhaps surprising, then, that they reveal little curiosity about cuisines other than their own. In part, that must be because the one they have is not only good, but virtually limitless in scope. Like the rest of their countrypeople, they eat just about anything that sprouts, swims, trots, flies, blooms or wriggles, and in thousands of permutations and combinations. However, unlike their counterparts in other regions of Spain, Catalan cooks frequently use herbs and spices and have a taste for tangier seasonings.

Emblematic are *romescu,* a sauce made of dried hot chili peppers, and *ali-oli,* a pungent garlic mayonnaise. Often a dab of the first is mixed into a cup of the second. Small bowls of either or both often accompany grilled or broiled fish, fowl, meat or game. Signature dishes are *zarzuela* and *bullabesa,* both magnificent seafood stews that mustn't be missed. The Catalan flair is also seen in rabbit cooked with snails, *xató* (a salad of endive, vinaigrette, almonds and hot peppers) and *botifarra amb mongetes* (sausage with white beans). *Crema catalana* is a Catalan version of the French *crème brulée,* a custard with a brittle caramel crust.

It is fortunate that the gastronomy of Catalunya is so variegated, for opportunities to sample alien dishes anywhere in the region are few, and largely unsatisfactory. Of almost anyone's list of the top 20 Barcelona restaurants, and very good they are, only one comes from over the seas or the Pyrenees to present avowedly foreign food. That is **Neichel**, the admirable creature of the eponymous chef-owner from Alsace, and even he must flesh out his menu with variations on Spanish favorites. So, while the selection provided below attempts to skip across the local scene from the traditional to *nueva cocina,* and from the rarefied to the economical, don't expect to find recommendations here for that cunning plate of curry, *enchiladas* or Szechuan *sam gap tee*. Only the occasional pizza or plate of ravioli will show up at most of these establishments.

Tapas **bars** (see page 38) aren't as ubiquitous as they are in Madrid, but neither can they be easily exhausted. Several of the restaurants mentioned here serve *tapas* at the bar inside the front door, a common arrangement. Two possibilities here are **Alt Heidelberg** (*Ronda Universitat 5*), which is German solely in that it serves sausages and beer, and **Gran Bodega** (*Valencia 193*), always full of happy nibblers and festooned with bottles and unrelated objects.

A distinguished example of the city's **tea shops** is **Casinet del Barri Gòtic** (*Freneria 6, behind the cathedral*), with a short menu that concentrates on pastries, ice cream and tasty light sandwiches. A further variation on how to pass the time between meals is represented by **Bon Vivant** (*Aribau 292*): point at items in the glass case and they'll make up a combination plate of the pâtés and cheeses of your choice and bring it to your sidewalk table.

For **fast-food**, the Spanish **Pokin's** chain, with several outlets around the city, competes with American interlopers. Along the **Moll de la Fusta** on the waterfront, several restaurants line up in similar quarters. The best bet is **Gamberinus**, at the E end. To distinguish it from the others, the owners commissioned a giant, smiling, semiabstract lobster to be placed above the roof. The artist was the same man who created the "Cobi" mascot for the Olympics.

No corner of the city center is more than a few paces from sustenance of some kind, and some streets positively bristle with choices. One of the most colorful and most ethnic (counter to the comments above) is **Carrer Santaló**. It runs uphill from Travessera de Gràcia, near the uptown Plaça de Francesc Macià, and every meal for a week could be eaten here without using the same restaurant twice. Among them are **El Pa Torrat** (*#68*), **Arcs de Sant Gervasi** (*#103*), **Casa Fernandez** (*#46*), the Italian **Bel Cavalletto** (*#125*), the Indian **Shahen Shah** (*no street number*), the Lebanese **Abou-Khalil** (*#88*) and the self-explanatory **Compañia General de Sandwiches** (*#153*), which offers 67 tasty versions of its stock-in-trade. None of these has an overarching reputation, but neither are they expensive. There are attractive bars and upscale shops along the route.

In the following selection, addresses, telephone and nearest metro stations are given, and symbols showing which restaurants are particularly luxurious (⌂) or simple (⌂). Other symbols show price categories, charge/credit cards and any other noteworthy points. See KEY TO SYMBOLS on page 5 for the full list of symbols. Times are specified when restaurants are **closed**.

Reservations rarely need be made more than a few hours in advance, although it is always wise to call ahead to be certain that a particular restaurant is open. Otherwise, persons arriving shortly before Spanish diners ordinarily do nearly always find a table — that is, before 2pm for lunch and 10pm for dinner.

AGUT D'AVIGNON ⌂
La Trinitat 3 ☎ 302-6034. Map 5D3 ▥▥ to ▥▥ ▭ ▦▦ ▭ ▦▦ ▥▥ ▭▭ ▥▥ Closed Holy Week. Metro: Jaume I.
Merely finding this honored restaurant is something of a feat

(look for the alley off the narrow Carrer d'Avinyó, which intersects Carrer de Ferran). The interior has the look of a hunting lodge, with tiles, stucco, fireplaces, balconies and evocative paintings.

Pollo con gambas (chicken with

shrimp), *salmón,* and such memorable exotica as fig blossoms with foie gras are among the selections from the Basque, Catalan and French cuisines. It is very popular, so it is wise to reserve ahead.

ALBA 🍴

Paris 168 ☎ *230-9119. Map 3C3* 💷 *to* 💷💷 🍽 *No cards. Closed Sat; Sun. Metro: Provença.*

Virtually every bar in Spain offers at least a short list of *tapas.* Here is a replication of the bountiful Madrid breed, its bi-winged zigzag bar laden with 40 platters of food from the endless *tapas* repertoire. The best strategy is to go with companions, order at least one *ración* for each person, and share. Consider peppers stuffed with cod, bread rubbed with ripe tomato and drizzled with oil (a must), the Catalan sausage *botifarra* with white beans, grilled fresh sardines, snails *marinera.*

No one speaks English there, but you only need to point to order the dishes you want. Be advised: eyes can get bigger than stomachs, so order with sensible caution and remember that crustaceans are very expensive.

Conventional meals are available at the tables at the back, surrounded by paintings executed by the very visible owner.

AMAYA

Rambla Santa Mònica 20-24 ☎ *302-1037. Map 5E2* 💷💷 🖵 🖿 🖾 🖾 🖾 🖾 *Metro: Drassanes.*

As plain and unpretentious as it can be, this thoroughly traditional restaurant has been settled in at the s end of the Rambles for years. That location makes it a better choice for lunch, when mid-level business and government people congregate, than at night, when the area has its less savory aspects. There are several rooms beyond the *tapas* bar in front, attended by a laconic lot of waiters who waste neither words nor motions.

Alleged to be Basque cooking "of the market," the menu actually includes regional specialties from all over Spain. Stick to the fish dishes, which are more expensive but invariably better prepared than the meats. The house wines are passable, and the bread is crusty and chewy. Keep Amaya in mind when other restaurants are closed: it's open from 1pm to 12.30am every day.

AZULETE 🍴

Via Augusta 281 ☎ *203-5943. Map 3B2* 💷💷 🖵 🖿 🖾 🖾 🖾 🖾 *Closed Sat lunch; Sun; first 2wks in Aug; Dec 23-Jan 6.*

Insider chic pertains here, a youthful hyper-cool that mitigates against the bellowing cigar-and-pinkie-ring crowd that befouls too many upper-crust Spanish restaurants. This very plainly isn't their kind of place.

The set is a renovated townhouse in a far northern precinct that barely makes it onto standard street maps (taxi required). It is the creation of Victoria Roque, a retiring sort who rarely makes forays into the dining area, though she has hung a large portrait of herself in the lounge. The entire main floor serves as the bar, filling early, by Spanish standards, with a big crowd of seemingly close friends. When even Catalan stomachs start to grumble, they exit down the stone staircase in the back leading to a glass-tented weatherproof garden, its tables arranged around a decorative pool. Attendance by the young staff is very proper and serious. The kitchen's daily specials are often the best choices, prepared with more dash than some of the items on the set menu.

BOTAFUMEIRO

Gran de Gràcia 81 ☎ *218-4230. Map 3B3* 💷💷 *to* 💷💷💷 🖵 🖿 🖾 🖾 🖾 🖾 *Closed Mon; Aug. Metro: Diagonal.*

Here is the traditional *tasca* taken to another, higher, plateau. No floor littered with shells and prawn skins, no greasy grill, and no jostling for a stand-up square foot of space. Occupy a bar stool with plenty of elbow room, and a linen place mat and flatware are laid before you in a wink. And, while the average corner tavern has two or three men furiously flinging dishes around, this one has an entire squad in white coats and gold braid.

That's just the bar. Beyond it is a ramble of rooms, which are appointed with much blond wood and brass and potted greenery. The problem? Some of the highest prices in town for classic Spanish dishes in utterly conventional guises, albeit with near-perfect preparation. You could always stick to a taste or two in the bar and have dinner elsewhere.

BRASSERIE FLO

Jonqueres 10 ☎ *317-8037. Map 5B3* 💷💷 *to* 💷💷💷 🖵 🖿 🖾 🖾 🖾 🖾

*Open daily for lunch and dinner.
Metro: Urquinaona.*

Several uses for Flo come to mind:
After a concert at the Palau de la
Música Catalana, less than two
blocks away. On a leisurely Sun
afternoon, when most restaurants
are closed or full. Or, as an antidote
to those Post-Modernist parade
grounds where food takes second
place to style.

The room resembles what the
name suggests: a sprawling, brightly
lit Left Bank emporium that
welcomes all, be they kids, trendies,
tourists, executives, oldsters, and
families in from the suburbs. The
pleasant waiting crew, buffitted as
you might expect in black vests and
white aprons, is adroit and
unflappable, even when a child gets
whiny or grandpa is cranky. The
taped music is a little too loud and
almost exclusively 30-year-old
American pop, but it only
contributes to the satisfied clamor
that reaches a crescendo during
peak hours. Tables are set
comfortably apart, with either
banquettes or upholstered chairs.
Even with all this and the utterly
predictable potted palms, Flo
manages to avoid looking like one
of those computer-imagined theme
eateries. French-Catalan dishes
comprise the menu, as, for example,
with the *sopa de peix,* a rich broth
that is the essence but not the flesh
of fish, and salmon tartare doused
with vodka. House wines are to be
recommended.

CA L'ISIDRE *(Casa Isidro)*
Les Flors 12 ☎ *241-1139. Map
3E3* //// ⬜ ■ ▦ ⬛ AE VISA
*Closed Sun; holidays; Holy
Week; Christmas; July 15-Aug
15. Metro: Paral-lel.*

The Gironés family doesn't need the
business few words might
bring it. For over 20yrs at the same
location (just off Avinguda del
Paral-lel), it has done quite well
indeed as a cherished retreat for
titled and artistic Barcelona. For
proof, ask to see the guest book, an
impressive roster that includes the
names of such luminaries as Joan
Miró. They are drawn by the
warmth and informality of a
family-run enterprise that features
cocina del mercado — cooking that
is determined by market availability.

Only 41 diners can be seated at
one time, and in rather snug
quarters at that, so reserve at least
two days ahead. Among possible
choices are the *surtido de verduritas*
(assorted grilled baby vegetables)

and *ensalada de mariscos* (shellfish
salad).

CAN SOLÉ
Sant Carles 4 ☎ *319-5012. Map
6F5* /// ⬜ ■ AE ⬛ VISA *Closed
Sat dinner; Sun. Metro:
Barceloneta.*

There was an open kitchen at Can
Solé 90yrs before that sort of layout
became an essential component of
the New Cooking. Clouds of smoke
and steam bear tantalizing aromas
from the pots to the eager diners.
Can Solé's customers wait at white
marble tables with cast-iron legs and
backless chairs (the latter provided
with the knowledge that Spaniards
always lean forward at meals). On
the walls are framed photos of
forgotten celebrities from the 1920s
to a few months ago.

Double rows of wine casks stand
behind the bar at the front door.
Their contents are drawn off into
porrones, fiendish devices that look
like pitchers with two spouts. In
theory, they are held by the neck
and raised above the head to direct
a thin stream of wine into the mouth
without touching the lips. In
practice, only those born Catalan
seem to be able to keep the wine off
their chins and shirtfronts. No
shame is attached to strangers who
simply pour into a glass. The food is
simple and abundant: most of the
appetizer courses are adequate
lunches in themselves. Nearly all of
the main courses involve seafood,
the sauces mopped up with bread
that Dalí would have painted before
he ate. Dinnertime is much quieter
than the midday meal.

CASA COSTA
Baluard 124 ☎ *319-4028. Map
6E5* /// to //// ⬜ ■ ▦ AE ⬛ ⬛
VISA *Metro: Barceloneta.*

Casa Costa dominates, in both
physical position and popularity, a
block of shoulder-to-shoulder
seafood eateries, each of which has
a hawker more persistent than a
Venetian gondolier. Its
neighborhood is the fisherman's
quarter of Barceloneta, the finger of
land that pokes into the sea below
the city proper. Up on the 1st and
2nd floors are simple rooms where
bountiful portions of *mariscos* and
pescados in every permutation are
the centerpieces.

THE CHICAGO PIZZA PIE
FACTORY
Provença 300 ☎ *215-9415. Map
4B4* // ⬜ VISA *Metro: Diagonal.*

This "deep-dish Chicago pizza" is

about as authentic as a flamenco *tablao* in Omaha, Nebraska. Never mind. The enterprise is directed at young people, almost all of them under 25, and they couldn't care less about the accuracy of the edibles or the surroundings. Half of everything is crimson, in a space that is big, loud, and plastered with assorted Windy City artifacts: street signs, sports pennants and posters. Placing an order can take 20-30mins; eating, paying and getting the change might take half that time.

Those familiar with American slang might be amused to see that the "johns" are named "Elton" and "Olivia Newton."

LA DAMA △

Diagonal 423-425 ☎ *202-0686. Map 3B3* ▮▮▮ *to* ▮▮▮ ☐ ■ ● *AE* ◉ ◉ *VISA Open daily for lunch and dinner. Metro: Provença.*
A marvelously Baroque elevator carries patrons to the second floor of this splendid *modernisme* building. The waiters sport black ties and wing collars, and sinuously carved lines inform door panels, window cornices, walls and etched glass. Toulouse-Lautrec wouldn't feel out of time. Tables are set far enough apart for privacy without that feeling of being adrift on a stadium floor.

Appetizer portions, be warned, are immense. On a visit during the autumn mushroom season, a 12-inch plate was covered rim-to-rim with a score of four different species. Main courses are more restrained, as a rule, in attractive, not prissy, arrangements. They arrive when ready, with no long, ceremonial waits between courses. The 6-course tasting menu is good value, especially since it won't be necessary to eat again for another day. An extra selling point is that La Dama is open for lunch and dinner every day of the week, unlike most in this category.

EGIPTE

Jerusalem 3 ☎ *317-7480. Map 5D2* ▮ ☐ ■ *No cards. Closed Sun. Metro: Liceu.*
Behind the Mercat de la Boqueria is a secret kept by a few hundred thousand natives and handfuls of venturesome tourists. No one seems to know how long the building has been there, but for at least a century, by the looks of it. Its armies of patrons observe no boundaries of class, from the impecunious young, to their prosperous parents, to elderly pensioners. They come

because it is possible to have a 3-course meal with wine for one and get out of the door only 2,000ptas poorer. That isn't easy these days.

In the front room, mismatched chairs are pulled up to tables with iron sewing-machine bases (the treadles still work). They are only inches apart, movement being further limited by the streams of customers and waiters squeezing past. Favored seats are on the balcony or in the rooms up the stairs at the back. The food is country Catalan, mostly in the adequate-to-good range. Fruits are often brought together with fish, fowl or game. The combinations can be delightful, although most of us could do without the maraschino cherry topping the mashed potatoes.

Observations: Lunch is cheaper than dinner, which is rarely the case in Spain. Arrive early or expect a wait. Wear whatever you wish. It's a couple of blocks into the Barri Xinés, so go during the day or with a large companion. And it isn't to be confused with the Bar Egipte a few doors away, or with the Egipte on Les Rambles.

ELDORADO PETIT △

Dolors Monserdà 51 ☎ *204-5153* ▮▮▮ ☐ ■ ● ● ▼ *AE* ◉ ◉ *VISA Closed Sun; 2wks in Aug.*
Overpraised by some, underrated by others, this always newsworthy restaurant continues that dual personality. Some of the dishes are traditional recipes in portions filling the plate; others adhere to the *nouvelle* conventions of tiny amounts of food cunningly arranged. Obviously they seek to please all comers, which they may do, although the high prices aren't really justified by the performance and surroundings. Choose the more animated ground floor of the converted mansion, unless the hush upstairs appeals. The restaurant is in the far NW precinct of the city, requiring a car or taxi.

FLASH-FLASH

La Granada del Penedès 25 ☎ *237-0990. Map 3B3* ▮ ☐ *AE* ◉ ◉ *VISA Closed Sun in July; Aug. Metro: Gràcia.*
Just the spot for a light lunch or a post-midnight repast before setting out for the *discoteca*-of-the-moment, this is a bouncy purveyor of omelets of both the sturdy Spanish and airy French varieties. Up to 75 combinations of ingredients can be

folded in, to order. There are meat dishes and salads for those not enamored of eggs.

FLORIAN ⌂
Bertrand i Serra 20 ☎ *212-4627* IIII *to* IIII □ ■ ▦ ◎ ▨ *Closed Sun; Holy Week; 2wks in Aug; Christmas. Metro: Les Tres Torres.*

A husband and wife run this fine restaurant, a common arrangement, except that he acts as host while she cooks. Possessed of a Bismarckian moustache and exuding self-assurance, he takes orders and oversees the work of his minions. He obviously doesn't consider smiling to be among his obligations, and although he speaks some English, he summons a waiter more competent in the language to deal with foreigners.

Rosa Grau, behind the swinging doors, adheres to certain conventions of the New Cuisine (such as large, unmatched plates of distinctive design), but her food is rarely of the froufrou cuteness that afflicts too many kitchens of that persuasion. Most dishes are Catalan recipes sifted through a contemporary vision. Characteristic is the one called *ricos y pobres* (white beans with shrimp and caviar). When it is mushroom season, ask to see what the owners have gathered. Of the several types that are often at hand, the most memorable are the meaty *setas* and *trompetas de la muerte* ("trumpets of death").

FONT DEL GAT
Passeig Santa Madrona s/n ☎ *424-0224. Map 3E2* IIII □ ■ ▦ ▨ ◎ ▨
One of the better choices for lunch on Montjuïc (but consider also the **cafeteria** in the FUNDACIÓ JOAN MIRÓ museum), this inn set among trees near the POBLE ESPANYOL provides uncomplicated Catalan cookery. Dining on the patio usually happens at night, beside a splashing fountain designed by Lluis Domènech i Montaner. The interior is in tile and stucco, with large windows opened to catch the breezes. Try the *habas a la Catalana* (beans) or *lenguado* (sole), lightly fried, with a garnish of pine nuts and raisins.

EL GRAN CAFÉ
Avinyó 9 ☎ *318-7986. Map 5D3* IIII *to* IIII □ ■ ▧ ▦ ▨ ◎ ◎ ▨ *Closed Sat lunch; Sun. Metro: Liceu.*
Grand, it is, summoning the *fin de*

siècle era when there was enough leisure and relative peace to hone the arts of living. Stairs spiral up from the ancient black-and-white tiled floor to the balcony near the high paneled ceiling; the service bar under the overhang is straddled by large bronze statues of plump females holding globular lamps. Wines are taken seriously by the management, with a card on each table rating vintages from the Rioja and Penedés wine regions from 1951 to the present. Uncommonly for this seaport, meats, such as the rare beef kebab with Béarnaise sauce, are carefully prepared.

NEICHEL ⌂
Av. Pedralbes 16 (at the back of) ☎ *203-8408* IIII □ ■ ▧ ▦ ▨ ▨ ◎ ◎ ▨ *Closed Sun; holidays; Aug; Christmas. Metro: Palau Reial or Maria Cristina.*
Never mind what is written elsewhere: *this* is the restaurant without equal in Barcelona. Alsatian chef Jean-Louis Neichel provides surcease from *paella, gazpacho* and wan pretenses to *nouvelle* flavors-of-the-week. He displays a wizardry that threads a line between pretty plates and supernal marriages of flavor and texture. With his artistry at the stove and his obsession with every detail of service, this is a high-wire act that is a privilege to witness. The absence of a menu in English was once a minor flaw, given the international character of the clientele. That has been corrected, the better for Sony executives and unilingual Brits and Yanks to plumb the longish roster of seasonal offerings supplemented by monthly specials and the *menú degustación.*

Jean-Louis' restless creativity plucks a faddish whimsy from here, an age-old technique from there, and applies them to provender from the Spanish growing districts of Ampurdá, Prat and Cantábria. Alert to increasing impatience with food that was more art than victual, he now expends less energy on immaculate presentations than he once did.

NETWORK
Diagonal 616 ☎ *201-7238. Map 3B2* IIII □ ▦ ▨ ◎ ▨ *Metro: Hospital Clínic.*
What we have here is the disco-as-fast-food-temple. A guard at the door nods approval for entry. One floor down, past rotating models of Earth and the Moon rising and falling through a hole in the ceiling,

is the main room. A large oval bar in the center has a disc jockey playing pop-rock, and over each flanking table hovers a silent black-and-white TV. Thus can the target customer group do what most of them have done since birth: eat, chatter and laugh while ignoring the cacophony and flickering images all around them.

The management pretends to multinationalism, though most of the food is of the rapid American variety. Little of it is good for you, but most of it is tasty: barbecued spare ribs, chili, *tacos*, *nachos*, spicy chicken wings, cheeseburgers, pastas and pizzas. On the bar are bowls of popcorn, peanuts, potato chips and cheese doodles. Almost all of this is finger food that is meant to be picked up with the hands. Watching a young Spaniard try to eat barbecued ribs with knife and fork is to observe an exercise in cross-cultural futility.

One more floor down is another bar, four pool tables and a set of unisex toilet stalls.

LA ODISEA
Copons 7 ☎302-3692. *Map 5C3*
▥ to ▥ ☐ ▆ ▤ 🅰🄴 💰 🄲🄾 🆅🄸🅂🄰
Closed Sat lunch; Sun; Holy Week; Aug. Metro: Jaume I.
Husband-and-wife teams are common in the city, whether in elevated or plebeian environs. In this old town hideaway, Antonio Ferrer shakes the skillets and has his portrait on the menu cover, while his *señora* controls the dining room. The name they've chosen — "The Odyssey" — is full of portent, and they usually deliver. The entry off a short dark street hints of a romantic journey, opening as it does into a room filled with dusky tones, cushy chairs, a grand piano, and large abstract and figurative paintings with an emphasis on the female form. The effect is that of the salon of a rakish remittance man of artistic bent, and the scheme is carried through in the dining room at the back. Some of the staff speak a little English, helpful in deciphering the handwritten menu. Shellfish and lamb are especially good.

RENO △
Tuset 27 ☎200-9129. *Map 3B3*
▥ ☐ ▆ ▆ ▤ ▃ 🆈 🅰🄴 💰 🄲🄾
🆅🄸🅂🄰 *Metro: Diagonal.*
Although now forced to share the pinnacle of *haute cuisine* with such younger competitors as **Neichel**, this long-standing leader hasn't slipped an inch. The reception is as

warm as ever, the environment formal but unintimidating, the staff exceptionally polished, the French-Catalan menu faultless. Men will feel most comfortable in a jacket and tie. The salmon smoked on the premises is sublime, prawns are revelatory, the sole is cooked to perfection, and it is impossible not to be effusive about the wild strawberries splashed with sweet wine and sprinkled with sugar. Fortunately, they almost never close.

SET PORTES
Passeig d'Isabel II, 14 ☎319-3033. *Map 6D4* ▥ ☐ ▆ ▤ ♫
🅰🄴 💰 🄲🄾 🆅🄸🅂🄰 *Metro: Barceloneta.*
These "seven doors" lead into a rambling restaurant of several rooms lit by basket-sized hanging lamps with peach-colored cloth shades. Popular prices, attentive waiters, and the house specialties of *paella*, *arroz con sardinas*, *bacalao* and *conejo* contrive to attract the chic and the bourgeois, the old and the young, families, couples and groups of executives. All are made to feel comfortable, especially at lunch. In the evenings, dim lights and a piano player create a romantic mood.

TRAMONTI 1980
Diagonal 501 ☎410-1535. *Map 3B2* ▥ ☐ ▆ ▤ 🆈 🅰🄴 💰 🄲🄾 🆅🄸🅂🄰
Open daily. Metro: Hospital Clínic.
If there is a better Italian in town than this, it has yet to reveal itself. Pasta is a recent enthusiasm in many of Barcelona's restaurants, of whatever persuasion, but prepared no more inventively nor properly *al dente* than here. Variations include squid ink **fettucine** and *linguine* tossed with tender rings of cuttlefish. Veal is the real flavorful thing, not the bleached white stuff to which North Americans are accustomed, and its marriage here with mushrooms is noteworthy. An animated crowd arranges itself happily on two floors with peach-hued walls and unobtrusive contemporary prints — if not entirely comfortably on the iron garden chairs provided. Service is better than might be expected, given the limited number of waiters available and the countless times they must trot up and down the stairs. At least the owner isn't averse to clearing dishes and bringing dessert or coffee.

EL TUNEL
Ample 33-35 ☎315-2759. *Map 5E3* ▥ to ▥ ☐ ▆ 🅰🄴 💰 🄲🄾 🆅🄸🅂🄰

Closed Sun dinner; Mon. Metro: Drassanes.
Businesspeople and assorted functionaries, overwhelmingly male, make this traditional (1923) redoubt their own at lunch. That is the best time to go, for this is a forbidding street near the waterfront at night. An amiable young host bows patrons into the comfortably old-fashioned rooms, with their ceramic wall tiles and watercolors of Barcelona scenes.

A pre-appetizer arrives after ordering, often a sizeable ration of steamed baby clams. Almost anything that follows is capably done, including the starter of steamed asparagus with tangy *romescu* sauce and *ali-oli*, and the *canelones trufados*. The Spanish fondness for organ meats is also indulged, with *sesos* (brains) and *callos* (tripe). To be charitable, they are acquired tastes. Identifiable fish and beef dishes are better.

Bars and cafés in Barcelona

Barcelona's social engine is fueled at least as much by its bars as by its cafés and restaurants. This is not a city of inebriates: drunkenness, like jogging, is more often an activity engaged in by foreigners. But when it is understood that conversation is the pursuit preferred over all others, the lubrication provided by as many as a dozen bars per city block becomes understandable. Some sources estimate that at least a hundred new bars are added every year to a group that already numbers in the thousands.

Most bars and pubs are closed on Sunday; in our selection we specify those that remain open. Like many of the discos and clubs mentioned in NIGHTLIFE & THE PERFORMING ARTS, some pubs do not have a telephone.

Barcelonan bars come in many guises, catering to every stratum of class, age, work and leisure activity. Most evident are the old-fashioned neighborhood *tabernas*, with their rows of hanging hams and loud television sets. They are *de facto* clubs, where friends and neighbors meet for a quick morning coffee, a sandwich, an after-lunch card game, and pre- and postprandial *copas* of wine or brandy, all taken with copious rations of gossip and exchanges of robust opinion.

Our WHERE TO EAT section describes several possibilities, but also available is the classy **La Bodegueta** (*Rambla Catalunya 100*), which is down a few steps near the corner of Carrer de Provença. It looks older than it is, with oval sherry casks forming the back bar, and the blackened gimcracks and dusty bottles on the shelves. A couple of blocks N of the Passeig de Gràcia is a similar establishment, **La Barcelonina de Vins i Esperits** (*Valencia 304 ☎ 215-7083*), which claims to have 500 wines on hand to go with its pâtés, cheeses and smoked fish. The **Bar El Paraigua** (*Pas de l'Ensenyança 2 ☎ 302-1131*) is an Art Nouveau retreat that seems to be popular with female friends who can have lengthy and undisturbed conversations in a quiet, uncrowded place that doesn't attract rowdy men. It also has a brick-walled cellar with cushier seating. You should look for it near the Plaça Sant Jaume.

The next largest category of Barcelonan watering-hole is the bar that functions, in large measure, as a late afternoon and early evening stopping-off point between work and dinner. That can be quite a long interval in Spain, and surroundings that at least attempt a higher style are considered to be essential. These may take on the trappings of a Manhattan cocktail lounge, a Mayfair public house or a Milanese showroom, but in all of them, the

dispensing of alcohol in various forms is primary, and food, if
any, is an afterthought. Simulations of the British **pub** were
abundant at one time. While that vogue has ebbed, there is still
Taberna Inglesa Dirty Dick's (*Marc Aureli 2*), a half-accurate
reproduction with hanging dimpled pint mugs and two or three
British brews on tap.

Coctelerías on the American model often trumpet their
specialties in their names, as in the cases of **Gimlet** (*Rech 24*
☎ *310-1027*) and **El Dry Martini** (*Aribau 162*), in the
Eixample district. The latter claims to have over 80 brands of gin
in stock, and various recipes for the basic concoction are on
hand. Not far away is the suave English-style **Ideal Cocktail Bar**
(*Aribau 89* ☎ *253-1028*), which specializes in blended and malt
whisky, augmented by fruit drinks and canapés. **La Gasolinera**
(*Aribau 97*) is a whimsy with a gas pump in front, its barmen
willing to accept instruction on making a preferred drink. On a
corner of the Rambles is **Boadas** (*Tallers 1* ☎ *318-9592*), a
crowded, triangular room that has been stirring up beaded
pitchers of martinis for over half a century.

Passeig del Born (*map 6D4-C5*) is a short street near the
Museu Picasso where several bars have sprung up in recent
years. They are of gentle mien, unchic and largely unknown to
foreigners. **17 Bar** (*Passeig del Born 17* ☎ *319-0048*) is a
high-ceilinged room with bamboo and raffia furniture,
amateurish paintings and "serious" English rock on the stereo. **El
Copetín** (*Passeig del Born 19*) pours good Irish coffee (*café
Irlandés*) for the marble-topped tables at the end of its long
polished entrance bar. Taped blues and jazz constitute the
música ambiental. Across the street is **El Born** (*Passeig del Born
26*), slightly more ambitious, with a claustrophobic dining room
upstairs, a carved stone sink converted to a bar, and a compact
lounge, warmed by a coal stove in winter. Pâtés, cheeses and
recorded jazz are on the card at **Miramelindo** (*Passeig del Born
15*). These four are all open every night.

Cuba libres are featured at **Estebar** (*Consell de Cent 257*), for
an often arty crowd. Higher, both in elevation and pecking order,
is **Merbeyé** (*Plaça Dr. Andreu s/n*), halfway up Tibidabo near
the base of the funicular. Long a haven for the chic of all ages,
Estebar does not court tourists, which is why there is live music
only between Sept and May. A disc jockey operates between sets,
there is a terrace for warm evenings, and an upstairs hideaway.

A welcome phenomenon is the *champañería* or, in Catalan,
xampanyería, where the drink to sip is just what the name
suggests. The emphasis is on Spanish *cavas*, which are
good-to-excellent sparkling wines made by the champagne
method. **Xampu Xampany** (*Gran Via 702* ☎ *232-0716*) is
typical, with widely spaced tables in a sleek setting. Caviar and
smoked salmon canapés accompany fluted glasses of the bubbly.
Glenn Miller, heavy metal and Euro-synth are known to alternate
on the sound system. Other possibilities are **La Xampanyería**
(*Provença 236* ☎ *253-7455*), **La Cava del Palau** (*Verdaguer i
Callis 10* ☎ *310-0938*) and **Casablanca** (*Bonavista 6*
☎ *237-6399*).

Finally, there are the grandiose bars sometimes referred to as
multiespacios, large spaces resembling discotheques, usually
without the dancing. High-profile designers are paid extravagant
fees and encouraged to run amok. That they do, with waterfall
urinals, laser displays, fashion shows, underground movies, art
exhibits, swimming pools, miniature golf, rows of snooker tables
and, in one case, a live snake in a glass tank. Post-Modernism is

the prevailing mode, which often amounts to an *anti*-Modernist return from the future. In stark spaces full of unyielding surfaces are mingled the kitsch and detritus of past decades. Pinlights and tensor lamps dangling from thread-thin wires are the illumination of choice.

The investments are huge — over 70 million pesetas and 2yrs of construction, in one case — and profits and longevity are uncertain. For a relatively long time, **Nick Havanna** (*Rosselló 208* ☎ *215-6591*) ruled this roost, with its giant pendulum and wall of TV monitors flashing continuous music videos. When last seen, however, it was looking worn and a little empty, as if the in crowd had moved on. Probably they were making the scene at **Otto Zutz** (*Lincoln 15* ☎ *238-0722*). Imagine a 2-floored warehouse that once served as a car repair station or small prison, for a foretaste of the relentless Neo-Brutalist decor. Spaniards think it looks like an American high school, which says something about the images sent abroad by Hollywood. Should this sound at all endearing, go before 2am, when it becomes a membership club. **Universal** (*Marià Cubí 182-184* ☎ *201-4658*) appears to be thriving, at least at this very nanosecond of writing. Post-Modernist, yes — a big empty room on the ground floor with a bar and photos of lightly clad, mostly female people projected on the bare brick wall. Up the iron staircase is another bar in a quieter room slightly smaller than below but just as bleak. For ephemeral reasons, this pulls in large numbers of pretty people in the 20-40 age group, the observing of whom is the main reason for going.

For those who enjoy games with their chat and booze, there are the bowling lanes at the back of **Boliche** (*Diagonal 510*) and the billiard tables at **Best Sellers** (*Aribau 132* ☎ *323-7225*), **SiSiSi** (*Diagonal 442*), **Ticktacktoe** (*Roger de Llúria 40* ☎ *318-9770*) or, logically, **Snooker** (*Mallorca 350* ☎ *258-2131*). Also on the circuit, enjoying elastic degrees of fickle popularity, are **Yabba Dabba** (*Avenir 3*), **Velvet** (*Balmes 161* ☎ *217-6714*), **The End** (*Santaló 34* ☎ *200-3942*), **Ciento 13** (*Aribau 113*) and **La Fira** (*Provença 171* ☎ *323-7271*), the last of which employs antique penny machines and salvaged fairground contraptions.

Cafés are often the setting for the Spanish *tertulia* tradition, wherein friends or colleagues gather to discuss issues of the day or of the cosmos. Frequently they are among the oldest of such establishments, as is the **Café de l'Opera** (*Rambles 74* ☎ *317-7585*), said to date back to the early part of the last century, and **Els Quatre Gats** (*Montsió 5* ☎ *302-4140*), a resurrected Barri Gòtic tavern that was once the cherished hangout of the young Picasso, Utrillo, Miró, and their lovers and rivals. A far newer addition is the bi-level **José Luis** (*Diagonal 520* ☎ *200-8312*), one of a chain noted for its delectable open-faced sandwiches and exclusive clientele, a kind of posh *tapas* bar for the elite.

Nightlife & the performing arts

Only Madrid comes as alive at night as Barcelona, and a short survey can only hint at the wealth of diversions. As fast as new discos, clubs, bars and pubs spring up, others close down. Those recommended here (and above in BARS AND CAFÉS) seem likely to persevere, but policies, owners and clientele can alter overnight, so any survey is subject to unpredictable change.

A copy of the *Guía del Ocio*, available at most newsstands, is a useful guide, with notices and reviews of current movies, concerts, and theatrical and sports events, as well as comprehensive listings of bars, nightspots and restaurants. It is written in Spanish, but is fairly easily understood. Hotel *conserjes* usually have copies and can help decipher the contents. Another source is the opinionated glossy magazine *Barcelona Concept*, which also devotes a good deal of space to shopping and fashion.

Discos are usually closed on Monday, jazz clubs from Monday-Wednesday, and bars and pubs, as noted above, on Sunday. Many have no telephone.

An admission fee is charged at *discotecas*, which usually includes the first drink. They often have "afternoon" sessions for teenagers, from about 7-10pm. They then close briefly, reopening at 11pm or midnight; but don't expect to see much action until after 2am.

Few things are as transient as the cachet of a disco, and a common device to enhance desirability is to feign a "members only" policy. Not many are really that exclusive, but an exception is **Up & Down** (*Numancia 179* ☎ *204-8809*), which routinely turns away seemingly respectable supplicants. The doorkeepers permit entrance according to a volatile mix of mood, their need for custom on a given night, and the physical appearance of would-be patrons. It is no dishonor to be turned away, although it can't hurt to be young, gorgeous and/or visibly prosperous. All this naturally makes this club in a far NW district irresistible to upscale folk of all ages. The younger among them head downstairs, while the aged (over 30) prefer the upper level, with its relatively muted music and restaurant.

Studio 54 (*Av. Paral-lel 64* ☎ *329-5454*) is too big to be so picky. Even on a busy night, it provides vast stretches of welcome elbow room and one of the most imaginative light shows in town. Going strong too when last seen were **Trauma** (*Consell de Cent 288* ☎ *318-2084*), the new wave **Distrito Distinto** (*Aragó 615*) and **Centro Ciudad** (*Consell de Cent 294* ☎ *318-9356*), the last of which has a pool to go with its several bars.

In addition to the *discotecas*, there are dance halls known as *salas de fiesta*. Representative is **Sutton** (*Tuset 32* ☎ *209-0537*), where an orchestra plays mostly Latin American compositions for dancing the tango, cha cha cha, samba, and other such crazes, like the *lambada*, that may come and go.

There are few **nightclubs** of the Parisian-Las Vegas strain in Barcelona, but one that measures up fairly well is **Scala Barcelona** (*Passeig de Sant Joan 47* ☎ *232-6363*). **El Molino** (*Vila Vilá 99* ☎ *241-6383*) is a music hall modeled on the Moulin Rouge in Paris, complete with a fake windmill on the facade, which has been going almost continuously since 1909.

Flamenco has rarely been accorded its due this far from Andalucía, and shows pretending to do so invariably lack the spontaneity and fire of the real thing. It is better to wait for a visit to Madrid or Sevilla, which still have authentic *tablaos* (as the shows are called). But if those cities aren't on the itinerary, a fair substitute is to be found at **Las Vegas del Guadalquivir** (*Aribau 230* ☎ *209-4523*). At these three clubs, dinner and show (twice nightly) are included in one fairly reasonable price; drinks are extra.

Jazz is quite popular in Catalunya, highlighted by the annual **Festival Internacional de Jazz** (☎ *302-6870*) in Barcelona in

Nov and a comparable summer event in nearby Terrassa, but there are, strangely, few permanent venues. The most reliable and consistently rewarding are **Abraxas** (*Gelabert 26* ☎ *230-5922*) and **La Cova del Drac** (*Tuset 30*), usually featuring mainstream trios and quartets. Serious jazzophiles attend to the sounds at **Harlem** (*Comtessa de Sobradiel 8* ☎ *310-0700*) in the heart of the Barri Gòtic.

Pop and rock are more readily heard. Major stars of the order of Janet Jackson and Tina Turner and such heavy metal groups as Iron Maiden and Anthrax usually hold their concerts at either the **Palau d'Esport** (*Lleida 40* ☎ *424-2776*) or the **Plaça de Toros Monumental** (*Gran Via 747* ☎ *232-7158*). Of the many bars and clubs, **KGB** (*Alegre de Dalt 55* ☎ *210-5906*) presents live groups performing all across the music spectrum, with an emphasis on progressive and alternative forms. **The Piano Bar** (*Aribau 108*) and **Piano Cristal** (*Casanova 264*) make their preferences clear.

Opera and classical music are given often glorious realization at the **Gran Teatre del Liceu** (*Rambles 61* ☎ *302-6019*) and the **Palau de la Música Catalana** (*Amadeu Vives 1* ☎ *268-1000*). Both structures are lauded for their acoustics and are notable for their distinctive architecture (SEE SIGHTS A-Z). Opera, ballet and symphony are performed at the Liceu, which routinely plays host to those luminaries in demand at every great house from Milan's La Scala to New York's Metropolitan. Its season is from September to early July. The Palau has concerts only, perhaps because no theatrical set could compete with the fantastic *modernisme* decor. There are over a dozen theaters staging dramatic productions, but obviously they are of scant interest to anyone not fluent in Spanish or Catalan. Occasional chamber music concerts are held at the **Teatre Lliure** (*Montseny 47* ☎ *218-9251*).

Films, both popular and artistic, have a wide audience. Most are dubbed into Spanish. Look for the initials **V.O.** on posters and in advertisements, indicating a film that retains its original language, with Spanish subtitles. Committed movie buffs will want to look up the **Filmoteca de la Generalitat de Catalunya** (*Travessera de Gràcia 63* ☎ *201-2906*), housed in a glum building not far E of the Plaça de Francesc Macià. Its frequently changed bill features films that movie-goers of mainstream tastes might regard as justly obscure.

Shopping

The acquisitive impulse is abundantly served — no, provoked — in Barcelona, with boggling numbers of specialty stores along all but the meanest streets. A logical overview of what's available can be had at leading **department stores**. **El Corte Inglés** (The English Cut), on the E side of the Plaça de Catalunya, is a representative of Spain's most prominent department store chain. Its several floors address every imaginable need, with boutiques scattered among the larger sections devoted to clothing, fragrances, furniture, kitchen utensils and the like. The relationship between price and quality is reasonable, and the selection is ample. The capable *cafetería* at the top has surprising views of the city.

Its principal rival is **Galerías Preciados** (*Av. Portal de l'Angel*), just S of El Corte Inglés. At the government-run **Artespaña**

(*Rambla de Catalunya 121*) are all kinds of Spanish handicrafts: ceramics, leather goods, silverwork, woodcarvings, clothing, furniture and accessories. Everything is in excellent taste — but there are no bargains.

In the **Barri Gòtic** (*map 5 C-D3*) there are specialty stores around every corner. Confectioners, tobacconists, and dealers in antiques, old books, leather goods and crafts predominate. For antiques, seek out Carrer del Banys Nous and Carrer de la Palla. Also worth trying are Carrer Freneria, which runs along the E wall of the cathedral (watch for the kitchenware and pottery store **La Caixa de Frang**); Carrer Portaferrisa, connecting the *plaça* in front of the cathedral with Les Rambles; or Carrer Ferrán, between Plaça Sant Jaume and Les Rambles. On the last street is **Itaca**, a shop full of pottery from many regions of Spain and Morocco. One of the owners speaks some English, and they will ship purchases anywhere (just don't expect the packages to arrive in the optimistically short time they predict). On the Plaça Sant Josep Oriol is a equally enticing ceramic and folk art boutique, **Molsa**.

The suggested walk on page 44 takes you past many of the shops mentioned above, as well as other possibilities.

International chic reigns along the **Passeig de Gràcia**, the broad boulevard between the Plaça de Catalunya and El Diagonal (*map 4 C4*). Many of the names found there are familiar from other fashionable capitals, including the celebrated Spanish firms dealing in various leather goods, such as **Loewe**.

Serious shoppers can begin by facing N at the SE corner of the Plaça de Catalunya: walk along the right-hand side of the *passeig*, cross W at the corner with Rosselló, and return S along the opposite side. Following that route, you will encounter the men's clothier **E. Furest**, the custom tailor **Pellicer** (for both men and women), and, in the famous Gaudí building, La Pedrera, the women's boutique **Parera**. Farther along the *passeig*, **Yanko** deals in superb Spanish shoes, handbags, purses and belts, and **A. Gratacos** in fine fabrics of great variety.

Crossing to the W side of the *passeig*, the pipes, lighters and pen displays of **Gimeno** catch the eye. Head S for **Carlos Torrents**, which focuses on stylish men's clothing of the Armani creed, and down the adjacent Ptge Concepció you'll find **Pierre Cardin**. Between Valencia and Aragó, an arcade cuts through to Rambla de Catalunya, called **El Bulevard Rosa**, an inviting arrangement of trendy boutiques, quality clothing stores, a bar-restaurant and a courtyard. It is a refreshing change of mood from the sedate aspect of the *passeig*.

Increasingly prosperous Spain offers few bargains, but **spices** can be found at irresistible prices. Avid cooks will want to consider taking home a cache of the world's costliest spice: saffron. Far cheaper here, in one of its few countries of origin, it can be had in several packaged quantities from **Angel Jobal** (*Princesa 38*). Patrons get giddy upon walking off the street into the thick, mingled aromas of dozens of teas and spices: cardamon, anis, dried peppers, nutmeg, oregano, and bins of more kinds of paprika than most people knew existed.

English-language **magazines** and limited selections of paperback **books** are sold at the all-night newsdealers along Les Rambles. Far more extensive numbers of English titles in all categories are available at the **Come In Bookshop** (*Provença 203* ☎ *253-1204*). In stock are reference works, computer manuals, travel guides, nonfiction, bestsellers, audio language cassettes... even birthday cards and comic books.

Sports in Barcelona

Ambitious construction programs leading up to the Olympics have bestowed on the city a remarkably diverse array of athletic facilities, including those as specialized as a velodrome and a canal for boat races. Their disposition after 1992 is not clear in all cases, but it is certain that Barcelona is now blessed with an abundance of recreational arenas, pools and gymnasia.

Basketball

A professional league with players drawn from all over Europe and North America plays in a number of venues during the winter season. For details, you should consult the hotel *conserje* (hall porter).

Boating

Rowboats are available to rent at the lake in **Ciutadella Park**. The **Royal Maritime Club of Barcelona** at the **Moll d'Espanya** on the waterfront provides services to visiting yachtsmen, including fuel, repairs, and sailing and navigation schools. For information about yacht and boat rental, contact the **Centre Informatiu Nàutic** (*Santaló 136 ☎ 200-8261*).

Bowling

The **Pedralbes Bowling Alley** (*Av. Dr. Marañón 11 ☎ 333-0352*) is open 10am-1.30am, and the **AMFF Bowling Centre** (*Sabino de Arana 6 ☎ 330-5048*) from 11am-1.30am. Both are near the University. Closer to downtown is **Boliche** (*Diagonal 508 ☎ 237-9098*), which is as much a bar as a bowling alley.

Bullfighting

Catalans insist they don't care for the *arte taurino*, and it is true that foreign spectators often seem to outnumber Spaniards at the bullring N of the center, the **Plaça de Toros Monumental** (*Gran Via 743 ☎ 245-5804*). There is a box office at **Muntaner 24**, or the *conserje* can obtain tickets for a commission. The season is from Mar-Sept.

Cycling

Bicycles can be rented at **Bicitram** (*Aragó 19*). Open Sat, Sun 10am-9pm.

Fitness centers

Health clubs are multiplying, but most are for members only. Some hotels have arrangements with private fitness centers, while others have installed equipment on their premises. Two with elaborate facilities, including saunas and aerobics classes, are the **Princesa Sofía** and the **Meliá Barcelona Sarrià**. Look for the ⚜ symbol in the hotel listings.

Fishing and hunting

For contacts, see page 124.

Football (American)

Amateur teams have been playing the American brand of football in the Barcelona area for several years, using such English names as the Eagles, Broncos, Boxers, Rebels and Giants. In 1991, the so-called World League of American Football began competition with ten teams in Europe and North America, including one in Barcelona called the Dragons. Its future is uncertain.

Football (soccer)

The world's favorite spectator sport is ably demonstrated by the city's successful team, FC Barcelona ("Barça," as it's known locally). They usually play at the **Nou Camp** stadium (*Av. Aristides Maillol s/n* ☎ 330-9411), which was enlarged to contain 125,000 people for the Olympics.

Golf

While there are no courses inside the city limits, there are five within 40km (25 miles) of downtown: **Prat Royal Golf Club** (*El Prat de Llobregat* ☎ 379-0278), **Vallromanes Golf Club** (*Montornès del Vallès* ☎ 568-0362), **Terramar Golf Club** (*Sitges* ☎ 894-0580), **Sant Cugat Golf Club** (*Sant Cugat del Vallès* ☎ 674-3958) and **Llavaneres Golf Club** (*Sant Andreu de Llavaneres* ☎ 792-6050).

Skating

Available ice skating rinks are at **Roger de Flor 168** (☎ 245-2800) and next to the stadium on **Av. Aristides Maillol** (☎ 330-9411). Skates can be hired and lessons arranged at both locations.

Skiing

The nearest ski resort is at **Núria** in the Eastern Pyrenees. They have an office in the city at **Passeig de Gràcia 26** (☎ 301-9777).

Swimming

A few hotels have pools: look for the 🏊 symbol. Public pools are in Barceloneta (*Passeig Marítim s/n* ☎ 309-3412), the **Can Caralleu** sports complex (*Esports s/n* ☎ 204-6905) and on Montjuïc (*Plaça Folch i Torres s/n* ☎ 241-0122).

Tennis

The **Can Caralleu** sports complex (*Esports s/n* ☎ 203-7874) is open to the public.

Barcelona for children

Children — anyone's children — are prized in Catalunya, as they are throughout Spain. One result is that they are less often set apart from the adult world than in more northerly parts of the Western world. Visitors are often surprised to see Spanish children up and participating in fiestas that roll on past midnight. That isn't to say that there aren't activities to excite and enthrall kids, just that their associated adults are likely to enjoy them, too.

Barcelona has not one, but two, amusement parks, one each atop MONTJUÏC and TIBIDABO, the highest hills. Disney had no hand in either, and their rides and game booths can be exhausted rather quickly, but younger children are almost certain to be engaged for an hour or two. Getting up either hill is also a treat, unless the child is Swiss or acrophobic. Tibidabo has an antique **tram** clanging halfway up, followed by a **funicular**. Montjuïc has a funicular (the FUNICULAR AEREO) *and* a **cable car** that glides to the summit and down, swinging over the **Parc d'Atracciones** on the way. Also atop Montjuïc is a 17thc **fort**, sure to hold the attention of any boy-child who hasn't seen one, with the bonus of the sizeable MUSEU MILITAR inside displaying antique weaponry, uniforms and regiments of lead soldiers.

Other museums that might lengthen attention spans are the MUSEU MARITÍM, with its ship models and full-sized vessels, and, not far away, the replica of Columbus' SANTA MARÍA and the MUSEU DE CERA (wax museum), at the end of a passage off the lower Rambles. Finally, there are the fair-sized ZOO DE BARCELONA and its aquarium in the PARC DE LA CIUTADELLA, about as certain a distraction for young minds as has been devised. For descriptions, see SIGHTS A-Z.

An excursion through Catalunya

Catalunya is blessed with miles of beaches, fertile valleys, pine-covered uplands and the craggy Pyrenees. Set out to the NE along the Gran Via, which quickly becomes the A-19 *autopista*. After about 28km (18 miles), this highway merges with the N11, which hugs the coast through several beach towns of little interest. Just beyond **Calella**, the N11 bends inland. Turn right toward **Blanes** on the C253 for the beginning of the Costa Brava. The corniche twists and curls along the indented shoreline, with repeated viewpoints over rocky coves and crescent beaches. The principal resorts along the way — clogged with buses and tourists from June to Sept — are **Lloret de Mar**, **Tossa de Mar** and **Sant Feliú de Guixols**.

〓 In **Sant Feliú de Guixols** is a branch of the highly regarded Barcelona restaurant, **Eldorado Petit** (*Rambla Vidal 23* ☎ *(972) 321-818* ▐▐▐▐).

❧ Nearby, in the planned community of **S'Agaro**, is one of Spain's finest resort hotels, **Hostal de la Gavina** (*Plaça de la Rosaleda* ☎ *(972) 321-100* ▐▐▐▐).

From there, find the C250, the inland road for **Girona**. That provincial capital is an unappreciated city, boasting the world's widest Gothic cathedral and some beautiful Romanesque churches. Ignored by tourists from the N intent on reaching Barcelona and the southern beaches, it is worth at least 2 or 3hrs of exploration.

Pick up the N11 N of the city, continuing to **Figueres**, 27km (17 miles) to the north. That is the home of the arresting (or outlandish) **Fundació Gala-Salvador Dalí** (*closed Mon*), the celebrated Surrealist's monument to himself and the love of his life, the Russian-born Gala.

〓 On the outskirts of town is the highly regarded restaurant, **Ampurdán** (*Ctra. N-II, km 763* ☎ *(972) 500-562* ▐▐ *to* ▐▐▐▐).

From the center of Figueres, take the C252 NE toward **Llança** (Llansa). From there, head SE for 17km (11 miles) through rocky hills to Cadaqués. Situated at the rim of a horseshoe bay, it still functions as a fishing port despite its popularity as a summer resort. Partly due to the long-term presence of Dalí, who kept a home nearby, Cadaqués is an important center for the visual arts: an exhibition held there is nearly as important to artists as one in Barcelona or Madrid. The town retains an attractive *plaza mayor* with a 17thC church.

Return to the road branching toward **Roses**, another combination of fishermen's village and resort, which began as the Greek colony of Rhoda. Continue w on the C260, passing once again through Figueres and following the signs for **Olot** (to

the w). The C260 soon joins the C150 at the pretty village of
Besalú. Continue on this road through pleasant countryside,
through Olot to **Ripoll**, which is the location of a notable
medieval Benedictine monastery.

From Ripoll, Barcelona is about 100km (63 miles) to the s, on
the N152.

🍴 You might perhaps break the journey for lunch or for the night at the
Parador de Vic (*no street address, 14km/9 miles NE of Vic* ☎ *(93)
888-7211* ▮▯).

Otherwise, continue N on the N152. Near **Ribes de Freser**, a
rack railway climbs through exciting alpine scenery to the winter
resort of **Núria**. This method of transportation (the only way to
reach it) takes about 1hr (round trip) and is worth the fairly
expensive fare; schedules vary with the season. Continuing along
the winding N152 requires diligent attention by the driver, but
passengers are treated to splendid views of the valley below. The
road leads past **La Molina** with its two winter resorts that have
attracted international sports competitions, and on to **Puigcerdà**,
on the French border. That geopolitical curiosity, **Llívia**, a
Spanish village entirely within French territory, lies 6km (4 miles)
farther N, at the end of a connecting road that is technically
neutral. Only that oddity really makes a detour worthwhile.

From Puigcerdà, take the C1313 sw for 50km (31 miles), past
lovely scenery and through the mountain villages of **Bellver de
Cerdanya** and **Prullans**, to **La Seu d'Urgell**.

🛏 While there is nothing special about the in-town **Parador la Seo de
Urgel** (*Santo Domingo s/n* ☎ *(973) 352-000* ▮▯), it is adequate for a
night's stay.

From here, the C145 climbs N into **Andorra** and its capital city,
Andorra la Vella, 20km (13 miles) away. The trip takes longer
than might be imagined, for the road is nearly always thick with

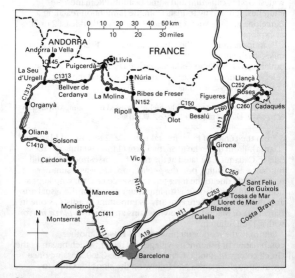

cars full of bargain-seekers. All manner of goods are available at substantial tax-free discounts in the mountain principality. That is the main reason for going there.

From La Seu d'Urgell, continue s along the C1313, following the Segre river. Just beyond **Organyá**, the road skirts the w bank of a man-made lake, then crosses E to the village of **Oliana**. After 10km (6 miles), turn left (E) and follow the C1410 to **Solsona**, which has a 13thC castle and 12thC cathedral. The road descends for 20km (13 miles) to **Cardona** and *its* castle.

✥ ☰ This castle is now the **Parador de Cardona** (*no street address* ☎ *(93) 869-1275* ▮▮▯). It serves as a good lunch stop and a romantic place to stay.

Continue s for 32km (20 miles) to **Manresa**, noted for the exceptionally wide vaulting of its 14th-16thC cathedral. At **Monistrol**, a further 15km (9 miles) s, either turn right (W) onto a twisting road leading to the **monastery of Montserrat**, or park at the railroad station and take the rack railway there.

Montserrat is the name of both the famous monastery and the mountain range in which it is cradled. Faithful Catholics come here to pay homage to the fabled **Black Madonna**, a wooden statue of the Virgin alleged to have been brought to Barcelona by St Peter and rediscovered in the 9thC. (In fact, its origins are probably 12thC.) Others come for the views or to hear the boys' choir in the basilica. The 19thC monastery is a replacement for a 10thC complex of structures destroyed by the French in 1812. Much of the area is gaudily commercial, but the shrine is still important to Spaniards.

From Monistrol, proceed s to the N11, and thence to Barcelona, 51km (32 miles) away.

Madrid

By European standards, Madrid is a young capital. Although settlements existed here from prehistoric times and most of Iberia's successive conquerors occupied it for various periods, it remained a minor farming community while the seat of government was moved from Toledo to Valladolid to Burgos at the whims of monarchs currently in power. Only when Felipe II chose the unheralded backwater as his capital in 1561 did it begin to receive the royal largesse that was to make it Spain's largest city and repository of most of its greatest works of art. Rarely — and briefly — thereafter did it lose its status.

In selecting Madrid, Felipe II had more in mind than the clear, dry climate. He hoped that a capital at the geographical center of Spain would help to keep the volatile outlying regions in check. As it happened, centrifugal forces have often been as powerful.

Through almost the whole of the national tragedy that was the Civil War, Loyalist Madrid was held in siege by Franco's Nationalists. Much of the city was destroyed or damaged during those 2½ years, through constant shelling and bombardment. Parks became bivouacs, churches were desecrated, palaces and museums plundered. Most have been restored or replaced, and the great monuments of the 17th and 18th century survive. There are sweeping plazas and grand boulevards, fountains and palaces, elegant Neoclassical buildings and more than forty museums. Long cloaked in an authoritarian shroud of repression and insularity, the suddenly cosmopolitan city crackles with vivacity and innovation, in a way that recalls the "swinging London" of the 1960s. Its designers challenge those of Milan, its artists and film-makers have an international reputation, and a palpable "Madrid Style" is taking shape. Its avatars and their acolytes crowd the hosts of ultrafashionable restaurants, cafés and clubs found in every *barrio*.

Old Madrid spreads to the south and west of the Puerta del Sol and the Plaza Mayor, built in the 17th century. Two European dynasties, the Hapsburgs and Bourbons, have provided Spain with most of its monarchs over the last 300 years. The succession of Felipes and Carloses only rarely displayed brilliance or even competence in leadership. However, they did command, or permit, the making of a number of impressive royal residences, monasteries, gardens and parks, and they commissioned or purchased the works of art that form the foundations of the important collections now on public view.

Since the Civil War, and especially in the last two decades, expansion has been primarily to the north, along both sides of the broad Paseo de la Castellana. A virtual new city of spreading apartment blocks and office buildings has been created, and the northeast precinct is now a grid of international banks, skyscrapers and corporate headquarters, little of which existed 30 years ago.

Madrid occupies the heart of the high central plateau called the Meseta, which is made up of low rolling plains for the most part, but broken by the granite peaks of the Sierra de Guadarrama and sparsely watered by the Tajo River. A logical base from which to explore a ring of smaller, older cities in the surrounding area, including Toledo, Segovia and El Escorial, it is also within easy reach of numerous summer country palaces and skiing in the Gredos Mountains.

Madrileños leave the city to visitors in August, when many shops and restaurants close. The principal events of the year, in a calendar festooned with activities, are the Fiestas de la Primavera and of San Isidro. Together, they take up much of the month of May, with bullfights, outdoor jazz and rock concerts, *zarzuelas*, the neighborhood street fairs called *verbenas*, and other celebrations.

Getting around

From the airport to the city

Barajas Airport has separate domestic and international terminals, which are both being extended at the time of writing. The trip to the city center takes as little as 20mins, or as many as 60mins, depending on traffic. The least expensive means of transportation is the yellow airport bus, which, for a fare below 300ptas, drops passengers at the depot on **Plaza Colón** on the Paseo de la Castellana. Buses stop at each terminal four times an hour from early in the morning until after midnight. Many major hotels are within a walk or short taxi ride of the Plaza Colón.

Taxi rides from the airport are more expensive than the bus, of course, but aren't unusually costly, except during rush hours. You should make certain that the meter has been turned back following the last fare. Supplements apply for luggage, trips to or from the airport, and between 11pm and 6am.

If renting a car at the airport, obtain a road map and careful directions to your hotel or other destination before leaving the terminal, for police and pedestrians encountered along the way are unlikely to speak English.

Public transportation

Said to be patterned after the Paris subway, Madrid's **metro** is relatively modern, but less extensive and with longer distances between stops than its model. Still, the system is kept fairly clean and reasonably safe, fares are still moderate, and the route maps are easy to decipher by passengers who don't speak Spanish. Stations can be identified by a diamond-shaped sign with the word **Metro** in the center.

Fares are charged per ride, not by distance. Discounts are available with a book (called a *taco*) of ten tickets and the unlimited-use *Metrotour* ticket, which is good for 3 or 5 days. Trains run from early morning until after midnight.

Red **buses** fill in many of the gaps in the metro system. Route maps can be obtained at the booths marked **EMT** near the bus stops on the Plaza de Cibeles and Puerta del Sol, the tourist office on the Plaza Mayor and, in theory, at branches of the bank called Caja de Ahorros de Madrid.

Discounts are available with the purchase of a *Bonobus* multiticket, good for ten rides, which can be obtained at the Cibeles or Sol metro stations: when you board the bus, insert the cardboard ticket into the punch machine located beside the driver. One bus route, called the **Circular**, serves as a de facto

---

Emergency information

Police (*Policía*) ☎091
Fire (*Cuerpo de bomberos*) ☎080
Ambulance (*Ambulancia*) ☎230-7144

Hospitals
British American Hospital Paseo de Juan XXIII ☎234-6700. Many English-speaking staff members.
Enfermedades Cardíacas Av. de la Reina Victoria 22 ☎234-8866. For suspected heart attacks.
Hospital La Paz Paseo de la Castellana 261 ☎734-5500 or 734-2600.

General emergencies.
Primero de Octubre Ctra Andalucía, km 5.4 ☎469-7600

Dental emergencies
Contact your embassy or consulate for a list of English-speaking dentists.

Late-night pharmacies
Pharmacies operate a late-night rota, each store taking a turn (the *farmacias de guardia*). For shops on duty that night ☎098; or check the sign on the door of the nearest pharmacy.

Help lines
Alcoholics Anonymous ☎222-6824
Drug addiction ☎430-6077
Lost property Plaza de Legazpi 7 ☎588-4346, or Santa Engracia 120 ☎441-0214

tour of the city, and for a low fare; central stops include the Plaza de Cibeles and Puerta del Sol.

Taxis
Metered taxis are black with a horizontal red band, or white with a diagonal colored band. They can be hailed in the street or found parked at stands near hotels or major attractions. During the day, the window sign *libre* indicates that a taxi is available for hire; at night, a green roof light is also illuminated. Fares are moderate; an average ride within the city costs 250-350ptas. Extra charges apply for trips after 11pm and to and from the airport and bullring. Don't accept rides in taxis without meters.

Cars
Traffic is heavy throughout the day and well into the evening. Street parking is extremely limited, especially in the older districts. Visitors with their own cars would be wise to park them in hotel garages and confine their use to excursions out of the city. Visitors intending to rent cars for day trips or extended tours can have them delivered to the hotel on the day of departure, saving parking fees.

Useful addresses

☎ The **telephone prefix (area code)** for Madrid is **91**.

Tourist information
There is a tourist office desk at **Barajas Airport** (☎ *205-8656*) and on the s side of the **Plaza Mayor** (*Oficina de Información, Plaza Mayor 3* ☎ *266-5477, map* **9** *D3, open (usually) Mon-Sat 9am-1.30pm, 4.30-8pm*).

   American Express Travel Service has its main office at Plaza de las Cortes 2 (☎ *222-1180, map* **10** *D4*). It is a valuable source of information for travelers in need of help, advice or emergency services.

Main post office
Plaza de la Cibeles 1 ☎221-8195. Map **10**C5. Open 8am-1am; limited services outside normal business hours.

Telephone services
Alarm call   ☎096
News   ☎095
Road conditions (outside Madrid)   ☎441-7222
Speaking clock   ☎093
Weather   ☎094

Tour operators
American Express   Plaza de las Cortes 2 ☎222-1180. Map **10**D4.
Compañía Internacional de Coches-Cammas (Wagon-Lits Cooks)   Marqués de Urquijo 28 ☎248-3000.
Juliá Tours   Capitán Haya 38 ☎270-4600. Variety of city tours, available in English.
Pullmantur   Plaza de Oriente 8 ☎241-1807. Map **9**D2. City tours.
Trapsatur   San Bernardo 23 ☎266-9900. Map **9**C3. City tours.
Viajes Meliá   Princesa 25 ☎247-5500. Map **9**B2.

Orientation

Europe's highest capital occupies the heart of a windswept, virtually treeless tableland. Viewed from above, Madrid appears to follow no grand plan, with streets radiating from central plazas in some neighborhoods, lined up in tidy grids in others, and meandering where they wish in still others.

Order can be discerned, however, in the wide north-south boulevard usually referred to as the **Paseo de la Castellana** or, simply, by the generic name **El Paseo**, despite the fact that the lower contiguous lengths of it are officially designated the **Paseo del Prado** and the **Paseo de Recoletos**. It is intersected by the east-west **Calle de Alcalá** at the **Plaza de Cibeles**, which is marked, for some reason, by a sumptuous statue and fountain honoring the goddess Cybele.

Within five streets of the plaza to the north or south are several prominent museums, including the famed **Prado** and the **Museo Arqueológico**. The **Parque del Retiro** is four streets east, and the **Jardín Botánico** (botanical garden) adjoins the Prado at the southern end. Within this orbit are several of the city's most luxurious hotels, including the **Ritz**, **Palace** and, a little farther north, the **Villa Magna**.

Business visitors are likely to spend a great deal of their time on the upper, northern reaches of the **Paseo de la Castellana**, which is fast becoming a teeming valley flanked by modestly proportioned skyscrapers. No Manhattan this, not with ample room in which to spread horizontally, but the sun strikes sparks from glass cubes housing scores of foreign banks and outposts of ubiquitous multinationals — IBM, Barclays, Citibank, JVC, Xerox, Bundesbank and Sony, among the many. Facing the Paseo are most of the big international-style hotels, including the **Meliá Castilla**, **Eurobuilding**, **Miguel Angel**, **Holiday Inn** and **Intercontinental**. Along the quieter side streets are many ambitious, stately restaurants devoted to the same expense-account crowd, notably **Zalacaín**, **Fortuny**, **Jockey** and **El Bodegón**.

In this glittery part of town, sightseeing attractions are few. For things to look at between meals, much time may be spent along or near Calle Alcalá, which, with its extensions Mayor and Arenal, cuts roughly from east to west through the center of the older districts of the city, sweeping through the **Puerta del Sol** (the point from which all roads in Spain were once measured), past the irresistible **Plaza Mayor** and the newly refurbished **Teatro Real**, and ending up in front of Madrid's second biggest attraction (after the Prado, that is), the **Palacio Real** (Royal Palace).

Short detours north off these avenues reach the monasteries of **Descalzas Reales** and **Encarnación**, while strolls south of the Plaza Mayor carry you past the *tascas*, cafés, flamenco clubs and family-style restaurants of oldest Madrid. This is the best area in which to pinch pesetas on lodgings, as at the **Llabeny**, near the **El Corte Inglés** department store.

That hardly exhausts the possibilities. Continue south down the **Paseo del Prado** to reach the upgraded **Atocha** district, with its important eponymous railroad station and the constantly improving **Reina Sofía cultural center**. And to the northwest of the Palacio Real is the **Parque de la Montaña**, which contains the reassembled Egyptian Temple of Debod, with its hilltop view of the semiwild recreational nature preserve, known as the **Casa del Campo**

A walk in Madrid

A city composed of scores of small neighborhoods consolidated into several large *distritos* — including **Centro**, **Salamanca** and **Retiro**, among the most frequently visited — Madrid's sprawling scope can be dismaying at first. While relatively few of its streets are without interest, aimless meandering is less rewarding than getting happily lost in Venice or Paris. Its museums and restaurants are scattered widely over the map, so visitors are often better served by taking the metro or a taxi to a specific destination, then using it as a point of reference for exploring the nearby blocks.

However, the oldest parts of Madrid are in a fairly compact area to the south and west of the PUERTA DEL SOL, so this suggested walk provides an introduction to the Madrid of the Bourbons and the Hapsburgs.

LA CIUDAD ANTIGUA
See map 9D3 and map opposite. Metro: Sol.

Standing beside the statue of **Felipe III** in the center of the PLAZA MAYOR, face the building with the heraldic crest, on the N side, the only facade painted white on a square of otherwise brick-red exteriors. That is the **Casa Panadería**, or bakery, a humble name for the place from which monarchs once chose to view the parades, pageants, bullfights and ritualized tortures staged for their subjects' edification and amusement.

Turn around to face the **Junta Municipal del Distrito Centro**, which has two lesser towers and an arched arcade. Go toward the far right (SW) corner, through the portal known as the **Arco de Cuchilleros**, and down the staircase past the restaurant **Las Cuevas de Luis Canelas**, with its doormen costumed as brigands.

The street at the bottom is Calle Cuchilleros. It is lined with the *tascas* and restaurants, including **Botín** (see page 112), down on the left, to which many visitors will want to return. For now, cross over to Calle del Maestro Villa, which opens, after a few strides, into the suddenly quieter **Plaza del Conde de Barajas**. A café in the middle is shaded by trees. Turn left, down Calle Gomez de Mora, then left again at the next corner.

Ahead is a marble cross, in the middle of the small square called **Puerta Cerrada** — "Closed Gate." On the formerly blank walls of six of the surrounding buildings are elaborately realized murals, which incorporate, among other things, *trompe l'oeil* windows and a surrealistic cornucopia.

Cross into Calle Cava Baja, which in effect is a continuation of Cuchilleros, with yet more *mesónes* and *tabernas*, as well as two restaurants that are worth remembering: **Julian de Tolosa**, shortly on the right, and **Casa Lucio** (see page 112), farther along on the left. The narrow, unprepossessing bar **La Solea** (#27 ☎ 265-3308) is the nightly scene of exuberant flamenco guitar and song performed by the homesick Andalucían patrons. (There are limits, though; a sign on the wall reads, "Don't dance or stamp your feet.")

Cava Baja soon empties into the **Plaza del Humilladero**. Cross the plaza, toward the monumental building with three towers straight ahead. The plaza is now called the **Puerta de Moros**. Up toward the right is seen the back of the 16thC **Capilla del Obispo** (Bishop's Chapel): under restoration at the time of writing, it contains a tomb carved with intricate Plateresque detail, and a fine altar.

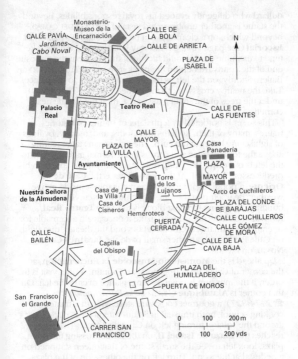

Continue down the Carrera San Francisco toward the 18thC
San Francisco el Grande church. It isn't all that "grand,"
actually, a fact that ongoing renovations won't significantly alter.
There are tours available, conducted by half-hearted Spanish-
speaking guides. Save yourself the time and pesetas by turning
right in front of the church along heavily-trafficked but tree-lined
Calle Bailén. A few streets along, on the left just before the
viaduct, is the restaurant **Ventorrillo**. While the food is nothing
special, it has many outdoor tables shaded by trees, with views of
the low hills and extensive parklands of CASA DEL CAMPO.

After a snack or a drink, continue N along Bailén. On the other
side of the viaduct, on the left, is a large gray-and-white church,
Nuestra Señora de la Almudena, begun late in the last century.
When completed, it will become Madrid's officially designated
cathedral. (The CATEDRAL DE SAN ISIDRO REAL, on Calle de Toledo
near the Plaza Mayor, presently serves that function.) It will not
take on that task in a particularly distinguished manner, from the
looks of it.

One short block farther, at the corner on the right, is **El
Anciano Rey de los Vinos**, one of the oldest and most famous
of the capital's *tabernas*. A tumbler of draft cider (*sidra*) is a
refreshing excuse to take a look inside.

Cross — with caution — to the opposite (W) side of Bailén and
proceed N to the far end of the incomplete cathedral. Turn left
into the narrow strip of park between the cathedral and the
fenced court of the PALACIO REAL. At the far end is an heroic statue
of **Felipe III**, a 16thC king who was in reality a far-from-intrepid

89

dullard who diligently evaded his royal responsibilities. Beyond the statue is another unobstructed vista of the CASA DEL CAMPO, beyond which, on a clear day, can be seen Felipe II's palace, **El Escorial** (see page 127). On the way back to Calle Bailén, take time to examine the splendid facade of the palace at the opposite end of the courtyard behind the black iron fence. Turn left (N) on Bailén. Shortly, on the left, is the visitor's entrance to the palace. Take the nearby crosswalk to the E side of Bailén. Turn left (N) under the trees of the small grassy area, then right at the next corner.

This street is bordered by a phalanx of statues of historic figures, many of them Romans and Goths, and, usually, by lines of sightseeing buses at the curb. The equestrian statue rearing above the topiary trees and shrubs in the formal garden-plaza to the left is of **Felipe IV**, a king only marginally more able than his predecessor, Felipe III. At the next corner is the **Café de Oriente**, a popular gathering place with tables outside in fine weather. Bear left past the café along the now-curving road. The building occupying the next block is the 1850 **Teatro Real**, renovated over recent years to make it once again acceptable for operatic performances. One street beyond the theater, turn right on Calle Pavía, with another small park, the **Jardines Cabo Noval**, on the left.

Up ahead is the **Monasterio-Museo de la Encarnación**, at the corner of Calles de la Bola and San Quintin. A brief visit is in order, if the museum is open. Exiting, glance over to the left. On that corner is **Alambique** (*Plaza de la Encarnación 2* ☎ *247-8827*), a gourmet cookware store with an affiliated cooking school, both unusual in Spain. After a look, circle back around the square, turning left on Calle de Arrieta. That soon reaches the **Plaza de Isabel II**, on the right. Crossing the open plaza, look left to see the small statue of that queen stationed on a pedestal at the E end. Turn left on the other side of the plaza, then right into Calle de las Fuentes. This rises to another major thoroughfare, Calle Mayor. Cross over and turn right.

A little over two streets down Mayor is the well-preserved **Plaza de la Villa**, enclosed on three sides by buildings dating from the city's earliest days as capital. The tower on the left is the 15thC **Torre de los Lujanos**, an occasional prison for captured enemy leaders, adjoining the Gothic **Hemeroteca**, a library. On the left is the 1670 **Casa de la Villa** (City Hall), containing a Goya canvas and attractive patio (*open Mon-Fri 9am-2pm*). Joined to the City Hall on the S side is the **Casa de Cisneros**, portions of which date to 1537.

Back on Mayor, turn right. At the next corner is a roofed **food market**, most interesting in the morning, when stocks are full. To return to the Plaza Mayor, cross the street and enter under the high arched portal.

Sights and places of interest

As its capital, Madrid has gathered to itself a lion's share of Spain's national patrimony. Apart from the presence of definitive gatherings of the works of Velázquez and Goya, Spain's two greatest painters before the 20thC, the more than 50 museums contain such wondrous relics of the Celtiberian past as the 5thC BC *Dama de Elche*, mosaics and statuary of the long Roman era, the sword of the semimythic El Cid, and the booty extracted from an empire that once nearly girdled the globe. The presence of these treasures is due in large measure to the Hapsburg and Bourbon monarchs who ruled, with widely varying degrees of aptitude, from the sixteenth century to the early twentieth century. The MUSEO DEL PRADO, which has enhanced its world-class stature with its recent acquisitions and reorganization, was created by kings and filled with their gifts and collections, as was the 2,000-room PALACIO REAL.

Those are mandatory sights numbers one and two, but there are others in the front row of the second rank. Among these must be the MUSEO ARQUEOLÓGICO NACIONAL, the MONASTERIO-MUSEO DE LAS DESCALZAS REALES and the MUSEO LÁZARO GALDIANO. Important among the several art centers created or refurbished in recent years are the Museo Thyssen-Bornemisza (an annex to the Prado) and the MUSEO NACIONAL CENTRO DE ARTE REINA SOFÍA.

All these compensate for what must be regarded as one of Madrid's touristic deficiencies. With its relatively short existence, it cannot claim the historical density or architectural heritage of either Sevilla or its arch-rival, Barcelona. Its oldest extant structures date back only as far as the sixteenth century, and there are few enough even of those. Most of them are in the Asturias area around the PLAZA MAYOR, and are included in A WALK IN MADRID (see page 88).

Following each street address in the listings below, in parentheses, is the cross street or prominent landmark nearest to the described site. Look for the ★ symbol against the most important sights and 🏛 for buildings of architectural interest. Places of special interest for children (✱) are also indicated.

If you only know the name of a museum, say, in English, and cannot find it in the following A-Z, try looking it up in the INDEX. Some lesser sights do not have their own entries but are included within other entries: look these up in the INDEX too.

When plotting a day's sightseeing, please remember that few things change as quickly or with less predictability in this ever-transmuting city as telephone numbers and opening hours. The wise visitor will always confirm opening times before setting out.

CASA DEL CAMPO ✱

This substantial area of heath and woodland was once a royal park and hunting ground for Felipe II, laid out in 1562 and extended and improved by subsequent monarchs. Its 1,747 hectares (4,370 acres) lie W of the canalized Manzanares River, which forms the western edge of the city center. They contain a **parque de atracciones** (amusement park) (☎ 463-2900 ☎ *open Apr-Oct Tues-Fri 11am-4pm, Sat-Sun 11am-1pm, closed Mon; Nov-Mar Sat-Sun 11am-8pm, closed Mon-Fri*) and a **zoo** (☎ *open Apr-Sept 10am-9pm; Oct-Mar 10am-sunset*). The latter facility is Spain's best, admittedly less than high praise in a country not known for the glories of its zoos. There is a dispirited quality to the place, but over 2,000 creatures are on display, among them a famous panda couple.

Check ahead for current opening hours before setting out, since they are subject to seasonal changes and caprices that cannot be anticipated here. A cable car carries visitors into the park from the station on Paseo del Pintor Rosales, near the intersection with Marqués de Urquijo, seven blocks W of the Argüelles metro station. It leaves passengers at some distance from either the zoo or the amusement park, however. For them, use the Batán metro station.

CASA-MUSEO DE LOPE DE VEGA
Cervantes 11 (Paseo del Prado) ☎ *429-9216. Map 10D4*
🚇 *Open Tues, Thurs 10am-2pm. Closed Fri-Mon; Wed;*
July 15-Sept 15. Metro: Antón Martin.

Félix Lope de Vega Carpio lived from 1562-1635, many of those years in this painstakingly reconstructed home. Considered one of the fathers of the modern theater — Shakespeare was a contemporary — he is believed to have written over 1,800 plays during a tempestuous life of frequent scandal and repeated amorous affairs. He even had time to sail with the Spanish Armada. The house is more intriguing for the larger-than-life character it sheltered than for the objects it contains.

CASÓN DEL BUEN RETIRO
Felipe IV 13 (Alfonso XII) ☎ *468-0481. Map 10D5* 🚇
Open Tues-Sat 9am-7pm; Sun and holidays 9am-2pm.
Closed Mon. Metro: Retiro.

An annex to the MUSEO DEL PRADO, four streets w, this 17thC building with an ugly 19thC Neoclassical overlay faces the PARQUE DEL RETIRO. Its principal attraction is the celebrated Picasso painting *Guernica* (★). A savage condemnation of the terror bombing of that Basque city during the Civil War, the anguished study in grays and blacks was held at the Museum of Modern Art in New York for over 40yrs. It was only brought back to Spain, according to the artist's wishes, when democracy returned after Franco's death. (For the *Guernica* alone, enter from Alfonso XII 28.) The rest of the collection is concerned with 19thC Spanish painting after Goya, a largely fallow period that produced few artists of even secondary distinction. Works by Sorolla, Fortuny and Rusinol are of some interest.

CATEDRAL DE SAN ISIDRO REAL
Toledo 37 (Plaza Mayor). Map 9E3. Metro: Sol.

Distinguished primarily as the burial place of the city's patron saint, this otherwise ordinary 17thC church is the provisional cathedral of Madrid, so designated in 1885. That status will last only until the completion of the intended official cathedral, **Nuestra Señora de la Almudena**, S of the PALACIO REAL.

CIUDAD UNIVERSITARIA *(University City)*
Metro: Moncloa.

This is the campus of the University of Madrid, one of Spain's most prestigious institutions of higher education. Opened to students in 1927, it became a major battlefield less than ten years later, during the Civil War. Severely damaged, it was rebuilt in an esthetically undistinguished manner, so there have been only two good reasons to make the longish trip from downtown: the MUSEO ESPAÑOL DE ARTE CONTEMPORÁNEO and the MUSEO DE AMÉRICA. The collection of the former has been moved to the MUSEO NACIONAL CENTRO DE ARTE REINA SOFÍA, and there are rumors that the latter will eventually be transferred, too, although extensive renovations were recently completed. Check its current status before setting out.

ERMITA DE SAN ANTONIO DE LA FLORIDA
Glorieta de San Antonio de la Florida s/n (Paseo de la Florida) ☎ *247-7921* 🚇 *Open July-Sept Mon, Tues,*
Thurs-Sat 10am-1.30pm, 4-7pm, Sun 10am-1.30pm;
Oct-May Mon-Tues, Thurs-Sat 11am-1.30pm, 3-6pm, Sun
11am-1.30pm. Closed Wed. Metro: Norte.

Completed in 1797, this youngest of three Madrid hermitages was ordered to be built by Carlos IV. He commissioned Francisco de Goya to paint the unusual dome fresco, the *Miracle of St Anthony of Padua*, which the artist finished in 1798, along with related scenes in the cross vault. In the depiction of the crowd witnessing the Saint's resurrection of a dead man, many of the onlookers were actual personages of the Spanish court and high society, while the models for some of the angels were said to be women of less than savory reputation. Goya did have his not very private jokes, often at the expense of his patrons, yet he retained royal favor for many years.

The building now functions as a de facto shrine to the artist, whose body is buried here. His remains had to be repatriated in 1888 from France, where he died, a voluntary exile, in 1828. They did not include his head, which disappeared from his Bordeaux tomb during the interim.

ESTUDIO Y MUSEO SOROLLA

Paseo General Martínez Campos 37 (Paseo de la Castellana) ☎ *410-1584* 📷 *Open Tues-Sat 10am-3pm. Closed Mon. Metro: Rubén Darío.*

The home of the Valencian artist Joaquín Sorolla y Bastida is preserved essentially as it was during his creative lifetime, which ended in 1923. His large landscapes and figurative paintings are well displayed in the rooms in which he lived and worked. Works by other popular artists supplement the collection.

MONASTERIO-MUSEO DE LAS DESCALZAS REALES ★

Plaza de las Descalzas Reales 3 (Arenal) ☎ *222-0687. Map 9C3* 📷 ✗ *compulsory. Open Tues, Wed, Fri, Sat 10.30am-12.30pm, 4-5.30pm; Thurs 10.30am-12.30pm; Sun 11am-1.30pm. Closed Mon. Metro: Sol.*

Aristocratic benefactors who sought spiritual retreat here clearly saw no need to condemn themselves to the unrelenting sobriety normally associated with such establishments. The 16thC building was first, after all, a palace, the birthplace of a daughter of Carlos V, the Holy Roman Emperor. It was she, Juana of Austria, who in the 16thC turned it into a profitable retreat for bluebloods, sheltering aristocrats whose families showered the convent with riches. The sumptuous collection on view includes Flemish tapestries, embroidered vestments, paintings, sculptures, 32 profusely decorated chapels (16 of which can be viewed), and a splendid Baroque staircase, its landings crowded with polychrome decorative carving and lined with rare marble veneers. A series of 1st-floor galleries displays canvases by Titian, Rubens, Fra Angelico and Zurbarán, among many works by lesser artists.

Few of the artworks are labeled, and the mandatory guided tour is conducted only in Spanish — not very helpful for the largely foreign visitors. But soldier on, for this is one of the more compelling repositories of religious art in the capital.

MONASTERIO-MUSEO DE LA ENCARNACIÓN

Plaza de la Encarnación 1 (Bailén) ☎ *247-0510. Map 9C2* ✗ *compulsory* 📷 *(but* 📷 *Wed). Open Tues-Thurs, Sat 10am-12.30pm, 4-5.30pm; Fri 10am-12.30pm; Sun 11am-1.30pm. Closed Mon; holidays.*

Construction of the monastery began in 1616, during the reign of Felipe III. Its collection of religious paintings and relics reflects his sponsorship and that of his Queen Margarita, although the monastery is not as richly endowed as the larger MONASTERIO-MUSEO DE LAS DESCALZAS REALES, which was built several decades earlier. The most important artist represented is José de Ribera, a Renaissance painter who was given his own gallery in the MUSEO DEL PRADO.

More impressive is the **reliquary room**, which is decorated in lavish Baroque style to display over 1,500 relics, mostly of rather obscure saints. The obligatory guided tour is conducted in Spanish only.

MUSEO DE AMÉRICA
Reyes Católicos 6 (Av. Arco de la Victoria) ☎ *243-9537*
☒ *Open 10am-7pm. Closed Mon; some holidays. Metro: Moncloa.*

Spanish America produced the bulk of this collection, especially pre-Columbian Peru and Mexico, but the name is sufficiently elastic to include arts and crafts from the Philippines. Mayan Palenque is represented by steles, and by a calendar more accurate than the European version; Incan Peru by funerary relics; Colombia by boisterous clay figurines; and all the colonies by folk art that preceded and followed the arrival of the conquistadors. All is shown to greater advantage since the recent renovation. Call ahead to confirm opening times.

MUSEO ARQUEOLÓGICO NACIONAL ★
Serrano 13 (Paseo de Recoletos) ☎ *403-6607. Map **10**B5*
☒ *Open Tues-Sat 9.30am-8.30pm; Sun 9.30am-2.30pm. Closed Mon; holidays. Metro: Colón.*

To the left of the street entrance and downstairs into an artificial cave is a reproduction of the paintings at Altamira (near Santillana del Mar, in the NW Cantabria region). It is not an especially compelling display, but is worth a visit, as access to the original requires special permission.

Inside the museum itself, galleries to the right are concerned primarily with Iberian and Roman artifacts. First encountered are ceramic figures of the 2nd and 3rdC BC found on the Balearic island of Ibiza, and urns from the necropolis of Villaricos in Almería, in Andalucía. The pride of the collection is the centerpiece of the next room. It is the life-sized bust of the **Dama de Elche**, a woman of rare sophistication, with an unusual disc headdress and serpent-head necklace. Dating back to the 4thC BC, before the Roman colonization, it is undiminished in impact by the glass case recently installed to protect it. The sculpture is flanked by the **Dama de Baza**, a more crudely wrought depiction of a full body on a throne.

The galleries that follow have sculpture, mosaics, jewelry, pottery and minor arts of the Roman epoch. Proceeding counter-clockwise, the next room has Roman statuary from Mérida and Cádiz and a 3rdC BC mosaic floor from Albacete. Galleries with two more such floors follow, along with cases of bronzes and glassware and several headless draped figures. These lead to the revamped Visigothic section, with striking installations of clothing, jewelry, glasswork and architectural fragments. Relatively little remains of the race that ruled Iberia for over 200yrs, but here, in hanging cases, are the elaborately fashioned and bejeweled gold crowns of Reccesvinth, from Toledo. Next, a scalloped 11thC gateway introduces the Moorish section and the arts of the Arab conquerors, with tiles and other ceramics predominating.

Iberian prehistory is illustrated in the basement, with reconstructed human and animal skeletons and models. Particularly intriguing are exhibits dealing with ancient ceremonial and domestic structures still to be seen in the Balearic Islands. Other rooms contain substantial displays of Greek pottery and Egyptian funerary objects.

On the first floor, the museum's definition is stretched to include decorative arts — tapestries, furnishings, bronzes — as well as arms and armor of the Middle Ages and the Renaissance. Reorganization of the collections continues.

MUSEO DE CARRUAJES
Paseo del Virgen del Puerto s/n (Campo del Moro)
☎ *276-2564. Off map 9D1. Open Mon-Sat 10am-12.45pm, 4-5.45pm; Sun, holidays 10am-1.30pm. Metro: Norte.*
Ornate horsedrawn carriages, saddles, harnesses and related implements of the age of royalty are the concern of this small museum in the **Campo del Moro**, the parkland immediately w of the PALACIO REAL. Most are of the 17thC and 18thC, including the one in which Alfonso XIII and his new bride were riding in 1906 when a bomb-throwing assassin made an unsuccessful attempt on their lives.

MUSEO DE CERA *(Wax Museum)*
Paseo de Recoletos 41 (Plaza de Colón) ☎ *419-2282. Map 10B5* 🔳 ✱ *Open 10.30am-2pm, 4-9pm. Metro: Colón.*
Those who find wax museums enlightening or entertaining discover here over 300 figures representing famous personalities from Spanish and world history. Many of them are kings, queens and ministers of state, a juiceless procession unlikely to engage for long a younger generation brought up on music videos and Elvis imitators. They are drawn, raptly, to the characterizations of Mick Jagger, Michael Jackson, Batman and the Beatles, not to mention the requisite grisly tableaux of assorted mayhem and tortures of the Inquisition. (Parents of subteenagers will want to avoid the latter. Needless to say, those are precisely the exhibits the kiddies will most want to see.) Most of the contemporary figures bear only passing resemblance to the people they supposedly replicate, that of the present King Juan Carlos being inexplicably among the least persuasive.

MUSEO CERRALBO
Ventura Rodríguez 17 (Plaza de España) ☎ *247-3646. Map 9B2* 🔳 *Open Tues-Sun 10am-3pm. Closed Mon; Aug. Metro: Plaza de España or Ventura Rodriguez.*
The Marqués de Cerralbo was a voracious collector, and this, his mansion, is filled with artworks that he left to the country after his death in 1922. His catholic tastes drew him to Celtiberian weaponry, Greek ceramics, Flemish tapestries, jewelry, clocks, porcelain, paintings by Zurbarán, Van Dyck, Titian and El Greco, and drawings by Goya and Tintoretto. Although lacking in scholarly discipline, it is a stunning collection.

MUSEO DE CIENCIAS NATURALES
José Gutiérrez Abascal 2 (Vitruvio) ☎ *261-8600* 🔳 *Open Tues-Sat 10am-6pm; Sun 10am-2pm. Closed Mon; Aug. Metro: República Argentina.*
Part of a scientific research complex off the Paseo de la Castellana, this museum contains exhibits concerned with

geology, entomology, paleontology and zoology, including stuffed animals.

MUSEO DEL EJÉRCITO *(Army Museum)*
Méndez Núñez 1 (Alfonso XII) ☎ *222-0628. Map* **10D5** *☒ Open Tues-Sun 10am-2pm. Closed Mon. Metro: Banco.*

Thousands of weapons and related implements are well displayed in the 17thC CASÓN DEL BUEN RETIRO. Under the sponsorship and direction of the Army, it is one of the few public places left in Spain where Generalissimo Franco and the Falange movement are not reviled or ignored, especially in the rooms concerned with the 1936-39 Civil War.

Most of the exhibits are of interest primarily to military buffs and scholars, but there are displays of Moorish ivory and silver daggers, toy soldiers, firearms, uniforms, armor, battle pennants and flags, letters written by Napoleon and Wellington, and *La Tizona*, the reputed sword of El Cid, who apparently had a very dainty hand for an epic hero. The collection may soon be moved elsewhere, for the all-powerful Museo del Prado, in desperate need of gallery space, has cast covetous eyes on this building.

MUSEO ESPAÑOL DE ARTE CONTEMPORÁNEO
The entire collection of this CIUDAD UNIVERSITARIA museum has been transferred to the MUSEO NACIONAL CENTRO DE ARTE REINA SOFÍA, and the building has been converted to other (unspecified) uses.

MUSEO LÁZARO GALDIANO
Serrano 122 (María de Molina) ☎ *261-6084* ☒ *Open 10am-2pm. Closed Mon; Aug. Metro: Rubén Darío.*

This impressive 19thC mansion, given to the city by the well-known author-financier, is celebrated for its comprehensive display of enamels, ivories, and gold and silverwork, which spans the Middle Ages on three continents.

The museum also exhibits Renaissance jewelry and *objets*, as well as paintings by Gainsborough, Bosch, Murillo, Rembrandt, Velázquez, Goya, Constable and Turner. Unfortunately, many paintings are badly hung and almost invisible, and the staff can be surly.

MUSEO MUNICIPAL
Fuencarral 78 (Barceló) ☎ *221-6656. Map* **10B4** *☒ Open Tues-Sat 10am-2pm, 5-9pm; Sun 10am-3pm. Closed Mon. Metro: Tribunal.*

The former 18thC hospice of **San Fernando** has now been converted into the municipal museum. The wildly Baroque portal is in fierce contrast with the plain brick facade. Exhibitions concentrate on the history of the city, and the most interesting show maps and models of Madrid in earlier centuries.

MUSEO NACIONAL DE ARTES DECORATIVAS
Montalbán 12 (Alfonso XII) ☎ *221-3440. Map* **10D5** *☒ Open Tues-Sat 10am-3pm; Sun 10am-2pm. Closed Mon; Aug. Metro: Banco de España.*

Domestic arts and crafts of the last four centuries are captivatingly presented in period rooms reflecting Gothic, Baroque, Mudejar, Levantine and folk persuasions.

Included in the displays are ceramics, china, leatherwork, furniture, clothing, crystal, lace and jewelry. The sumptuously furnished rooms re-created on the 1st and 2nd floors deserve particular attention.

MUSEO NACIONAL CENTRO DE ARTE REINA SOFÍA

Santa Isabel 52 (Ronda de Atocha) ☎ *467-5062. Map 10F5* 🚇 *Open Wed-Mon 10am-9pm. Closed Tues. Metro: Atocha.*

The palatial but abandoned former 18thC hospital was resurrected as an exposition center in the mid-1980s and named for the present queen. It quickly became the city's principal venue for traveling exhibitions of such major international artists as Jasper Johns and Diego Rivera. A second wave of renovations, completed in 1990, prepared the building to receive 13,000 artworks from the MUSEO ESPAÑOL DE ARTE CONTEMPORÁNEO (which is being converted to other purposes). While that collection is not of the highest order, it does have many pieces by such notables as Miró and Picasso, and the Reina Sofía is in a far more convenient location.

"Contemporary" is defined here as ranging from the mid-19thC late Romantics onward, up to the Spanish Abstractionists who burst onto the scene in the 1960s. Works by Antonio Tàpies, Eduardo Vicente, Dalí, Juan de Echevarría, Solana and Rosales, among many, represent most major modern art movements of that period, but the collection is sketchy in parts and therefore less illuminating than might be hoped. An art library of over 50,000 volumes has been installed on the 3rd floor.

MUSEO DEL PRADO ★

Paseo del Prado s/n (Felipe IV) ☎ *420-2836 and 420-1768. Map 10D5* 🚇 *(but* 🖼 *on Sat)* 𝄞 🍴 *Open Tues-Sat 9am-7pm; Sun 9am-1.45pm. Closed Mon. Metro: Antón Martín.*

Whatever their many deficiencies as rulers, such monarchs as Felipe IV and Carlos V and their aides had true collectors' eyes for the artistic achievements of their times. Felipe II is responsible for the outstanding Flemish paintings and the peerless collection of Titians. And Fernando VII, at best an otherwise ineffectual monarch, was responsible for transforming what had been intended as a natural history museum into what became one of the greatest repositories of art in the Western world. The Prado, opened in 1819, contains the cream of the royal collections. Although the Spanish masters Velázquez, Goya, Murillo, El Greco and Zurbarán are abundantly represented, there are also numerous favorites of the various foreign courts. Particularly evident are the Flemish Baroque painter Rubens, the Italians Titian, Bellini, Tintoretto, Botticelli and Fra Angelico, the Dutch Van der Weyden, Van Dyck and Rembrandt, and the Germans Dürer and Holbein.

An extensive, multimillion-peseta renovation is in its final stages, a principal objective being the installation of air conditioning for canvases in danger of deterioration from the often extreme temperature changes of the capital. In addition, the Baron Hans Heinrich Thyssen-Bornemisza has agreed to a long-term loan to the Prado of his private collection, considered one of the most important in the world.

The 18thC **Palacio de Villahermosa**, diagonally across the Plaza Cánovas del Castillo from the Prado, is being restored to accept these works. There is also talk of moving there all the Goyas and many of the 18thC paintings from the main building, or, possibly, expanding into the nearby MUSEO DEL EJÉRCITO. With these continuing changes, artworks are moved frequently, and it

97

is not possible to provide more than a sketchy guide to the galleries.

Entrance to the undistinguished late 18thC Neoclassical building is made at street level, beyond the statue of a seated Velázquez. This floor and the one above are where the principal galleries are located, with an additional smaller space below.

Turn right (s) into a wing dominated by the vast 17thC allegorical and religious canvases of **Rubens**. In the far right-hand corner is his powerful *Death of Seneca*, and beyond, a circular salon of **Greek sculptures**. Return to the main hall, and turn right (E) into a series of galleries, which also highlight Rubens but phase into Dutch still-lifes and landscapes. A sampling of **Goyas** is found in two galleries down to the right, the larger number to be found (at the time of writing) in the rooms directly above. The so-called "black" paintings are here — huddled, despairing figures expressively grouped in unknown terror. Most of these were lifted from the walls of Goya's country home. Less well-known than his earlier paintings, they are his most profoundly moving works.

Return to the main vestibule, continuing into the N hall and a glorious profusion of **early Gothic panels** surrounded by astonishing gilt frames. These artists' successors from the early Renaissance, notably **Ribera** and **Ribalta**, are seen in the rooms beyond.

The first-floor vaulted central hall is devoted to **Velázquez**, with equestrian portraits of royalty and lavish historical and mythological scenes. Velázquez knew which side of his bread was buttered. Unlike Goya, who was also a court painter, he did not tweak the sensibilities of his royal patrons or display an overt satirical bent. Instead, he concentrated on perfecting his painterly techniques and the masterly use of light, which is reminiscent of Rembrandt. The huge painting of *Las Meninas* (Maids of Honor) is accorded a room of its own, as it should be. Like *Las Lanzas* (The Surrender of Breda), it is unforgettable.

A portal in the E wall leads to a gallery showing work by **El Greco**. None of his most famous pictures are here, for he was not in favor until relatively recently, and many of his canvases were taken abroad. However, those displayed are representative of his expressive style. In the next chambers hang the famous portrayal by **Goya** of a massacre of peasants by a Napoleonic firing squad, and, in an opposite corner, a portrait of *Fernando VII* — a subject the artist clearly held in contempt. Also on view are the side-by-side nude and clothed portraits of the Maja, a noblewoman who was probably Goya's mistress at the time. Continuing, viewers come upon his scathing group portrait of the family of Carlos IV, whose members were presumably unaware that they were being portrayed as buffoons and simpletons. That Goya remained in royal favor after paintings such as this is remarkable.

This account serves merely as an introduction, highlighting some of the most memorable works. The Prado repays repeated visits, to explore on different occasions such varied delights as **Romanesque murals**, fine inlaid **Florentine furniture**, the florid works of **Watteau** and other artists of the **18th-19thC Romantic** period, the splendid collections of **Titian** and the **Venetian school**, and the mysterious paintings of **Hieronymus Bosch**.

The best advice is to be organized: decide before you set out what you want to see and arrive early or during lunchtime (the museum is open through the siesta period) to avoid as much as possible the daily crush of visitors. The main entrance is always crowded and there is an inevitable wait. Try the less-used doors at the N or s ends of the building. The entrance fee includes admission to CASÓN DEL BUEN RETIRO, three blocks E.

MUSEO NAVAL
Montalbán 2 (Paseo del Prado) ☎ 221-0419. Map 10D5 ▨ (but ▣ on Thurs). Open Tues-Sun 10.30am-1.30pm. Closed Mon; Aug. Metro: Banco de España.
On display are delightful ship models, navigation instruments, and a chart of the New World made by Juan de la Cosa in 1500. Particular attention is given to the Battle of Lepanto of 1571, in which an allied Christian fleet of over 200 galleons soundly defeated the Turkish force. It was the greatest victory in the annals of Spanish sea power, one that might have contributed to the misplaced confidence in the Armada launched against England 17yrs later.

MUSEO DE LA REAL ACADEMIA DE BELLAS ARTES DE SAN FERNANDO
Alcalá 13 (Puerta del Sol) ☎ 276-2564. Map 10D4 ▨ Open Mon-Sat 10am-2pm. Closed Sun. Metro: Sevilla.
This recently restored building contains paintings and other artworks gathered by the Academy since the middle of the 18thC. While the cream of the collection was long ago skimmed off for the Prado, on display are works by Velázquez, Murillo, Zurbarán, El Greco, Vicente López, Ribera and Sorolla, as well as such non-Spaniards as Rubens and Bellini. Powerful Goya canvases of his expressionistic later years dominate some galleries, while Pablo Picasso is represented by a number of his prints. Opening hours are to be expanded in the course of the continuing reclamation.

MUSEO ROMÁNTICO
San Mateo 13 ☎ 448-1045. Map 10B4 ▨ Open Tues-Sun 10am-3pm. Closed Mon; Aug 1 to mid-Sept.
The mid-19thC mini-*palacio* of the **Marqués de la Vega-Inclán** was given with the family collection of paintings and furnishings. These date from before 1800 but are dominated by objects of the latter part of the Romantic era. Although the collection is a bit of a mishmash, it is most agreeable to stroll through, noting such charming accessories as Victorian dollhouses between canvases by Goya and Zurbarán.

MUSEO TAURINO
Alcalá 237 (Av. de la Paz) ☎ 255-1857 ▨ Open Tues-Fri, Sun 9am-2.30pm. Closed Mon; Sat.
An annex of the Las Ventas Plaza de Toros (bullring) chronicles the history of the *corrida* in carefully organized pictorial exhibits showing the careers of the great matadors. Unfortunately, it is too small and too far E of the center for any but confirmed *aficionados* to make the special trip, and it closes hours before scheduled bullfights.

PALACIO REAL *(Royal Palace)* 🏛
Plaza de Oriente s/n (Bailén) ☎ 248-7404. Map 9C2 ▨ (but ▣ on Wed). Four separate tickets are required to see the official apartments, painting galleries, library and armory ✗ compulsory ✿ Open May-Sept Mon-Sat 9.30am-12.45pm, 4-6.30pm, Sun and holidays 9.30am-

1.30pm; Oct-Apr Mon-Sat 9.30am-12.45pm, 3.30- 5.15pm, Sun and holidays 9.30am-1.30pm. Closed for occasions of state. Metro: Opera.

Putting aside its potential as a persuasive antimonarchist argument, the Royal Palace is, with the Prado Museum, one of the two mandatory sights of Madrid. This huge Renaissance Neoclassical building lies N of a great courtyard formed by colonnaded halls and ancillary structures. It was completed in 1764, the same year that Carlos III took up residence. Clearly, the Spanish Bourbons did not regard excess as a vice: the palace has no fewer than *2,000* rooms, although only 50 are accessible to visitors. By contrast, London's Buckingham Palace has fewer than 600 rooms.

The main facade is comparatively restrained, the ground floor of plain granite blocks being surmounted by Corinthian columns and pilasters and a balustraded balcony. Originally the statues of kings and generals that circle the adjacent Plaza de Oriente were to be arrayed along this roofline, but they proved too heavy. The interior, however, shows all the extravagance of the last flamboyant flame-out of Rococo.

Visitors wait in the lobby for tour groups to be assembled. Guides are available who speak English and the major European languages, and when five or more persons who speak one of those languages are on hand, they are summoned to the portal of the Grand Staircase. (If it is winter, keep your coat, for the palace is chilly. Disabled people in wheelchairs need assistance to get upstairs.) As the guided tour is compulsory, there is no need to attempt a room-by-room description. Hints and highlights follow of what you will see.

The double marble staircase ascends to the first floor beneath a florid ceiling painting by the 18thC Italian Conrado Giaquinto. Circular windows and arches pierce the domed ceiling, encrusted with medallions, stucco cherubim, and white and gold carved garlands. The **Salón de Alabarderos** is next, named after the royal guards whose quarters were once here. Spanish tapestries of the 18thC illustrate episodes from the lives of Solomon, Joseph and David. The following rooms include the **Salón de Columnas** and the apartments that constituted the principal residence of Carlos III and his family. The **Saleta de Gasparni**, named after the designer, is in lavish Rococo style, with fine chandeliers (now electrified), gilt-framed mirrors, and a circular sofa with an extravagant candelabra, a gift from the French monarchs. An antechamber contains portraits of *Carlos IV* and *Queen María Luisa* by Goya. The **Salón de Gasparini** has a fantastic profusion of entwined tendrils and garlands in high painted relief leaping up the walls and across the arched ceiling.

Nearly as astonishing is the **Sala de Porcelana**, in which 400 panels of exquisitely modeled and hand-painted scenes in porcelain are joined to cover all the walls and the ceiling. Even these are surpassed in grandeur by the **state dining room**, its single long table set for 145 guests, the gold-edged china glinting beneath 15 ornate chandeliers. The present king uses the hall for ceremonial dinners.

After rooms devoted to collections of fans, clocks and silverware, the tour leads to the **Capilla Real** (Royal Chapel), completed in 1757. Beneath the dome are columns of veined black marble with gilded capitals, statues of saints, paintings by Giaquinto and an image of the 10yr-old St Félix. Finally, there is the **Salón del Trono** (Throne Room). Used occasionally by the present monarchs (who don't live in the palace), it contains chairs bearing their carved profiles. The **painting galleries** contain nothing that isn't surpassed by the Prado collections, but there are two curiosities: a portrait with the face and hands rendered by El Greco but completed by his son, and a rearing horse by Velázquez that was to be an equestrian portrait. The artist died before he could paint his royal subject.

The tour ends in the waiting room. As you leave through the w door, bear right (N) toward the **Biblioteca Real** (Royal Library), which is interesting for its maps, engravings, Renaissance musical instruments and collection of 300,000 books. Turning left (s) from the waiting room, walk across the courtyard to the **Armería Real** (Royal Armory). A superb display of over 100 suits of armor, many mounted on horseback, with plumed helmets, is supplemented by crossbows, lances, shields, swords, wheel-lock pistols and rifles. Somehow poignant are the suits of armor made for the royal progeny at various stages of childhood, to train them to wear in adulthood as much as 80lbs of metal plate.

PARQUE DEL OESTE
Metro: Plaza de España or Norte.

The "Park of the West" has the loveliest plants of any in Madrid, especially in the gardens at the corner of Irún and Ferraz and near the Casa del Campo cable-car station off Paseo Pintor Rosales. The elevated land at the SE end of the park contains the reconstructed Egyptian **Templo de Debod** (☒ *open 10am-1pm, 5-8pm, holidays 10am-3pm*), which dates from the 4thC BC and was moved here to save it from the rising waters created by the Aswan Dam.

PARQUE DEL RETIRO
Map 10D-E6 ☀ Closed Nov-Feb 10.30pm-6am. Metro: Retiro.

This large, well-used park of over 320 acres was once the grounds of a palace that belonged to Felipe IV but no longer exists. There are flower gardens, tree-shaded walks, lagoons and ponds, fountains, an extravagant pavilion and a glass-domed conservatory.

The main entrance is from the Plaza de la Independencia, from which a pedestrian mall cuts diagonally to the Plaza de Nicaragua and the artificial lake — **El Estanque Grande** — that fronts the grandiose pavilion commemorating Alfonso XII. He is represented by the equestrian statue that tops the high central pedestal. Passing along the w edge of the lake, you eventually arrive at the path leading to the **Palacio de Cristal**, a glass-domed Victorian conservatory recently restored and now used as a cultural center. To the E is another exhibition hall, the **Palacio de Velázquez**, also newly restored to its original purpose.

Warm weekends are busiest in the park, with couples renting rowboats on El Estanque, gypsies with performing dogs and monkeys, rows of tables with tarot card readers, and several kiosks for drinks and snacks. To see the formal gardens, exit bearing w, toward Calle Alfonso XII and the CASÓN DEL BUEN RETIRO.

PLAZA DE ESPAÑA
Map 9C2. Metro: Plaza de España.

This busy square, at the point where Grand Vía becomes Calle Princesa, is now hemmed in by two of Madrid's tallest buildings. A monument to Cervantes has the author gazing down upon his protagonists, Don Quixote and Sancho Panza.

PLAZA DE LA CIBELES
Map 10C5. Metro: Banco de España.
This busy intersection of Calle Alcalá and Paseo del Prado is
given a marked grandeur by the presence of the most handsome
of the capital's many fountains. It celebrates the Greek goddess
Cybele, who commands a chariot and team of horses. On the SE
side is the wedding-cake **Palacio de Comunicaciónes**, a
neo-Baroque extravaganza that houses the main post office.
Occupying the NW corner is the fenced-in estate of the **Palacio
de Vistahermosa**, now headquarters of the Army's general staff.
Opposite it, to the S, is the massive, somber **Bank of Spain**.

PLAZA MAYOR ★ 🏛
Map 9D3. Metro: Sol.
One of the capital's most harmonious public spaces, this
enclosed square gave focus to the rambling village that was
17thC Madrid. The equestrian statue in the center is of Felipe III,
during whose reign the surrounding structures were built. They
were designed by Juan Gómez de Mora, largely uniform in
height, with balconies above arcaded walkways bordered with
shops, tapas bars and restaurants. Cafés with outdoor tables on
all four sides provide observation stations for the pedestrians-
only traffic (but nurse the expensive drinks and sit in the middle
to reduce the entreaties of persistent beggars).

At #3 on the S side is a municipal tourist office. The turreted
building on the N side is the **Casa Panadería**, once a municipal
bakery. The conical turrets on either side were designed by the
quintessential Hapsburg architect, Juan de Herrera, who was
responsible in part for Felipe II's El Escorial. Kings and queens
once witnessed the activities in the square below from the
balcony of the Panadería. These included such entertainments as
bullfights, executions and *autos-da-fé*, the inventive acts of
death-by-torture favored by the masters of the Inquisition.

The plaza remains the setting for carnivals, music festivals,
fireworks and plays. What you might see: women selling flowers
table-to-table; musicians of many persuasions and levels of
aptitude performing in front of the cafés; a pride of caricaturists at
their easels; latter-day hippies passing around a hashish pipe;
youngsters whirling in impromptu *sevillanas*; the people called
chulos, who dress in vaguely Edwardian suits and vividly colored
tiered dresses; rock concerts; *zarzuelas*; symphony orchestras;
and pageants with horsemen in 18thC regalia.

PUERTA DE ALCALÁ
Map 10C6. Metro: Retiro.
The 18thC triumphal arch, erected in honor of Carlos III, stands
in the center of the Plaza de la Independencia, on the S side of
which is the main entrance to the PARQUE DEL RETIRO. The
monument has three central archways and two squared end
portals, the five divided by Ionic columns, while the pediment
supports seated stone figures. Unprepossessing during daylight,
despite its bulk, it assumes a decided air of grandeur when
illuminated at night.

PUERTA DEL SOL
Map 9D3. Metro: Sol.
A triumphal arch once stood in this plaza, whose name translates
as "The Gate of the Sun." That disappeared centuries ago, and in
more recent decades the half-moon-shaped plaza was known for
the lively cafés that spilled across its sidewalks. Those, too, are

gone, replaced largely by American and Spanish fast-food chain restaurants. In the late 1980s, the plaza was reorganized to deal in a less chaotic manner with the traffic caused by the ten streets that meet there. Buses are now channeled into several bays to complement the refurbished metro station directly below. New street lamps and a fountain were installed; several newsstands sell foreign-language publications. The late 19thC buildings enclosing the plaza were painted a pale pink with white trim (already starting to accumulate new coats of grime).

The dominant structure on the S side is the 18thC headquarters of the *policía nacional*, a fact less evident now that the guards no longer carry submachine guns. Inside the door is a tablet proclaiming that point to be **kilométrico zero**, the point from which all the roads radiating from Madrid are measured. The clock high on the facade was installed in 1866 and draws all eyes as it moves toward midnight on New Year's Eve, when Madrileños gather in the plaza to watch the gold ball fall to the roofline. When the clock starts to strike 12, onlookers, according to custom, pop one grape in their mouths for every stroke.

REAL FÁBRICA DE TAPICES *(Royal Tapestry Factory)*
Fuenterrabia 2 (Av. de Menéndez y Pelayo) ☎ *251-3400* ▨ *Open Mon-Fri 9.30am-12.30pm. Closed Sat; Sun; Aug. Metro: Menéndez Pelayo.*

Goya once worked for this royal factory, which was founded by a Flemish master in 1720 and has been at this site since 1889. He and other noted artists produced the drawings — called cartoons — that artisans followed in creating the superb tapestries for which Spain became famous. His cartoons are now in the MUSEO DEL PRADO, but the still-functioning factory continues to use the designs. The workshops and exhibition hall can be visited.

REAL JARDÍN BOTÁNICO *(Royal Botanical Garden)*
Paseo del Prado (Plaza Murillo) ☎ *468-2025. Map 10E5* ▨ *Open 10pm-dusk. Metro: Atocha.*

Initiated by Fernando VI in 1755, but completed in 1783 during the reign of Carlos III, the royal botanical garden lies immediately S of the MUSEO DEL PRADO. It was designed by Juan de Villanueva in the formal French manner, the plots laid out in grids and each section bordered by low shrubs. Reportedly a shadow of its original self, following 200yrs of war, bad weather and neglect, it was restored in 1978 and remains a pleasant refuge from the city's traffic and noise. Obviously, it is at its best in late spring and early summer, with its ordered profusion of day lilies, peonies and multicolored roses.

ROYAL PALACE   See PALACIO REAL.

Where to stay in Madrid

Despite virtual economic parity with northern European capitals, and the high prices that implies, it is still possible to find lodgings in Madrid at budget levels. That's the good news. On the other hand, none of the lower-cost *hostals* can be compared for charm or warmth with even a middling London bed-and-breakfast or a *pensione* in Florence. At the economy level, therefore, expect no-frills fixtures, dark halls, creaking elevators and sagging mattresses. Air conditioning and reliable heating are not necessarily to be expected. What you *can* take comfort in is the assurance that at least the Spaniards hold to a higher standard of cleanliness than do most of their neighbors along the Mediterranean rim.

The most desirable accommodations in this category are found on or within a few streets of the **Grand Vía** or the **Puerta del Sol**, or near one of the two railroad stations, **Chamartín** and **Atocha**. That means most are in inherently noisy locations, so a room backing onto an airshaft may be preferable to one facing the street. Look out for our ■ symbol for a couple of decent recommendations in this category.

At the opposite, luxury end of the scale, Madrid's Edwardian-era **Ritz** and its contemporary equivalent, the **Villa Magna**, are the equals of nearly anything on the Continent. They adhere to the most rarefied standards of service and surroundings; but it must also be said that their tariffs outstrip both inflation and reason. Most visitors will be more than satisfied with hotels in the 4-star category (look for the ▦ symbol for our recommendations) and, with greater care in selection, some of those that have been awarded 3 stars.

Always be prepared to request another room if the first one shown is unsatisfactory. Madrid hotels tend to assign their least desirable quarters to strangers, and often have more acceptable rooms at no difference in rate.

The larger, international-style hotels are located primarily on or near the middle and upper reaches of the **Paseo de la Castellana**, in the newer, northerly part of the city. They are largely indistinguishable inside from their cousins in Singapore or Stuttgart, which happily suits their executive clients. Many of them, such as the **Miguel Angel**, **Meliá Castilla** and **Holiday Inn,** have swimming pools, saunas and fitness clubs. Check the symbols at the end of individual entries below (see KEY TO SYMBOLS on page 5 for the full list of symbols). All of the listed hotels accept two or more major charge/credit cards. Metro stations are mentioned only if they are within easy walking distance of the hotel in question. If no station is given, it can be assumed that a taxi will be necessary for all but resolute backpackers. Following each street address, in parentheses, is the nearest cross street or prominent landmark to the described site.

Given the number and diversity of Madrid hotels, it is nearly always possible to obtain satisfactory accommodations on short notice — a statement that cannot truthfully be made about most cities in Spain.

It is preferable, however, to have written confirmation of reservations, especially at Christmas, Easter, and from late May through August. To facilitate this, nearly all the hotels mentioned here have telex and fax numbers and English-speaking personnel attending them. The postal service is not to be trusted for this purpose, being far too slow. In extremis, there are hotel reservation booths at the domestic and international airport terminals and at the railroad stations.

☎ The **telephone prefix (area code)** for Madrid is **91**.

Hotels classified by price

Very expensive (▥▥▥▥): **Eurobuilding**, **Meliá Madrid**, **Miguel Angel** ▦, **Palace** ▦, **Ritz** ▦, **Villa Magna** ▦, **Villa Real** ▦
Expensive to very expensive (▥▥▥▥ to ▥▥▥▥): **Wellington**
Expensive (▥▥▥▥): **Barajas**, **Holiday Inn**, **Meliá Castella**, **Sanvy**

Moderately priced to expensive (*IIIⵔ* to *IIIIⵔ*): **Suecia**
Moderately priced (*IIIⵔ*): **Aitana, Carlton, Chamartín, Emperatriz,
Reina Victoria**
Inexpensive to moderately priced (*Iⵔ* to *IIIⵔ*): **Liabeny, Serrano** 🏨
Inexpensive (*Iⵔ*): **Carlos V** 🏨

AITANA
*Paseo de la Castellana 152
(General Yagüe), 28046 Madrid*
☎ 250-4840 ⊕ 49186 *IIIⵔ* 111 rms
🛏 111 ▦ Metro: Lima.
*Location: Near the Bernabeu soccer
stadium.* Businesspeople who must
watch expenses favor the tidy
Aitana for its proximity to the
multinational companies
headquartered in the burgeoning
northern sector. Nothing thrilling,
but minimal conveniences are in
place. It lacks a dining room, but
there are many good restaurants in
the immediate vicinity.
‡ ▢ 🗎 🦞

BARAJAS
*Av. de Logroño 305, 28042
Barajas* ☎ 747-7700 ⊕ 22255
⊛ 747-8717 *IIIIⵔ* 230 rms 🛏 230
▦ 🍽 🍷
*Location: Near the airport, 14km (9
miles) from the city center.* Were it
in town, this hotel would rank
among the more desirable. It
possesses many amenities and
recreational facilities, including a
pool, gymnasium and convenient
golf course. As it is, it mostly suits
visitors who have chauffeured
limousines, expense accounts for
taxis or very early flights from the
nearby airport.
🖂 ⅙ 🦞 🛱 ✒/ 💓 ‡ ▢ 🗎

CARLOS V 🏨
*Maestro Vitoria 5 (Plaza
Descalzas Reales), 28013 Madrid*
☎ 531-4100 ⊕ 48704. Map 9D3
Iⵔ 67 rms 🛏 67 ▦ Metro: Sol
or Callao.
*Location: In shopping district N of
Puerta del Sol.* Around one corner is
the MONASTERIO-MUSEO DE LAS
DESCALZAS REALES, one of the city's
more important historical sites, and
around the other is a branch of the
Galerías Preciados, a prominent
department store chain. The turn-of-
the-century structure has the high
ceilings and close walls of the
period, with evidence of many
renovations over the years.
Relatively low rates and the
convenient location — the PLAZA
MAYOR and PALACIO REAL are within
walking distance — offset any
complaints about the less-than-
fetching decor and lack of
a dining room.
‡ ▢ 🗎 🦞

CARLTON ✿
*Paseo de las Delicias 26
(Vizcaya), 28045 Madrid*
☎ 239-7100 ⊕ 44571 ⊛ 227-8510.
Map 10F6 *IIIⵔ* 112 rms 🛏 112 ▦
🍽 Metro: Atocha or Palos de la
Frontera.
*Location: Near Atocha railroad
station.* Extensive recent
renovations have made this a more
desirable stop than ever. Its
location, in an unfashionable but
entirely acceptable retail and
residential neighborhood, keeps
rates below those charged by many
of its only slightly more central
rivals. Yet the MUSEO REINA SOFÍA and
MUSEO DEL PRADO are both within
walking distance, and few comforts
have been neglected. Room TV, for
example, has channels in five
languages, including English.
Bathrooms have hairdryers; each
closet has a strongbox; windows are
double-glazed to reduce traffic noise
to a low hum. Weekend rates
(*Fri-Sun*) are 50 percent less than
Mon-Thurs.
🖂 ‡ ▢ 🗎 🦞

CHAMARTÍN
*Agustín de Foxá s/n (Hiedra),
28036 Madrid* ☎ 733-9011
⊕ 492012 ⊛ 733-0214 *IIIⵔ* 378 rms
🛏 378 ▦ 🍽 🍷 Metro:
Chamartín.
*Location: Next to Chamartín
railroad station.* Persons arriving by
train from Barcelona or France, or
leaving for those destinations, might
find this contemporary hotel
convenient, although it is at the far
northern edge of the city. And
visitors planning driving tours in
those directions can avoid the stress
of downtown traffic when
departing. Otherwise, expect
nothing out of the ordinary.
‡ ▢ 🗎 💓 🍽

EMPERATRIZ
*López de Hoyos 4 (Paseo de la
Castellana), 28006 Madrid*
☎ 563-8088 ⊕ 43640 ⊛ 563-9804
IIIⵔ 170 rms 🛏 170 ▦ 🍽
*Location: Quiet street off the Paseo
de Castellana.* It isn't easy to find
affection for a place that relies for its
color scheme on gradations of olive
drab and mustard. Nor, come to
think of it, for one that entices more
than its share of package tours. But
the groups are gotten out early each

105

day, and there is a pretty, private garden with a fountain across the way that gets the morning off on the right foot. The best thing about the place is the rotating corps of competent *conserjes*, especially the impishly avuncular Juan Muñoz. Single travelers should definitely choose to spend a few pesetas extra for the use of a double room. The singles are cramped, to put it mildly, with cot-like beds and drizzly showerheads. Buffet breakfasts downstairs aren't bad, if you can stand the wallpaper.

🏡 💙 ⚡ 🔲 📷 🏄 ➡️ ▣

EUROBUILDING

Padre Damián 23 (Alberto Alcocer), 28036 Madrid ☎ 457-3100 ⊚ 22548 ⊗ 457-9729 ⅢⅢ 520 rms 🖵 412 ▦ ➡ ▣ ☕ *Metro: Tetuán.*

Location: In the northern commercial district, near the Bernabeu soccer stadium. The theory of this modern twin high-rise, block-square hostelry was that clients on expense accounts could have relative quiet and a degree of posh in one tower, while those on group tours would be content with the lesser comforts of the other. That original intention has been displaced, and the price range has narrowed into the upper brackets. Expect neither warmth nor charm, but once you are ensconced there is little reason to leave. There are two entrances, two swimming pools, a gym, saunas, a gallery of shops, hairdressers, barbers, four bars and four restaurants. Bedrooms have terry robes, hairdryers, shower massage and satellite TV. Down below is the long-lived **Mau-Mau** disco. The principal liability is the distance from the capital's most important tourist attractions.

💙 ≋ 🙌 🌴 ⚡ 🔲 🏄 ⊙ ▣

HOLIDAY INN

Plaza Carlos Trias Bertrán 4 (General Perón), 28020 ☎ 597-0102 ⊚ 44709 ⊗ 597-0292 ⅢⅢ 313 rms 🖵 313 ▦ ➡ ▣ ☕ *Metro: Lima.*

Location: W of the upper reaches of Paseo de Castellana. Familiarity has its virtues, especially in a foreign land, and many North Americans are comforted by the no-surprises predictability of this outpost of the chain that is so ubiquitous in their homeland. They are startled, however, by the hefty room rates, which are substantially higher than they probably expect. In exchange, they get the use of a pool, fitness

center, sauna and satellite TV. Rooms are ordinary but more spacious than the Spanish norm.

≋ 🙌 🌴 ⚡ 🔲 ▣

LIABENY ♣

Salud 3 (Gran Vía), 28013 Madrid ☎ 532-5306 ⊚ 49024. Map 9C3 ⅢⅠ to ⅢⅢ 160 rms 🖵 160 ▦ ➡ ▣ ☕ ▤ *Metro: Sol.*

Location: Near the Puerta del Sol. Refreshed with new paint, baths and beds, the comfortable rooms carry out the promise of the spacious wood-paneled lobby. Individual air conditioning and heating controls are provided; the TV has channels in several languages. Colors are mostly tones of brown, a somber scheme belied by the animated cocktail bar as well as the restaurant and cafeteria. The situation couldn't be better, with the PLAZA MAYOR, the **Gran Vía**, the big department stores, and the lively *tapas* district of **Plaza Santa Ana** all close at hand. On all those counts, along with the relatively low price, there isn't a more desirable stop for the peseta-watching traveler who's unwilling to make wrenching sacrifices in the name of economy.

⚡ 🔲 🏄 🏄 ▤

MELIÁ CASTILLA

Capitán Haya 43 (Francisco Gervás), 28036 Madrid ☎ 571-2211 ⊚ 23142 ⊗ 571-2210 ⅢⅢ 921 rms 🖵 921 ▦ ➡ ▣ ☕ *Metro: Cuzco.*

Location: One block W of the Paseo de la Castellana, in the northerly office district. The management say this is the largest hotel in Iberia, although there are other claimants. More important, it manages to satisfy the expectations of both businesspeople and tourists, with taste and big-city efficiency. The garage, a somewhat rare facility in Madrid hotels, is welcome, as are the health club and sauna. Three restaurants are augmented by the **Scala** supper club, its shows reminiscent of the Folies Bergères.

💙 ≋ 🙌 🌴 ⚡ 🔲 🏄 ⊙ 🎵 ▣

MELIÁ MADRID

Princesa 27 (Luisa Fernanda), 28008 Madrid ☎ 241-8200 ⊚ 22537 ⊗ 241-1988. Map 9B2 ⅢⅢ 265 rms 🖵 265 ▦ ➡ ▣ ☕ *Metro: Ventura Rodríguez.*

Location: Near the Plaza de España and the Palacio Real. Although both architecture and staff are rather chilly, the Meliá Madrid strives to overcome these deficiencies. It is the only 5-star hotel in this busy west-central neighborhood, handily near to many prominent corporate offices as well as the restaurants and nighttime diversions near the **Plaza de Oriente**. In addition to the expected amenities, there is a projection room, hairdresser, barber, gymnasium, sauna, and substantial conference space with the latest types of audiovisual devices.

🌿 ≋ ⴄ ☞ ✆ ☐ ✉ ⚓ ● ▣

MIGUEL ANGEL 🏨
Miguel Angel 31 (José Abascal),
28010 Madrid ☎ 442-0022
⑭ 44235 ⑳ 442-5320 ∭ 278 rms
▣ 278 ▦ ⚓ ✉ ⌲ Metro:
Rubén Darío.
Location: *N of the city center, beside the Paseo de la Castellana.* No reasonable facility or amenity is denied guests of this 5-star luxury mid-rise in the Paseo de Castellana corporate district, assuming one doesn't demand charm. Prominent on that list is the only indoor swimming pool in any Madrid hotel, augmented by a workout room with sauna. The satellite TV antenna pulls in channels in several languages, including English. Staff attend quickly to client needs. Bedrooms are decorated in mellow, darker hues and the furniture is carefully chosen. Reserve well ahead.

🌿 ≋ ⴄ ☞ ☐ ✉ ⚓ ⵣ ● ▣

PALACE 🏨
Plaza de las Cortes 7 (Paseo del
Prado), 28014 Madrid
☎ 429-7551 ⑭ 23903 ⑳ 429-8266.
Map **10D4** ∭ 520 rms ▣ 520 ▦
⚓ ✉ ⌲ Metro: Sevilla.
Location: *Three streets from the Prado.* Second only to the **Ritz** among the capital's *grande dame* hotels, the Palace continues to polish its image. Glamor, intrigue, diplomacy and statecraft have long been associated with its stately halls and bedchambers. Regular guests include star bullfighters, rock musicians, politicians, artists and executives. Perhaps because it is three times the size of its principal competitor, service can seem chilly and offhand. (At these prices, they should do something about that.) An impressive glass dome shelters the busy reception salon, up the stairs at the back of the lobby. Adjoining it is the courtly lounge, a prime venue for the city's movers and shakers. Renovations underway will add a swimming pool, sauna and squash court.

ⵣ ☐ ✉ ▣

REINA VICTORIA
Plaza del Angel 7 (Calle del
Prado), 28012 Madrid
☎ 531-4500 ⑭ 42920 ⑳ 522-0307.
Map **10D4** ∭ 201 rms ▣ 201 ▦
⚓ ✉ ⌲ Metro: Antón Martín.
Location: *Opposite the Teatro Español, 5mins from Puerta del Sol.* Long a favorite of the bullfighting clique, this once-proud hotel had deteriorated as sadly and surely as the Plaza Santa Ana it faces. Now the decline of both has been reversed. A bronze bust of the eponymous monarch presides over a handsome lobby with overstuffed sofas and glass chandeliers. Off to one side is the tranquil, pretty dining room, where a substantial buffet breakfast is available each morning. All bedrooms have strongboxes with programmable combinations, and a satellite dish antenna pulls in TV channels in several languages. The desirable doubles are those facing the plaza, with their large bay windows providing both greater floor space and light than the same-priced doubles in the back. One of Madrid's most tantalizing *tapas* districts beckons just outside the door.

ⵣ ☐ ✉ ⵣ

RITZ 🏨
Plaza de la Lealtad 5 (Paseo del
Prado), 28014 Madrid
☎ 521-2857 ⑭ 43986 ⑳ 532-8776.
Map **10D5** ∭ 156 rms ▣ 156 ▦
⚓ ⌲ Metro: Banco de España.
Location: *Two streets N of the Prado.* Since 1910, when it was built at the behest of Alfonso XIII, the Ritz has cosseted the cultured and wealthy elite with exquisitely precise service and lavish Edwardian-style appointments. With a capacity of only 306 guests, the staff of 230 is rarely unable to attend to needs with quicksilver grace. They make it a practice to learn clients' names upon registration, which permits the doorman to hand over the correct room key and the elevator operator to press the appropriate floor button without a word. The bedcovers are turned back at night; a butler will bring a nightcap in a blink. Hand shoes over to the valet and they are returned brilliantly shined — and with the laces ironed. To maintain the proper atmosphere, adult males are expected to wear jacket and tie in the restaurant and public rooms. Those who habitually travel in shorts, T-shirts and sneakers will be happier elsewhere. There aren't ten hotels in the whole of Spain that can

match the Ritz experience. Indeed, poll after poll places it among the best ten in the *world*.
♥ ‡ □ ☎ ▣

SANVY
Goya 3 (Serrano), 28001 Madrid
☎ 276-0800 ☎ 44994 ☎ 275-2443.
Map 10B5 ▥ 147 rms ▭ 147 ▦
━ ▣ ≍ *Metro: Colón.*
Location: Facing the Plaza de Colón and Paseo de la Castellana. The top-floor swimming pool is one attraction, and the nearby fashionable **Calle Serrano** is another. The **Belagua** dining room is better than the usual hotel average, and there are several good restaurants nearby. Recent renovations have made this a more desirable stop than ever.
≈ ‡ □ ☎ ⅍ ▣

SERRANO 🏠
Marqués de Villamejor 8 (Serrano), 28006 Madrid
☎ 435-5200 ☎ 27521 ▥ to ▥ 34 rms ▭ 34 ▦ ━ ≍
Location: Quiet street between Paseo de la Castellana and Calle Serrano. Its colors and furnishings are a bit of a jumble, but things are kept tidy, and the hotel is too small to host the clamorous tour groups that are the lifeblood of most establishments in its price category. The bar-salon on the main floor is also the setting for the decent buffet breakfast. They recently replaced the drooping old mattresses with firm new ones, and retrofitted the baths with marble, shower massages and hairdryers. No glamor, just good value, enhanced by the desirable **Salamanca** neighborhood.
⌂ ‡ □ ☎ ⅍ ♈ ▣

SUECIA
Marqués de Casa Riera 4 (Alcalá), 28014 Madrid
☎ 531-6900 ☎ 22313 ☎ 521-7141.
Map 10D4 ▥ to ▥ 128 rms ▭ 128 ▦ ≍ *Metro: Banco de España or Sevilla.*
Location: Near the Teatro de la Zarzuela. The **Bellman** restaurant of the "Sweden" offers Madrid's only authentic *smörgåsbord* on Fri and Sat. Ernest Hemingway lived in a 5th-floor suite, now equipped with a Jacuzzi, during his last stay in the city. The quiet yet central situation remains popular with business groups and visitors of a cultural bent.
‡ □ ☎ ▣

VILLA MAGNA 🏠
Paseo de la Castellana 22 (Zurbarán), 28046 Madrid

☎ 578-2000 ☎ 22914 ☎ 575-9504.
Map 10A5 ▥ 192 rms ▭ 192 ▦ ━ ▣ ≍
Location: Halfway between the northern commercial district and the city center. It strives to be a contemporary manifestation of the aristocratic **Ritz**, and nearly succeeds. The horseshoe front drive looks like a Mercedes-Benz parking lot, with an occasional Ferrari thrown in for color and dash. Scrupulously tended gardens set off the otherwise bland exterior of the gleaming mid-rise tower. The decorative preferences of 18th and 19thC French and English kings inform the plush salons and dining areas: a little Regency here, the Sun King there, a touch of Second Empire beneath the cut-glass chandeliers. Afternoon tea is taken in these surroundings, a piano tinkling behind the clink of silver on bone china.

Opulence pertains in the guestrooms, as well, with Irish linen on the beds and terry-cloth robes hanging on the doors. Satellite TV has channels in several languages, although a teenager might be required to decipher the complex remote control.
♥ ‡ □ ☎ ▣

VILLA REAL 🏠
Plaza de las Cortes 10 (San Jerónimo), 28014 Madrid
☎ 420-3767 ☎ 44600 ☎ 420-2547.
Map 10D4 ▥ 115 rms ▭ 115 ▦ ━ ≍ *Metro: Sol.*
Location: 5mins' walk from the Prado museum. The capital's newest luxury hotel is a pocket version of the **Ritz**, which can be seen from the front door. The lobby is impeccably furnished with Louis XIV reproductions and antiques, glowing Oriental carpets and bowls of flowers. The young charmers at the front desk contrast refreshingly with the sullen functionaries who usually hold that position. One of them shows each guest his or her room, explaining its features — the new-fangled card-keys, for example. and the multilingual, many-channeled TV. Room service is available at any time. Perhaps because rooms are rather compact, the tariffs, while certainly steep, aren't what they are at others of its class... yet.
⌂ ‡ □ ☎ ⅍ ▣

WELLINGTON
Velázquez 8 (Alcalá), 28001 Madrid ☎ 275-4400 ☎ 22700 ☎ 276-4164 ▥ to ▥ 258 rms

⌨258 ▦ ➤ ➾ *Metro: Retiro.*
*Location: Near Puerto de Alcalá
and Parque del Retiro.* Given a
soupçon more polish here, a dash of
creativity there, this stately
medium-sized entry could be
among Madrid's highest tier of
hotels.

Lacking that extra care, it
nevertheless remains among the
most desirable in the **Salamanca**
district, especially with participants
and followers of bullfighting.
Parents with children should note
that there is a pool.

🐾 ➤ ⬧ ☐ ⬜ 🐾 ☿

Where to eat in Madrid

As the capital of Spain, Madrid has always had representatives of
the nation's several regional cuisines. Purveyors of *non*-Spanish
cooking were until recently, however, few in number and rarely
distinctive. As the city has grown more cosmopolitan, so have its
tastes in food begun to broaden. While still far less diverse in its
offerings than London or New York, there are now credible and
even exemplary versions of Indian, Chinese, Middle Eastern and
Italian repertoires. Food and travel writers have been slow to
remark upon this, a faintly patronizing double standard in which
only Spanish restaurants are named, denying the growing
richness of the Madrid dining experience. Imagine, by extension,
if they mentioned only steakhouses in Manhattan or pub grub in
Mayfair.

So, by all means sample the native strains — the foods of
Catalunya, the Basque Country, Galicia, Asturias, Valencia and
Andalucía — but don't neglect the savory curries of **Annapurna**
and **Baisakhi**, the pastas of **Spaghetti & Bollicine**, the tastes of
Asia at **Suntory** and **Hang Zhou**, and the new-wave inventions
of **La Gamella** and **El Mentidero de la Villa**.

Most of the restaurants considered to occupy the peak positions
in the local pecking order are mentioned below: they include
such worthies as **Zalacaín**, **Cabo Mayor** and **Juan de Alzate**.
However, it will come as no surprise to read that these are
invariably expensive, and therefore a number of satisfying,
lower-priced establishments are also described. Together, they
are only a small sampling of the thousands of restaurateurs and
taberna owners who are contending to feed the permanent and
transient populace. And at least our suggestions should point the
way to rewarding neighborhoods.

In the following selection, addresses, telephone and nearest
metro stations are given, with symbols showing particularly
luxurious (△) or simple (⊜) restaurants, and those that
represent good value (✿). Other symbols show price categories,
charge and credit cards and other noteworthy points. See KEY TO
SYMBOLS on page 5 for the full list of symbols. Times are specified
when restaurants are **closed**.

Except in the cases of such gastronomic landmarks as Zalacaín
and El Bodegón, advance reservations are rarely necessary. Since
Madrileños rarely sit down to lunch before 2pm or to dinner
before 10.30pm, patrons arriving before those hours can nearly
always get a table.

Fast food

As noted in WHAT TO EAT AND DRINK (page 36), there is always a
place nearby in which to get a snack or a meal, never mind the
late and restricted hours of the formal restaurants. Cafés and bars
serving food are around every corner. Fast-food outlets have long

had a foothold, with such US companies as **McDonald's**, **Wendy's** and **Burger King** abetted by the Spanish chains: **Vips**, **Bob's** and **Foster's of Hollywood**. While they all traffic in the usual sandwiches and burgers, the locals at least have the virtue of being less predictable, and they provide complete meals, as well. No culinary ground-breaking here, of course, but generally inexpensive sustenance is made available at just about any hour, even on Sunday, when most conventional restaurants are closed. But it must be said that, whatever their virtues, such places are essentially fueling stations.

Tapas

To satisfy both the social impulse and appetites either peckish or raging, there is no more gratifying solution than a *tapas* crawl. These characteristic bar snacks (described on page 38) are found in no more glorious profusion than here, the putative city of their invention. While there is no limit to the *mesónes* and *tabernas* in which to sample *tapas*, many knowledgeable enthusiasts point neophytes directly to the **Plaza de Santa Ana**, not far from the Puerta del Sol.

Stand in the middle of that square, lively on all but the dankest days. Face the Teatro Español, at the opposite end from the Hotel Victoria. On the right-hand side of the plaza are four possible starting points for a *tapas* excursion. The **Cervecería Alemaña** (*#6*) was one of many Hemingway haunts in the 1930s. On the same side are the **Cervecería La Plaza** (*#2*), the new **Naturbier** (*#9*) and **Cervecería Santa Ana** (*#10*). The featured tipple at all of these is obvious from their names: beer, available on draft. On the left-hand side of the square, try the baked mussels at **Viña P** (*#3*), a large bar-restaurant; or step into **Platerías** (*#11*).

Any of these will spark an appetite. To continue, walk to the corner of the plaza to the immediate left of the Teatro. After a few steps along Principe, turn right down pedestrians-only Manuel Fernández y González. On the left is **La Trucha** (*#3*), noted for its smoked fish platters, and at the far corner is **La Chuleta** (*#10*), which produces heaps of delicately fried sea creatures. Note, while on this street, the presence of **Viva Madrid** (*#7*) and **Los Gabrieles** (*Echegaray 17*). Neither serves food, but both are very old, and layered with magnificent picture tiles.

Return to the Plaza Santa Ana and walk toward the Hotel Victoria, turning right at the corner on Núñez de Arce. At #12 is **La Casa del Abuelo**, specializing in seafood, and opposite is a smaller branch of the aforementioned **La Trucha**. This is a good place to sample *pimientos de Padrón*, the grilled green peppers from Galicia. At the next corner, turn left on Cruz, then immediately right on Victoria. Along this block, virtually every storefront is a *tapas* bar. Two of the best are at the far end, **Casa Vasca** (*#2*), with its stuffed peppers and grilled sardines, and **Museo del Jamón** (*San Jerónimo 6*), a "museum of ham" hung with ranks of air-cured haunches from every region of Spain.

EL AMPARO ⌂
Callejón de Puigcerdá 8
☎ *431-6456* ▢ ⬜ ▤ 🚗 ☕ AE
⬛ *Closed Sat lunch; Sun; Holy Week; Aug. Metro: Wellington.*
El Amparo hides its considerable light down a mews off Calle Jorge Juan (E of the intersection with Calle

de Claudio Coello). Carriage lights, a vine-cloaked wall and a brass plate announce its presence. As often as not, you have to knock for entrance. It is worth the effort, for this is among the elite of Madrid's culinary temples. Its largely French Basque offerings include *scallops de foie gras a las pimientas con mango* and *hojaldre de cigalas* (crayfish in puff pastry), distributed by a staff whose professionalism is a joy to witness.

ANNAPURNA
Zurbano 5 ☎ 410-7727
╟╟ ▭ ▦▦ ● ▼ ᴁ *Closed Sun; holidays; Aug.* Metro: Colón.

Indian cuisine was poorly represented in the city until Annapurna launched its resounding assault. First impressions are of modish elegance. The ingratiating bar-lounge in front sets the tone with tub chairs, statuettes of Hindu gods, touches of gleaming brass and ancient scenes rendered in batik. There is a short card of Indian appetizers there, variations on *tapas* that include fragrant chicken chunks on skewers accompanied by bowls of a mild tamarind sauce and a fiery dip.

Full meals are prepared in a spotless kitchen with two tandoori ovens, whence come such pleasers as chicken *murgh tandoor* and lamb *rogan josh*. The L-shaped dining room has a glassed view of the garden at the rear.

ARMSTRONGS
Jovellanos 5 ☎ 522-4230. Map 10D4 ╟╟ to ╟╟ ▭ ▦▦ ᴁ ● ●
ᴠᴵˢᴬ Metro: Sevilla.

Ken Armstrong used to be a London lawyer. Traveling through the United States, he kept seeing signs that read, "No Soliciting." He took that as divine guidance, he insists, quit the law, and opened this restaurant across the street from the Teatro de la Zarzuela. At first, it featured profoundly American food (chili, burgers, Waldorf salad), and waiters and waitresses chosen more for their looks than their aptitudes. Their majesties Juan Carlos and Sofia came to see what was going on. They were followed by a stream of actors, aristocrats, singers and politicians.

Eventually Armstrong stepped back from his early nose-thumbing, internationalized his menu and hired careerists to replace the disco dollies. The several rooms are now even more lovely than at the start, the vestibule alive with flowers and hanging and potted plants. Many dishes, such as salmon crepes, are large enough to share, and the weekend brunch, which Armstrong introduced to Madrid, is cheaper than other meals. Even budget-watchers will want to take that opportunity to experience what has evolved into one of Madrid's best restaurants.

BAISAKHI ✿
Agastia 75 ☎ 431-1534 ╟╟ ▦▦ ▭
▰▰ ᴁ ● ● ᴠᴵˢᴬ *Closed Sun.*

After helping make **Annapurna** a success, Buphendra Gupta set out on his own. The space he selected isn't as sleekly stylish as his former digs, but it is airy and spacious, with sitar music on the stereo, and embroidered hangings and other objects from his Indian homeland to set the mood. In deference to the Spanish antipathy to fiery seasonings, he substitutes the intense, complex flavorings of exotic, but mild, spices. For the more adventurous foreigners who seek him out, he usually has a hotter dish or two on hand, such as pork *vindaloo* . Tandoori chicken arrives juicy and aromatic, not red and dry. Gupta, who greets guests, takes their orders and somehow still does most of the cooking, also takes on an educational role, carefully explaining ingredients and preparation. The difficult location, well E of the center, is worth finding. Agastia runs parallel to Calle de Arturo Soria, and the restaurant is at the junction with Calle Duque de Tamames.

BRASSERIE DE LISTA
José Ortega y Gasset 6
☎ 435-2818 ╟╟ ▭ ▰▰ ▦▦ ● ᴠᴵˢᴬ
Metro: Serrano.

With the potted palms sitting on veined marble floors, the faintly Art Nouveau scrolled woodwork, and waiters in aprons almost to their ankles, it looks every inch the Left Bank brasserie it intends to emulate. Nothing on the plate distracts overmuch from the spirited conversations taking place all around. But neither does it disappoint, or at least not often. Such appetizers as the mozzarella and tomato salad with anchovies and fresh oregano lead smoothly to, perhaps, the baked cod filets brightened by a napping of tangy Catalan *romescu* sauce. Splendid, no, but good enough to pack the place with suited executives at 2pm, and a younger, hipper crowd after 10pm. The sidewalk tables are especially popular.

EL BODEGÓN ⌂
Pinar 15 ☎ 262-3137 ╟╟ ▭ ▰▰
▰▰ ▦▦ ᴁ ● ● ᴠᴵˢᴬ *Closed Sun; holidays; Aug.*

Time and tide cause no ripples at this classic. A gracious welcome awaits patrons at a converted townhouse in a tranquil neighborhood near fashionable Calle Serrano. The understated decor draws the eye to the radiant garden behind. Tables are large, and chairs upholstered. Well-schooled waiters guide diners through the elaborate selections and ceremonially whisk away the silver bells that cover each course. The *menú degustación* (changed frequently) might include baby lima beans and tiny string beans in pastry with just a wisp of sauce, *lenguado* with slivers of assorted mushrooms, tasty *filets de buey* drizzled with paprika sauce, and twin mounds of sorbet. Reserve for Fri and Sat evenings.

BOTÍN
Cuchilleros 17 ☎ 266-4217. Map 9D3 |||| ⊡ ▤ ▦ 𝐴𝐵 ⊙ ⊙ 𝘝𝘐𝘚𝘈 Metro: Tirso de Molina.
Successive managements have had since 1725 to pack these three floors, as well as a subterranean *bodega*, with enough picturesque detail for a dozen restaurants.

Ernest Hemingway was once a habitué, and every foreigner arriving in Madrid since has made a visit here as obligatory as a tour of the Prado museum. Roast meats and fowl are the specialties, the tastiest of which are chicken and kid. The dish for which Botín is most famous, however, is *cochinillo asado* (roast suckling pig). The place is always full, so expect a wait for a table.

CABO MAYOR
Juan Hurtado de Mendoza 11 (at the rear) ☎ 250-8776 |||| ⊡ ▤ ▦ 𝐴𝐵 ⊙ Closed Sun; Holy Week; last 2wks in Aug. Metro: Cuzco.
Nautical trappings of boat hulls and squared portholes belie the marked sophistication of the inspired kitchen. Disciplined young cooks under the direction of the celebrated Pedro Larumbe observe the essentials of the Basque tradition, but eschew thickened sauces and play with new combinations.

One example is the tender medallions of anglerfish (monkfish) showered with baby eels, bracketed with tiny clams and afloat in an aromatic saffron sauce. Others are *lomo de merluza* (loin of hake) and *cigalas y langostinos con verduras al jerez sibarita* (prawns, lobsters and vegetables in a sherry sauce). Desserts are well above the Spanish norm.

CAFÉ DE ORIENTE
Plaza Oriente 2 ☎ 541-3974. Map 9D2 |||| ⊡ ▤ ▦ 𝐴𝐵 ⊙ ⊙ 𝘝𝘐𝘚𝘈 Closed Sat lunch; Sun; Aug. Metro: Opera.
One of Madrid's most popular gathering places was the creation of an activist priest who began his parallel career as a restaurateur when he was seeking a way to put ex-convicts to work. On a plaza facing the Palacio Real, it attracts patrons from every stratum of society, from earnest music students and politicians to nightbirds and Japanese executives. They come for an ice cream on the terrace, a sandwich in the Edwardian bar, or a casual meal either in the crowded main room or downstairs in the brick-lined old cellar. No visitor should miss it, and just about any hour will do.

CASA LUCIO
Cava Baja 35 ☎ 265-3252. Map 9E2 |||| ⊡ ▤ 𝐴𝐵 𝘝𝘐𝘚𝘈 Closed Sat lunch; Aug. Metro: Latina.
There isn't a more traditional Castilian restaurant to be found, nor, apart from **Botín**, a few blocks away, a more popular one. It is filled when more famous competitors are half-empty, and Madrileños flock to it as eagerly as tourists do. Locals tend to be gathered downstairs, while the upper floor serves as a kind of foreign colony. No second-class treatment is to be implied, although the ground level is palpably livelier. Service is swift, efficient, and largely unsmiling wherever one is seated. Overhead are heavy dark beams (actually, simulations of their hand-hewn models), beneath the feet are terra cotta tiles, and the chairs are slung leather. The menu is just as predictable, detailing, in three languages, such standards as *cocido* (a 3-course boiled dinner) and roast meats. The difference is that they are done exceptionally well. The large joint of lamb, for one, is as succulent and sturdy in flavor as could be asked for. Order vegetables as a first or side course, though, for main dishes arrive alone or with fried potatoes only. Reservations are always necessary.

CASA MARTA ☙
Santa Clara 10 ☎ 248-2825. Map 9D2 |||| ⊡ ▤ 𝘝𝘐𝘚𝘈 Closed Sun; holidays. Metro: Opera.
Still quite new on the scene, it looks every bit the sort of extension of a family kitchen once found on every corner of Madrid's *barrios*. That

was before the city became chic, and this kind of enterprise ran into danger of becoming extinct. It is small — two rooms — with tiled dados and curtains at the windows, crisp and bright as a new penny. That isn't really Mamma back at the stove, but the food looks and tastes as if she is. The recipes are drawn from every corner of the peninsula, executed with a refreshing lack of artifice and in substantial portions. It's a little difficult to find: look for the Calle de la Union on the s side of the Opera house, walk up one block, and turn left.

FORTUNY ⌂
Fortuny 34 ☎ *308-3267. Map* **10A5** ▥ ▢ ▤▤ ⚓ ❖ *AE* ⦿ *VISA Closed Sat lunch; Sun; holidays. Metro: Rubén Dario.*
On the basis of pure grandeur, Fortuny leads the pack. It takes up all floors of a late 19thC mansion situated in a stately residential neighborhood just w of the Paseo de la Castellana. The handsome structure is bordered on two sides by courtyards and enclosed by a high wall, with a top-hatted attendant manning the gate. There are nine dining salons on two levels, each decorated in distinct period styles, as well as an extravagantly appointed bar off the reception area. Fellow diners have the glossy appearance and burnished manners of those accustomed to being in such places, attended to by a staff that nearly outnumbers them. Apart from somewhat timid seasonings, the food is memorably inventive, leaning to such concoctions as sliced rare duck presented inside a ring of raviolis stuffed with puréed figs. It's quite pretentious, heaven knows, and not a nightly event for most people, but it is certainly a possibility for a celebration or a farewell to Madrid.

LA GAMELLA
Alfonso XII 4 ☎ *532-4509. Map* **10C6** ▥ ▢ ▤▤ *AE* ⦿ *VISA Closed Sat lunch; weekends in July; Aug. Metro: Retiro.*
US-born Dick Stevens has been in Spain over 25yrs. He has taken it upon himself to introduce Madrileños to Californian/New American cooking techniques, most recently at this location near the Puerta de Alcalá and Parque del Retiro. Interestingly, his closest competitor is the prestigious but over-praised Horcher, with a kitchen he easily eclipses in both creativity and execution. For proof,

try the deceptively humble three-bean salad, with its nuggets of smoked salmon and a vinegar scented with English lavender. Or consider the refreshing melon *gazpacho*, the fried goat cheese with sweet beets and grapefruit *confit*, or the thin slices of rare duck garnished with a complex sauce of fruit, onions, cardamom and cumin. The menu is changed seasonally. Stevens is a constant presence in the dining room, advising, taking orders, and retiring behind the kitchen doors to prepare the food. He can give this kind of personal attention because only 38 persons can be seated at a time.

HANG ZHOU ❀
Lopéz de Hoyos 14 ☎ *563-1172* ▢ ▢ ▤▤ *AE* ⦿ *VISA*
It feels odd, somehow, ordering shark's fin soup in Spanish from a Chinese waitress in Madrid. The menu, to be sure, has English translations, most about as enlightening as this one: "Kan trou with three delicias." Nothing served here would win awards in Hong Kong or London, nor, for that matter, in Kansas City. But in a country slow to accept foreign cuisines, the food is credibly done, and isn't the attack of the blands produced by most Chinese eateries in the capital. Dishes described as *picante*, for example, actually *are* spicy-hot, a virtually epochal circumstance. Prices, on the other hand, are very gentle. Even Peking duck, the most expensive item by far, costs no more than a far less interesting combination plate at a Puerta del Sol cafeteria. Apart from the brass light fixtures festooned with red tassels, the decor is relatively restrained. Service is dour but efficient.

JOCKEY ⌂
Amador de los Rios 6 ☎ *319-1003. Map* **10B5** ▥ ▢ ▤▤ ⚓ *AE* ⦿ *VISA Closed Sun; holidays; Aug. Metro: Colón.*
For decades this was called the "Jockey Club," but the second word was eventually dropped to eliminate the suggestion of exclusivity. It is certainly one of the top places in Madrid, but decidedly not, as has been proclaimed in print, one of the "great restaurants of the world." An unbroken banquette covered in emerald velvet runs from the curtained entrance past the far service bar. Equestrian prints from the 19thC hang on polished wood paneling, and curb and snaffle bits

and Toby mugs enhance the intended sport-of-kings ambience. Tables are snugly spaced, for it is a small room. The host will be suavely anxious about your well-being. Regulars understandably receive closer attention, but newcomers are not made to feel like orphans. Everything on the menu is likely to please, most of it Spanish in origin but with a light French touch. The cellar is excellent.

JOSÉ LUIS
Serrano 89 ☎ *563-0959* ⫘ *to* ⫘.
⫘ ⫘ AE ⫘ ⫘ VISA
Meals *are* served, but what this and the four other José Luis branches are known for are *tapas*. Primarily open-faced sandwiches — smoked salmon, veal cutlets, caviar on toast — they are set out on the bar, and instead of ordering, customers simply take the ones they want. Barmen keep track of who ate what. The clientele is mostly upscale, and, because of the prices, largely past 35. Silver-haired men who wear their suit coats draped about their shoulders smoke furiously but suavely and expound to women with large amounts of well-tended hair and earrings as long as their necks. (*Additional branches at Salgado 11, Sambara 153, Paseo de la Habana, Paseo Alcobendas 10.*)

JUAN DE ALZATE ⌂
Princesa 18 ☎ *247-0010.* Map
9B2 ⫘ ⫘ ⫘ AE ⫘ ⫘ VISA
Metro: *Ventura Rodríguez.*
Flamboyant Iñaki Izaguirre dominates a room with his wild moustache, considerable height and girth, and, not least, his robust manner. He has been described as the Dalí of contemporary Spanish cooking, not too excessive a designation given the art applied to his creations. While his food follows certain *nouvelle* conventions — outsized plates; food resting atop, not under, sauces — he doesn't for a moment forget flavor and texture. Nor are the portions of that dainty order that leaves wallets depleted and hunger pangs unassuaged. His young waiters, in full white tie and tails, look like they are playing dress-up in their grandfathers' clothes, but they are obviously carefully trained and perform their duties with a touch of welcome insouciance. Characteristic of the whimsies they are called upon to serve is the swirl of spaghetti squash mimicking pasta tumbled with tendrils of zucchini and a cool, tangy tomato dressing. To get a better sense of Sr. Izaguirre's achievements, choose the *menú degustación*, which gives tastes of several items.

LHARDY
San Jerónimo 8 ☎ *521-3385.*
Map **10D4** ⫘ ⫘ ⫘ ⫘
Closed Sun; holiday dinners; Aug. Metro: *Sevilla.*
Lhardy is a delightful throwback to gentler times. Downstairs there is a delicatessen-pastry store combined with a confectioner-tea room. Customers patiently wait for thin crustless sandwiches accompanied by thimbles of sherry or cups of consommé. Queen Isabel II was on the throne when the business started in 1839, and the upstairs dining room reflects these origins. Apart from the *cocido*, the cooking is routine, with such specialties as *crema de mariscos* (cream of shellfish — a soup) and roast beef. Atmosphere is Lhardy's appeal, and it is almost worth the high prices to soak it in.

LÚCULO
Génova 19 ☎ *319-4029.* Map
10B5 ⫘ ⫘ ⫘ ⫘ ⫘ ⫘ ⫘ AE
⫘ ⫘ VISA Closed Sat lunch; Sun; mid-Aug to mid-Sept. Metro: *Colón.*
An arched passageway leads to a tiled and columned patio, then into the restaurant proper. The welcome is gracious, the several rooms commodious. Chef-owner Garcia Ange Dalmer is French Catalan, a rotund, obsessive man who spends as much time attending directly to patrons as he does working in the kitchen. He bustles about, adjusting a plate here, clearing a table there, confirming the principle that we should never trust a chef who is too thin or too phlegmatic. His menu is changed too frequently to make it worthwhile to describe specific dishes. Suffice it to say that the direction is consistently forward, the product of a committed and tireless epicure.

EL MENTIDERO DE LA VILLA
Santo Tomé 6 ☎ *308-1285.* Map
10B5 ⫘ ⫘ ⫘ AE ⫘ ⫘ Closed
Sat lunch; Sun; last 2wks in Aug.
Metro: *Colón.*
At first, this vanguardist newcomer to the once staid gastronomic scene seemed likely to disappear as quietly as it arrived. For one thing, it's tricky to find (on Calle Santo *Tomé*, not Santo Tomás, and near the Palacio de Justicia). For another, the food is of the Franco-Asian

variety, almost ordinary in the US and certain other European capitals, but still radical for the local palate. Innovation makes most Spaniards jumpy. Acceptance is growing, however, as more people discover that artists are at work here. Owner Mario Martinéz and Ken Sato, his partner in the venture, are the culinary equivalents of Picasso painting two-headed women. The welcome is warm, the surroundings stylishly informal, the service gracious. Put yourself in Mario's hands.

O'PAZO
Reina Mercedes 20 ☎ 253-2333 ⅢⅢ 🗂 ■■ ▤▤ 🚗 ⓒⒹ ▨ *Closed Sun; Aug. Metro: Alvarado.*
Sometimes, Galician food improves in direct proportion to its distance from its region of origin. Here is a case in point. A busy, homey series of rooms is usually full for both lunch and dinner with well-dressed patrons intent on enjoying themselves.   The menu is strictly seafood, but of the highest quality. A plate of unbidden cold snails arrives to accompany the apéritif. Everything that follows, including *caldo a la marinera* (fisherman's soup), *besugo* (sea bream) and *cigalas a la plancha* (grilled prawns), is good to excellent. The fixed-price menu keeps the cost down. Service is brisk to the point of being overbearing.

PALACIO DE ANGLONA ♣
Segovia 13 ☎ 266-3753. *Map 9D2* ⅢⅢ 🗂 ▤▤ ▨ *Closed lunch.*
In a neighborhood starting to show signs of fashionability, this "palace" gets credit for leading the way. Rooms on three levels, while hardly palatial, are uncrowded, with agreeable Post-Modernist touches, including stippled rust-colored walls and arty Italianate halogen lamps strung above the tables. Students and artists comprise the visible staff, bringing such youthful offerings as pasta salads and semi-designer pizzas as well as full meals. They do not ask every three bites if everything is all right. The costliest item on the card is medallions of three meats with a trio of matching sauces, and there is no reason why a 3-course meal, with a glass or two of house wine, shouldn't be well under 2,000ptas. They stay open until 3am every night.

EL PESCADOR
José Ortega y Gasset 75 ☎ 402-1290 ⅢⅢ 🗂 ▤▤ 🚗 ▨

ⓒⒹ ▨ *Closed Sun, mid-Aug to mid-Sept. Metro: Núñez Balboa.*
Under the same management as **O'Pazo**, the quality of the seafood, the swift service and animated *ambiente* are comparable. The afternoon meal draws a crowd of considerable clout, including government ministers and, from time to time, the Prime Minister. *Zarzuela*, a fish stew, is special. If adhering to a budget, avoid the costlier prawns and lobsters. They now accept charge and credit cards.

SEÑORIO DE BERTIZ
Commandante Zorita 4 ☎ 533-2757 ⅢⅢ 🗂 ■■ ▤▤ 🚗 ▨ ⓒ ▨ *Closed Sat lunch; Sun; Aug. Metro: Nuevos Ministerios.*
Here, everything old is new again. Not long ago it was coasting on a medium-to-good reputation it barely deserved. The then-owners had, in the Spanish phrase, "stopped the watch," allowing things to slide into indifference.

Their energetic successors pulled down the heavy drapes, stripped the wallpaper from the walls and replaced most of the yawning staff. Alert professionals were installed on both sides of the stove, and new life was breathed into the menu (mostly Basque) and the service (classical). The result is reassuringly conservative dining, best for those who use restaurants as extensions of their offices.

SIXTO GRAN MESÓN
Cervantes 28 ☎ 429-2255. *Map 10D4* ⅢⅢ 🗂 ■■ ▤▤ ▨ ⓒ ⓓ ▨ *Closed Sun dinner. Metro: Antón Martin.*
Beams, white plaster and terra cotta accurately reflect the thoroughly Castilian bias of this restaurant, in both surroundings and menu. The ground floor has a *taberna* atmosphere, with high-level *tapas*; the long dining room upstairs is more sedate. Up there, waiters speedily bring well-prepared classic dishes, such as *paella, chuletas de cordero* and *pollo asado*. Try to sit by the fireplace in chilly weather.

SPAGHETTI & BOLLICINE
Prim 15 ☎ 521-4515. *Map 10C5* ⅢⅢ 🗂 ▤▤ ▨ *Closed Sun.*
Although Spanish cooks have long prepared pastas, it was not until very recently that they learned the meaning of *al dente* and that sauces containing ingredients other than tomatoes were possible. This unassuming *trattoria* extends their

education, with over 30 different fabrications. Many of the names aren't generic, which makes selection difficult, but the perky waitresses serve complimentary glasses of sparkling wine to smooth the way. Grilled vegetables are excellent starters, with pasta, in substantial portions, for the main course.

SUNTORY
Paseo de la Castellana 36-38
☎ 577-3733 ▥▥ ▱ ▬ ▦ ஺ ▣
▣ ▨ *Closed Sun; holidays.*
Spaniards like their seafood very fresh and very well cooked. *Sushi* and *sashimi* obviously represent a critical departure from the latter convention. Even in this gastronomically still conservative city, however, there are enough people willing to try something — *anything* — new to make this Japanese import a rapid success. (Of course, there were also all those Sony and Mitsubishi executives in town eager for a home-uncooked meal.) The edible artistries of the chefs are as intriguing to watch being assembled as they are to eat. The basic raw fishes are super-fresh,

as they should be at what might be the highest prices in town for *any* kind of food.

ZALACAÍN ⌂
Alvarez de Baena 4 ☎ 261-4840
▥▥ ▱ ▬ ▦ ▰ ▨ *Closed Sat lunch; Sun; holidays; Holy Week; Aug.*
Mercedes and Lancias growl in the street outside as preliminary testimony to the reputation of a grand luxury restaurant. Zalacaín gathers awards in profusion. By any legitimate gauge, the creation of Jesus María Oyarbide has few peers in Spain. He has left little to chance. Patrons are received graciously. Tables shimmer with gleaming glasses, polished silverware and arrangements of fresh flowers, fruit or even dried vegetables. Ingredients are top quality and purchased daily. Any selection of specialties is hopelessly inadequate, for no dish will disappoint. The only reservation is the size of the bill, which is stunning even by Parisian standards. Vintage wines are very expensive, but the house versions are more than adequate and more affordable.

≡ Among other restaurants worth trying are **La Dorada** (*Orense 64* ☎ *270-2004* ▥▯); **Principe de Viana** (*Manuel de Falla 5* ☎ *259-1448* ▥▥▯); **Viridiana** (*Fundadores 23* ☎ *246-9040* ▥▥▯); **Currito** (*Pabellón de Vizcaya, Casa de Campo* ☎ *464-5704* ▥▯); **Nicolas** (*Cardenal Cisneros 82* ☎ *448-3634* ▥▯); **Pinocchio** (*Padre Damián 37* ☎ *259-3189* ▯); and **El Cuchi** (*Cuchilleros 3* ☎ *266-4424* ▯ *to* ▥▯ *map 9 D3*).

Bars and cafés

When work ends for the day in Madrid, sometime between 7 and 8pm, everyone gets out and about, stopping in favorite taverns for *tapas* and small glasses of wine or beer. In this, the birthplace of that singular culinary invention, there are *tapas* bars, called **tascas**, in virtually every neighborhood. They are typically announced by trays of raw ingredients or cooked food in their windows and, often, by lists of specialties painted on the windows. (For a suggested *tapas*-crawl, known as a *tapeo*, see page 110.)

These traditional bar-cafés serve several distinct functions, with regulars popping in for *café con leche* and a roll before work, then for a late-morning snack called a *merienda*, followed by a prelunch thimble of *tinto*, a couple of before-dinner *tapas*, and, later still, coffee and brandy. Given this all-day operation and the early-morning opening, this type of bar usually closes around midnight.

Closely related are the traditional **cafés**, some of them in operation since the last century, others as young as yesterday. The distinctions between them and the type of bar described above are elusive, but have most to do with the fact that patrons are prone to linger longer in cafés. This is partly because there are often more diversions, the oldest being the *tertulia*. The word refers to a discussion group, in its ancient manifestations formal and structured, with restricted membership and regular meeting times (usually 5pm). It has also been applied, with less accuracy, to casual gatherings occurring frequently but not necessarily on a predetermined schedule. Topics under discussion range from the frivolous to the profound, from soccer to ecology, but the meeting place is most often a café.

One of the oldest of these is across the street from the main post office, the landmark **Café Lyon** (*Alcalá 57*). Favored by academicians and other intellectuals, it has a well-worn, earnest air. Not far away, on a service road parallel to the W side of the Castellana, is the famous **Café Gijón** (*Paseo de Recoletos 21*). Big, wood-paneled, with large gilt-framed mirrors, it is filled with smoke and loud conversation from early to late, as it has been for over a century. Ideas and avant-garde esthetic concepts still ricochet around the room. It isn't necessarily a place in which to eat, although meals are available and complimentary *tapas* usually come with drinks.

A few steps N is the far more attractive and inviting **El Espejo** (*Paseo de Recoletos 31* ☎ *308-2347*). Barely a decade old, it looks as if it was around in 1900, with its crystal chandelier and marble-topped tables in the front-room bar, and the elaborate Art Nouveau detailing of walls and ceiling. Air conditioning vents the clouds of cigarette smoke in summer, and the dining room at the back is above-average for the breed. **Café Commercial** (*Glorieta de Bilbao 10*) has long had a seriously left-wing, radical, Bohemian image, although most of its usually youngish customers don't appear to fit that description at all. Another classic is the **Cuevas de Sésamo** (*Príncipe 7*), near Plaza Santa Ana, which often has live piano or accordion music. Similar is the **Café Libertad 8** (*Libertad 8*), a theatrical hangout which features art exhibitions and small-scale concerts.

In fine weather, Madrileños want to be outside, and they are accommodated by an ever-increasing number of sidewalk cafés, or *terrazas*. These al fresco extensions of existing bars and cafés are found throughout the city. Both the **Gijón** and **El Espejo**, mentioned above, have them, laid out with greater dash in the latter's case. A glassed Art Nouveau pavilion is the centerpiece, potted plants surround the tables, and a pianist or string quartet serenades the people-watchers. A few blocks N, on the opposite side of the boulevard, is the **Café Castellana** (*Paseo de la Castellana 21*), which has a very loud music system to drown out the traffic. Neither of these competing noises squelches conversation among the attractive young customers. One of the most popular *terrazas* is that of the **Café de Oriente**, opposite the Palacio Real (see pages 99-101), and, of course, the several establishments lining the sides of the **Plaza Mayor**. Prices are somewhat high at all of these, but not an eyebrow is cocked if a drink is nursed for an hour or more.

Another category of bar is the more sophisticated variety that opens in late afternoon or evening, which, for want of a better title, might be called a **cocktail lounge**, as they often are in North America. Its main function is as a place for conversation, particularly in the later hours; food is usually of minor consideration, if indeed it is even available. Such places declare their intentions and, in part, determine their patronage, by their hours, fixtures and even their names. Music is often a feature, sometimes live, more frequently on sound systems.

Hispano (*Paseo de la Castellana 78* ☎ *411-4876*) is filled with those Madrileños sufficiently interested in being perceived as "in" to ignore the inflated prices. An assortment of smoked fish can accompany capable renditions of such American-style cocktails as Dry Martinis, Margaritas, Bloody Marys and Daiquiris. At **The Sportsman** (*Alcalá 55* ☎ *276-6908*), burgundy velvet and polished wood paneling once served as backdrop for a space that strove to emulate a London club (complete with dart board). The new owners made it a shrine to the international movie and singing stars for whom one of the principals once played piano. Now he performs here, on occasion, and the place is as relaxing as ever, if rather less British in tone.

The bar of the **Palace** hotel (*Plaza de las Cortes 7* ☎ *429-7551*) is frequented by legions of politicians and journalists straining to hear each other's whispered intrigues. The barmen can whip together any cocktail you care to mention, as the long menu illustrates. Not far from the hotel is another old-timer, **Museo Chicote** (*Gran Vía 12* ☎ *532-6737*), a cocktail mecca that opened in 1931. Hemingway and Ava Gardner were among the notables who assaulted their livers here, in a vaguely Art Deco setting of no particular distinction other than its historical cocktail function. The gray-haired retainers behind the bar deftly shake up their Martinis, Bloody Marys, Manhattans, Rob Roys, Bullshots and dozens of other classics with the bored air of men who look as if they might have been around at the inaugural party. Chicote is a stripling compared to three other retreats in the older neighborhoods to the w. Just s and slightly e of the Plaza Santa Ana are two of Madrid's oldest, most colorful watering holes, **Viva Madrid** (*Manuel Fernández y González 7*) and, at the next corner, **Los Gabrieles** (*Echegaray 17* ☎ *429-6261*). Both are magnificently decorated with the pictographic tiles characteristic of 19thC *bodegas*, a word, in this context, that refers to wine cellars that are also drinking places. Wine and beer are the main tipples; taped jazz and Latin music dominate the eclectic stereo programs; there are no *tapas*, but much chatter.

Political gossip is topic *numero uno* at **Balmoral** (*Hermosilla 10* ☎ *431-4133*): not surprising, given its situation among the government ministries strung along the Paseo de la Castellano. Maturity and calm prevail in the atmosphere of a proper gentleman's club, complete with leather chairs and hunting trophy. Similar, but smaller and without Balmoral's panache, is **St Andrews Pub** (*Hermanos Bécquer 5* ☎ *563-1419*). Down the hill from the US Embassy, it has outdoor tables enclosed by a hedge and a stag's head over the door. Inside are red leather couches and chairs, and a dapper barman in a white dinner jacket caters to the over-40 crowd. The appeal of **Cock** (*Reina 16*) is baffling to many. It is, after all, down a forbidding street on the wrong side of the Gran Vía. But the glum, cavernous room, however inexplicably, remains a haunt of the youthful intelligentsia, in part because hot movie director Pedro Almodóvar has been known to drop by, trailing adoring acolytes.

On the other hand, the cachet of **Archy** (*Marqués de Riscal 11* ☎ *308-4374*) is readily understood even before entering the door. Out there, just watching the pretty, prosperous patrons is a treat, as they debark from models of every luxury car made since the Great Depression. Some just stop by for a preprandial apéritif (say, around midnight), while many stay for dinner (about 12.30), and are joined downstairs later by still others for dancing (until 4am). **Max** (*Aduana 24*) is equally *au courant*, and certainly as late, but isn't for dining or dancing.

Nightlife & the performing arts

Madrileños live for the night. Concerts and plays rarely begin before 10pm, dinner is at 11pm or later, and discos and nightclubs don't kick into high gear until 2am. This taste for burning the candle at both ends, combined with the recent prosperity of the young and the middle class, has given the city a billowing reputation for diverse, round-the-clock diversion. Visitors who wonder how the natives can work all day and play all night can solve the problem by doing as their hosts do: taking a long nap whenever the need arises and circumstances permit. Any time between 2pm and 10pm will do.

For comprehensive information about what's on and when, buy a copy of the weekly *Guía del Ocio* at any newsstand. This "leisure guide" recommends events and lists concerts, plays, movies, art exhibits, children's activities, bars, nightclubs and restaurants. It's in Spanish, but not difficult to decipher. The hotel *conserje* usually has a copy and can translate.

Jazz, rock, and pop can be heard in venues ranging from grim to posh, in many districts. One unlikely street is **Calle Huertas** (*map 9 D3- 10 E5*), which runs from the Paseo del Prado almost to the Plaza Mayor. All but deserted during the day, it blossoms after dark with bistros, music bars and dance clubs.

One magnet in this street is the **Café Jazz Populart** (*Huertas 22 ☎ 429-8407*), a spacious street-level room with a long marble-topped bar. Combos of three to five musicians explore a broad spectrum of sounds, including, but not confined to, Afro-tinged and mainstream jazz, reggae, salsa and blues. A short walk away is the larger and better-known **Café Central** (*Plaza del Angel 10 ☎ 468-0844*). While jazz is the primary attraction, any given night can focus on folksingers, blues shouters, Brazilian salsa, or whatever else strikes the management's fancy.

There's jazz in other parts of town too. One old reliable is the **Whisky Jazz Club** (*Diego de León 7 ☎ 261-1165*), which has been a center of live jazz for years. The minimum admission fee includes your first drink, is very reasonable, and is even cheaper from 8-10pm (*☎ in advance for current attractions*). **Segundo Jazz** (*Comandate Zorita 8 ☎ 254-9437*) is similar in character and longevity, but features Brazilian jazz and salsa.

On the burgeoning w side of the city, the new **Café del Mercado** (*Ronda de Toledo 1 ☎ 265-8739*) packs in customers in the later hours at the upscale shopping center, the Mercado Puerta de Toledo. The musical menu ranges over Latin American rhythms, American soul, and that intriguing new hybrid, flamenco rock. Live shows are on before midnight, dancing later.

Touring big-time rock and pop performers of the Madonna and Rolling Stones luminosity often alight for a night or two at the **Vicente Calderón Stadium** (*Paseo de los Melancólicos s/n ☎ 266-4707*). But for regular appearances by bands of equal enthusiasm, if lesser star-power, check out current attractions at the **Universal Club** (*Fundadores 7 ☎ 246-6157 or 246-9136*).

Candilejas (*Bailén 16 ☎ 265-5545*) mines a different musical vein. The name means "limelight," as might be guessed by the prominent posters of Charlie Chaplin in that role. He is joined by representations of such icons as Clark Gable, Vivian Leigh, Elizabeth Taylor, Humphrey Bogart and James Dean. From Sept-May, live **cabaret** is presented in the back room, mostly drawn from Broadway shows and Hollywood musicals.

A peculiarly Japanese import is the *karaoke* bar, in which songs of the last 50yrs are recorded without the main vocalist,

119

and patrons are invited to step up to the mike and fulfill their showbiz fantasies. **Karaoke Hakodate** (*Fortuny 47* ☎ *308-0355*) puts its own twist on the format. Videos are projected with the lyrics of a song shown in English, Japanese and Spanish. A song book lists offerings originally recorded by The Beatles, Andy Williams, Pat Boone, Neil Sedaka, Julio Iglesias, Willie Nelson, and many more. Just order up a video and be Elvis or Sinatra for three minutes. Don't show up in blue jeans.

Most **discos** in the capital flare and fade like fireflies, but a surprising number survive for years. The more ambitious *discotecas*, with elaborate fixtures and superior sound systems, are found primarily near the **Puerta del Sol** (*map 9 D3*) and in streets paralleling the middle reaches of the **Paseo de la Castellana** (*N of map 10 B5*). Standard practice is to charge an admission fee at the door, which usually includes the first (expensive) drink. Many discos have "afternoon" sessions, from about 7-9.30pm, closing for dinner and reopening at 11pm or later. At the "in" spots, business rarely picks up until well after 1am, and most close at 4 or 5am.

The white-hot **Teatriz** (*Hermosilla 15* ☎ *577-5379*) is almost painfully chic. International designer Phillipe Starck has concocted few environments so conspicuously *decorated* as this. Don't bother reaching for those attractive books on the shelves: they are bolted in place, leaning and stacked *just so*. Cocktails for two costs as much as a good dinner almost anywhere outside this building. Rational people are apt to be amused by everything save the prices, while habitués find nothing funny about any of it.

Many old movie theaters have been converted into discos. **Pacha** (*Barceló 11* ☎ *447-0128*) is one example. It has a square bar in the center, silver tubular seating at the sides, a disc jockey at the far left, several bristling light bars that rise and descend from the ceiling, and a dance floor. Another theater was turned into **Joy Eslava** (*Arenal 11* ☎ *266-5440*). The old dress-circle seats and the stage, from which the imaginative lightshow emanates, have been preserved. The large dance floor is installed where the stalls once were and, once the correct hour is reached, is always full. Up in the new northern sector of town, the Eurobuilding complex contains **Mau-Mau** (*José Lázaro Galdiano 3* ☎ *250-2757*), a spangled, vaulted disco where the seating is cushy, tall plants are dramatically spotlit, service is swift and there is rarely a crush on the dance floor or around the bar.

Madrid is one of the only cities in Spain where you can still witness an authentic performance of *flamenco*. At **Corral de la Morería** (*Morería 17* ☎ *265-8446*) the dancers are spirited and the musicians seem to draw inspiration from the enthusiasm of their audience. Go after midnight. **Café de Chinitas** (*Torija 7* ☎ *248-5135*) is not far from the Plaza de España, but ask for careful directions. The high-ceilinged, tunnel-like room has green flocked wallpaper for an impression of modest elegance. Both the drinks and the show measure up well.

Flamenco and its derivatives were long scorned by upwardly mobile Spaniards as an art form of low origin performed largely for tourists. A fresh nighttime rage, however, is for the *sevillanas*, a dance resembling familiar flamenco movements but performed by customers themselves, often to live bands who supplement their Andalucían music with Latin American rhythms. One of the first spots to resurrect this dance form, and still one of the most popular, is **Al Andalus** (*Capitán Haya 19* ☎ *456-1439*). The engaging backdrop for its band and dancers is a mock-up facade of an Andalucían "white village," the chairs typically straight-backed with raffia seats. Go well after midnight. The classiest *sala rociera*, as these clubs are known, is **El Porton** (*Lopéz de Hoyos 25* ☎ *262-4956*). Entrance policies are as restrictive as at some of the more exclusive discos, and as inconsistent. Try going around midnight early in the week — and dress up. Another possibility is **La Caseta** (*General Castaños 13* ☎ *419-0343*).

Nightclubs of a more conventional variety, with comedians, singers, chorus lines, dinner and dancing, are no thicker on the ground than in most cities in these penny-pinching days. The closest to the Montmartre-Las Vegas variety is **Scala** in the Hotel Meliá Castilla (*Capitán Haya 43* ☎ *571-4411*), which takes into account the international character of its audiences. There are two shows a night, the first with dinner. Most of the heavily advertised alternatives are distinctly Spanish, requiring a knowledge of the language to enjoy much of the entertainment. For those visitors with at least a rudimentary understanding, **Cleofas** (*Goya 7* ☎ *276-4523*) and **Las Noches del Cuple** (*La Palma 51* ☎ *532-7115*) are possibilities.

Classical music and opera are not neglected. The very large **Auditorio Nacional** (*Principe de Vergara 136* ☎ *337-0100*) and the medium-sized **Teatro Monumental** (*Atocha 65* ☎ *227-1214*) and **Teatro Albeniz** (*Paz 11* ☎ *522-0200*) are used by national and international orchestras of substantial reputation, while a number of smaller halls serve as settings for piano concerts, song recitals and chamber ensembles. Among these are **Aula de Cultura Mare Nostrum** (*Paseo de la Castellana 1* ☎ *410-7162*) and **Achna** (*San Bernardo 107* ☎ *447-1900*). At the time of writing, the **Teatro Real de la Opera** on Plaza de Oriente was undergoing extensive renovation, partly to soundproof it against the metro line that runs underneath, but started lining up talent for its 1992 reopening a year in advance. In the meantime, classical opera and the uniquely Spanish light opera known as *zarzuela* have been staged successfully at the **Teatro Lirico Nacional de la Zarzuela** (*Jovellanos 4* ☎ *429-8225*). In summer, and especially during the fiestas of May, municipally sponsored open-air concerts and *zarzuelas* are staged in the **Plaza Mayor**, the **Parque del Retiro** and in neighborhood squares around the city.

Ballet is given a full season at the **Centro Cultural de la Villa** (*Plaza de Colón s/n* ☎ *275-6080*), with visits by such stellar troupes as the National Ballet of Australia and the dance company of the Paris Opéra. Dance is presented frequently at the **Teatro Albeniz** and the **Teatro Lirico Nacional de la Zarzuela** (*see above*).

Comedy and drama are presented at over two dozen theaters. These won't be of interest to visitors who aren't fluent in Spanish, but those who are can find current information in the *Guía del Ocio*. **Film** is a staple entertainment for this city of movie-goers, from early silents to revivals to the latest Hollywood mega-hit (or disaster). Most are dubbed into Spanish, but some are subtitled, especially films with limited potential audiences. Look for the legend *V.O. Subtitulada* — "subtitled original version" — in newspaper ads or theater marquees. The notation is usually found at the end of individual movie listings, and under the subheadings *Reposiciones* and *Reestrenos* — "revivals" — in the very serious-minded *Filmoteca*. Since at least a third of all movies shown during any given week were produced in the US or Britain, speakers of English will have little difficulty in finding acceptable filmic diversions.

Shopping

Spain's arrival as a fire-breathing force on the European economic stage has demolished its former reputation as a bargain paradise. Just about anything one might want is available, but rarely now at prices lower than at home. Craftsmanship and quality should determine what are worthwhile purchases. As a rule, the best buys in those terms are in leather goods, perfumes, clothes, wines and liquor. Avoid fans, shawls, "Toledo" cutlery, and people who attempt to steer you to "factories" and "workshops" with reputedly unbelievable prices.

Some sources still suggest that the venerable **flea market** known as **El Rastro** is the place in which to ferret out bargains, but nowadays that is more of a sightseeing event than a shopping excursion. Every Sunday and holiday morning until 2pm stalls fill the center of the Ribera de Curtidores, a street that pitches sharply down through the edge of the old town toward the river. Most of the bordering stores sell flimsy ephemera and outright junk, but some have decent copper and brass objects, antiques and reproductions. Tales of Goya drawings and Roman coins, snatched from the grasp of unwary dealers for unbelievable prices, faded long ago into folklore. El Rastro is still a scene of amiable pandemonium, crowds of people shuffling patiently along past hawkers and Gypsy animal trainers. There are good buys — perhaps — among the disorderly heaps of audio cassettes, T-shirts and plastic toys, but an educated eye is essential. Bargaining is customary, but it rarely results in significant savings. Pickpockets find this a fruitful environment, so keep wallets and handbags under firm control.

There are two **department store** chains in Madrid, worth visiting if only to gain an idea of what goods and products are available. The ubiquitous rivals **El Corte Inglés** (*branches at Preciados, Goya, Castellana and Princesa*) and **Galerías Preciados** (*at Plaza Callao, Arapiles, and Goya*) are useful first stops. An expensive but high-quality selection of Spanish handicrafts and furnishings is available at **Artespaña** (*Plaza de las Cortes 3*).

The primary shopping districts bristle with boutiques, specialty shops, bookstores, custom tailors, *perfumerías*, shoe stores, arcades, art galleries and designer clothes stores. **Calle Serrano** (*map 10 B-C6*) heads the list, starting near Plaza de la Independencia and running N to about Calle Juan Bravo. International firms dealing in luxury items cluster along that stretch and its adjacent blocks to the E. In only the short walk from Plaza de la Independencia to the Museo de Arqueológico, an alert shopper encounters several art and Oriental rug galleries; **Charles Jourdan**; the shoes and leather goods of **Farrutux** and **Fernando Escudero**; haberdasher **Panería Inglesa**; the porcelains and dinnerware of **Domo**; leather articles of great diversity and style at **Loewe**; silverware and jewelry at century-old **Duran**; and the head-to-toe men's and women's clothier, **Alfredo**. Continuing N, in approximately ascending order, there are the semi-daring fashions of **Lady Charma**; the yuppie male clothing of **Cortefiel**; another branch of **Artespaña** (*E on Calle Hermosilla*); a **Marks & Spencer**; **Gucci**; **Versace** and **Vuitton** (*both on Calle de José Ortega y Gasset*); and the Spanish fashion designer **Don Carlos**, who, when last seen, was drawing inspiration from native folkloric themes.

Antique stores are everywhere, but **Antiquedades Linares** (*San Jerónimo 48*) has a large selection and central location near the Palace Hotel. **Casa del Libros** (*Gran Vía 29*) has several floors of books in many categories, with a section of fiction and nonfiction titles in English. An encyclopedic selection of cookware is on hand at **Alambique** (*Plaza de la Encarnación 2*). The managers conduct cooking classes of varying lengths, some with instruction in English. Those in the market find that guitars present rare bargain possibilities. There are racks of rosewood and spruce beauties at the **Union Musical Española** (*San Jerónimo 26*), along with pianos and other instruments.

Sports in Madrid

Athletic facilities aren't as comprehensive or as up-to-date as in Barcelona, which, after all, was preparing for the Olympics at the time of writing. Still, Madrid has a sufficiency of pools, courts and arenas in which to watch or participate in favorite sports.

Basketball
An increasingly popular professional sport, with teams featuring American and Eastern European players, basketball can be seen in a number of venues in winter. Consult the hotel *conserje.*

Boating
Rowboats are available to rent at the lakes in **Parque del Retiro** and **Casa del Campo**. Sailing and other water-sports can be arranged at reservoirs in the near countryside.

Bowling
La bolera has hardly taken Madrid by storm, but there are several bowling centers, including **Bowling Chamartín** (*Estación de Chamartín* ☎ *315-7119*), **Stadium** (*Alcalá 106* ☎ *276-0315*), **Winstar** (*Paseo de la Castellana 77* ☎ *455-5282*) and **Bilbao** (*Fuencarral 118* ☎ *447-2378*).

Bullfighting
The season runs from late Mar-early Oct, with *corridas* usually scheduled for Wed and Sun evenings at 6 or 7pm. During certain festivals, such as that of San Isidro, in May, they are held every night. There are two *plazas de toros* — bullrings — the larger and more important being **Las Ventas**, E of downtown. The other is **Vista Alegre**, on the W side of the Mantanzas River.

Fitness centers
Madrileños were late to embrace the 1980s enthusiasm for physical fitness. Health clubs are now proliferating, but most are for members only, so visitors desiring such facilities are wise to reserve at one of the several hotels offering them. **Barajas** is out near the airport, but has a well-equipped gym with sauna, as well as two pools, tennis, golf and squash. In town, consider **Eurobuilding**, **Meliá Castilla**, **Meliá Madrid**, **Miguel Angel** (see WHERE TO STAY IN MADRID for addresses and ☎ for all of these), **Castellana Intercontinental** (*Paseo de la Castellana* ☎ *410-0200*) or, the least expensive of the group, the **Convención** (*O'Donnell 53* ☎ *574-6800*). If not staying in any of these hotels, an alternative possibility is the **Gimnasio Argüelles** (*Andrés Mellado 21-23* ☎ *549-0040*). It advertises body-building equipment, squash, classes in karate, ballet, aerobics, and even the folkloric *sevillanas.*

Fishing and hunting

Opportunities for these activities are widespread, especially in the Gredos mountains, w of the city, but obtaining the proper permissions and licenses is a chore. For information, write at least 6mths in advance (and preferably a year ahead) to the **Instituto para la Conservación de la Naturaleza** (*Gran Vía 35, Madrid 28013*), or contact the nearest branch of the **National Tourist Office of Spain** (see page 23) for advice.

Football (soccer)

By far the most popular spectator sport, *fútbol* is at its best in the giant **Santiago Bernabeu** stadium (*Paseo de la Castellana 140* ☎ *250-0600*). Up to 130,000 fans can root for their team, Real Madrid, consistently one of Spain's most successful, on Sun from Sept-May. The smaller **Estadio Vicente Caledrón** (*Paseo de los Melancólicos s/n* ☎ *266-4707*) is the home of Atlético de Madrid, another major Spanish club.

Golf

There are ten courses within short drives. The nearest is **Golf de Somosaguas**, adjacent to Casa del Campo (☎ *212-1647*); **Nuevo Club de Golf** (*Carretera de La Coruña km 26* ☎ *630-0820*) does not require full membership. Some hotels have special arrangements with other clubs; ask the *conserje*.

Horse-racing

International entrants compete on Sun in spring and fall at the **Hipódromo de la Zarzuela** (*Carretera de La Coruña km 6.5* ☎ *207-0140*).

Running

Both **Casa del Campo** and **Parque del Retiro** have permanent tracks for recreational runners, some of whom also use the pedestrian malls that border the **Paseo de la Castellano**.

Skiing

Navacerrada is the closest ski resort, only 50km (31 miles) away and reachable by road and rail. It has one run of more than 3,500 meters. Only 7km (4 miles) farther is the **Cotos**, with runs as long as 2,300 meters.

Tennis

Casa del Campo (☎ *464-9617*) and the **Nuevo Club de Golf** (☎ *630-0820*) have courts, as does the **Hotel Barajas** (see WHERE TO STAY IN MADRID), near the airport.

Madrid for children

Madrileños dote on their children, as do all Spaniards. Since the kids are encouraged to participate in all family celebrations and community festivities, less reason is seen to create child-segregated entertainments. Expect no mini-Disneylands, nor much in the way of children's theaters and museums. All is not lost, however. High on the list is the **zoo** in the CASA DEL CAMPO, a large but uninspired facility with a pair of Chinese pandas among its many exhibits. Half the fun is getting there, via the **cable car** (*teleférico*) that departs from the terminal on Paseo de Pintor Rosales, not far from the **Temple of Debod**. To the E of the zoo is a rather tame amusement park, the **Parque de Atracciones** (☎ *463-2900*). In PARQUE DEL RETIRO, animal trainers put dogs and monkeys through their paces, and puppet shows are staged, all along the promenade that fronts the lake.

Since little effort is made by most museums to cater to the curiosity of youngsters, the majority will bore them into rampant fidgets within minutes. An exception might be the MUSEO DE CERA (wax museum). Parents will probably want to shield their progeny from the more bloodthirsty exhibits of homicides and torture chambers, which, of course, are exactly the ones the kids most want to see. The martial airs and weaponry of the MUSEO DEL EJÉRCITO may lengthen the attention spans of all but the youngest children, as might the ship models of the MUSEO NAVAL. The armory of the PALACIO REAL has not only knights on horseback but also child-sized suits of armor designed for the royal heirs.

No other country gratifies children's fantasies of daring knights and fierce dragons as does Spain. An excursion might be scheduled from Madrid to **Avila**, for example, which is surrounded by medieval walls. Overnight stays in castles are particularly enjoyable, as in the fairytale paradors at **Alarcón** and **Oropesa**, both within easy drives of Madrid. See EXCURSIONS TO CASTILLA AND LÉON for further inspiration.

Excursions to Castilla & Léon

The ancient towns around the capital can be seen in easy day trips, spending each night in Madrid. Alternatively, devote 4-7 days to a road trip circling Madrid, then return to contemplate your experiences. Follow *Route 1* (below). Those familiar with the inner ring of Segovia, Avila, Toledo and Aranjuez, or who wish to get off that beaten track, can choose *Route 2* (page 127), a triangular tour through Castilla and León. They encounter fewer foreigners, and gather insights into the region that sustained the Christian Reconquest before Madrid was made capital.

Several of the buildings referred to on the following pages are illustrated on pages 14-16.

ROUTE 1: A SPIRAL AROUND MADRID

Head N along the Paseo de la Castellana in Madrid, taking care to follow the turn toward Burgos where the highway branches to the E, just beyond the Chamartín railroad station. This connects with the route designated N1. Continue N for 66km (41 miles). About 2km (1¼ miles) beyond the town of **Lozoyuela**, turn left (W) onto the C604 toward **Rascafría** (25km/16 miles). This road runs to the foothills of the **Sierra de Guadarrama**, bending SW along the river Lozoya. 2km (1¼ miles) beyond Rascafría is the 14thC **Monasterio del Paular**, designed by the architect of Toledo cathedral; part of the monastery is now a first-class hotel, and part is occupied by Benedictine monks, who permit guided tours (*closed Thurs*).

Follow the C604 for a further 27km (17 miles) SW, then turn right (N) onto the N601 over the mountain pass of **Puerto de Navacerrada** (snow might close the pass in winter months). Descend through evergreen forests, leaving behind the mountains, which flatten for 17km (11 miles) to the town of **San Ildefonso** (also called **La Granja**). Felipe V commissioned a palace and extensive gardens here, reminiscent of Versailles.

Castilla and Léon

Segovia, with its functioning Roman aqueduct, a photogenic castle and a modern *parador*, is 11km (7 miles) farther on.

A beguiling spot for lunch is the **Mesón de Cándido** (*Plaza Azoguejo 5* ☎ *(911) 428-103 IIIⅠ*), in the very shadow of the aqueduct.

Take the N603, s out of Segovia, as far as the A6 *autopista* (30km). Head N on the A6, leaving at the next exit, onto the N501, and travel w to **Avila** (28km/17 miles). With its conspicuously intact walls and their 88 semicircular towers, the ancient walled town deserves an overnight stay.

The **Parador de Avila** (*Marqués de Canales de Chozas 16* ☎ *(918) 211-340 IIIⅠ*) fills that need admirably, and its restaurant is the best in town. A staircase from the extensive gardens leads directly up onto the parapets.

When you are ready to leave, drive w to the opposite side of town, picking up the N110 for a short distance before forking to the left on the C502 and continuing through **Solosancho**, across the Adaja river, and then into the **Sierra de Gredos**.

Near the crest, a road branches right (w) toward the **Parador de Gredos** (*no street address* ☎ *(918) 348-048 IIIⅠ*). This was the very first of the *paradores*, built to resemble a hunting lodge, with a dining room from which to observe the unspoiled mountains.

Afterwards, return to the C502, heading s over the Puerto del Pico (Pico Pass) and descending to **Talavera de la Reina**, known for its flourishing porcelain industry more than its charm. The road leading toward the town center is lined at the western outskirts with ceramics shops, crowded with vases, pitchers, plates and other pottery. Check several shops before buying.

Should an overnight stop be required, don't stay in Talavera. Instead, head w along the NV about 20km (13 miles) to Oropesa with its fine **Parador de Oropesa** (*Plaza del Palacio 1* ☎ *(925) 430-000 IIIⅠ*). Housed in a superb 14thC castle with vaulted halls and corridors leading past cozy inglenooks and crannies, it has magnificent views of the Sierra de Gredos and the Tajo Valley.

Continue 43km (27 miles) E from Talavera to **Maqueda**, then bear SE on the N403 to **Toledo**. The city does not disappoint. It stands boldly on its granite hill moated by the green Tajo, a medieval huddle of roofs, steeples and towers. There is much to see: the cathedral, the Casa y Museo del Greco (house of the painter El Greco) and two of the last few synagogues in Spain.

Since Toledo rewards an overnight stay, especially after the tour buses have left for Madrid, *the* place to stay is the **Parador de Toledo** (*Paseo de los Cigarrakes* ☎ *(925) 221-850 IIIIⅠ*), on a promontory on the opposite bank, overlooking the city. Advance reservations are essential, however, usually months in advance. The *parador* dining room is quite capable. In the town itself, an excellent choice is the **Hostal del Cardenal** (*Paseo de Recaredo 24* ☎ *(925) 220-862 IIIⅠ*), an 18thC baronial mansion with a shaded garden and 27 rooms.

When ready, pick up the N400 on the opposite side of the river and head E for **Aranjuez**, 44km (27 miles) away. The Spanish Bourbons had a palace here, damaged by war and fire, but now restored to a semblance of its former grandeur.

A succession of landscape architects has left a legacy of elaborate gardens, parks and elm-lined walks. The outlying fields

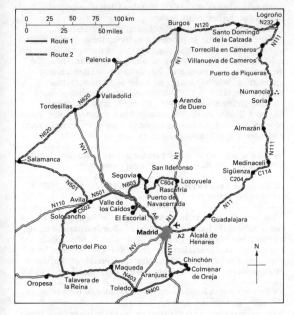

produce strawberries and asparagus that are prized throughout the country.

It is less than an hour N on the NVI to **Madrid**. If another day is available, however, take the unnumbered road E from Aranjuez to **Colmenar de Oreja**, and turn N for **Chinchón**. Two Gothic castles and a 16thC church in the charming *plaza mayor* justify the detour by themselves. From there, it is a short drive back to the NIV and 52km (32 miles) to **Madrid**.

⌁ There is a handsome new hotel in a refurbished former convent, the **Parador de Chinchón** (*Avenida del Generalísimo 1* ☎ (91) 849-0836 ▥□).

ROUTE 2: WEST AND NORTH OF MADRID

Follow the Gran Vía in Madrid W and NW after it becomes Calle Princesa. This soon leads to the NVI and on to the excellent A6 *autopista*, heading NW. After 21km (13 miles), make a detour to **El Escorial**, 11km (7 miles) to the SW. Here is the vast palace-monastery constructed for Felipe II in the 16thC to a design by Juan de Herrera. The reclusive, ascetic king governed the Spanish Empire from here for the last 14yrs of his life, dying within the monastery's walls in 1598. Hardly smaller than St Peter's and the Vatican, it breathes the spirit of the Counter-Reformation. Praised by some for its massive simplicity, it is also dismissed as glum and ponderous, especially when black storm clouds gather around the nearby mountain peaks and block the sun. The pleasant village nearby is not uncommonly touristy, and has several agreeable bars and cafés in which to pass an hour.

On the way back to the A6, an access road leads off to the left toward the **Valle de los Caídos** — the Valley of the Fallen — where Franco ordered a "basilica" to be dug into the side of the mountain in honor of the Civil War dead. It is an enterprise redolent of the pompous, hollow grandeur that so often characterizes the public works of long-lived tyrants.

Once back on the A6 proceed NW, taking the second exit, W toward **Avila** (see *Route 1*, page 125). From there, it is 100km (62 miles) on the N501 across tawny tableland to **Salamanca**. The medieval university city is a feast of Gothic and Renaissance architecture, with adjoining cathedrals and a peerless main square. Two faiths — Catholicism and intellectualism — have coexisted there since the 13thC, when the university was founded. That often uneasy relationship is manifest in the clumps of animated students and clerics moving along its ancient streets and lanes. Allow at least 24hrs to explore the city.

☞ Stay if possible at the modern **Parador de Salamanca** (*Teso de la Feria 2* ☎ (923) 268-700 **IIII**) on the N side of the Tormes river.

➤ For dinner, **Chez Victor** (*Espoz y Mina 26* ☎ (923) 213-123 **IIII**) outshines its competitors in all categories.

The next day, follow the Valladolid road — the N620 or E80 — out of Salamanca for 83km (52 miles) to **Tordesillas**, the small market town where the Treaty of Tordesillas, in which Spain and Portugal divided suzerainty over the just-discovered New World, was signed in 1494. Juana the Mad sequestered herself in the Monasterio de las Claras for 44yrs after her husband died in 1506.

➤ If it's time for lunch, there is the modest **Parador de Tordesillas** (☎ (983) 770-051 **IIII**), s of town.

Valladolid is 30km (19 miles) farther on the N620/E80. A frequent residence of noblemen and kings — Isabel and Fernando were married here — from its liberation from the Moors in the 12thC until its brief tenure as capital in the 16thC, Valladolid is now an industrial and agricultural center. Examples of important architectural modes of the early Renaissance are scattered throughout the city. The N620 continues NE, bypassing **Palencia** (as you should, too) and reaching **Burgos** after 121km (76 miles). This city also functioned intermittently as capital, and profited from that influence, with a magnificent cathedral commissioned by Fernando III. The old quarter surrounding it encourages strolling.

➤ Several traditional restaurants make Burgos a logical destination at lunchtime. Two possibilities are **Casa Ojeda** (*Victoria 5* ☎ (947) 209-052 **IIII**) and **Mesón del Cid** (*Plaza Santa Maria 8* ☎ (947) 205-971 **IIII**).

The tour will have taken a leisurely 3-5 days to this point. If it is time to get back to **Madrid**, the N1 heads due s. The trip of 245km (153 miles) can be completed in about 3hrs, with time for lunch in **Aranda de Duero**. But if you have another 3-4 days to spare, continue E on the N120 toward Logroño.

After 67km (42 miles) is **Santo Domingo de la Calzada**, a town with an unprepossessing main street, but charming alleys to the left (N) side, especially around the cathedral. This was a pilgrimage stop on the Way of St James. Visit the church to see the caged chickens.

☞ On the same small square is the **Parador Santo Domingo de la Calzada** (*Plaza del Santo 3* ☎ (941) 340-300 **IIII**), erected from the ruins of a medieval hospice.

Continue on the N120 and N232 to **Logroño**, the heart of the famous Rioja wine district.

⇌ Several fair-to-good restaurants provide venues for testing the principal local product, but heading the list is the **Mesón de la Merced** (*Mayor 109* ☎ *(941) 221-166* ▮▮▮). Set in a lavishly appointed mansion, it contains what might be the most comprehensive wine cellar in the region.

Heading S on the N111, the road slowly rises through vegetable fields and orchards along the Iregua river. After 30km (19 miles), an old stone bridge leads right (W) into **Torrecilla en Cameros**, backed by the peaks of the **Sierra de Cameros Nuevo**. It has an appealing little church. Continue S on the N111, through the charming village of **Villanueva de Cameros**, onto the twisting road that climbs up to the **Piqueras** pass, and then down to **Garray**. Off a side road to the S is the site of the ancient settlement of **Numancia**, where native Celtiberians held off the Romans for months in 134BC. Only some foundations and columns built by the eventual victors remain, since all significant archeological finds have been removed to museums. Back on the main road, it is 7km (4 miles) to medieval **Soria**.

✑ Soria has the small, modern **Parador de Soria** (*Parque del Castillo s/n* ☎ *(975) 213-445* ▮▮▮).

After 35km (22 miles), the N111 leads to **Almazán**, which retains vestiges of its medieval fortifications, and several buildings of the period during which it was a frontier outpost of the kingdom of Aragón. The attractive main square has a Romanesque church and a Renaissance palace. Another 40km (25 miles) farther S, turn into the village of **Medinaceli**, where a 2ndC Roman arch, several small *palacios* and a 13thC castle survive. Continuing S, turn right (SW) onto the N11 (not to be confused with the N111, which terminates slightly N). After 12km (7 miles), turn right onto the C114 to **Sigüenza**. The tidily picturesque town is dominated by a restored castle and bishop's residence. Among the worthwhile sights are the 12th-15thC cathedral next to the sloping, arcaded *plaza mayor*.

✑ The castle now houses the especially appealing **Parador de Sigüenza** (☎ *(911) 390-100* ▮▮▮).

A secondary road, the C204, leads through increasingly varied countryside to the N11, toward **Madrid**. The well-surfaced route fortunately bypasses **Guadalajara** (46km/29 miles). Another 25km (15 miles) farther on is the university town of **Alcalá de Henares**. Off to the left (S) is the bustling Plaza de Cervantes, named after the author, who was born here. Madrid is only 31km (19 miles) farther west.

⇌ To the S of the plaza is the **Hostería del Estudiante** (*Colegios 3* ☎ *(91)888-0330* ▮▮▮). A former college dining hall with origins in the 15thC, it is now a restaurant of the *parador* chain.

Sevilla *(Seville)*

If you would know Spain and have time for only one city, make that Sevilla. True, it is not the grandest nor loveliest nor most vibrant of Iberian provincial capitals. While it ranks high in those categories, other cities surpass it. What it does do is fulfill our romantic imaginings and lay before us the national heritage.

Staunch resistance to invasion has not been a constant theme in Sevillian history. Since the days of the Roman Empire, the aristocracy and merchant class have displayed an almost unseemly eagerness to embrace the beliefs of each new force that cast a covetous eye on their city. The overnight capitulation to Nationalist rebels in July 1936 was merely the most recent example.

Iberians — or possibly Phoenicians — founded the riverside settlement that Julius Caesar encountered on an excursion up the Guadalquivir in 45BC. Despite nearly six centuries of Roman occupation, transition of authority to the Vandals and then the Visigoths proceeded with little apparent turmoil in the 5thC AD. The Moors easily absorbed the city in 712, their first year on the peninsula, and various Arab factions ruled until the triumph of the Christians under Fernando III of Castilla in 1248.

In the 14thC, Pedro the Cruel made a lasting impact, manifest in the **Alcázar**, a palace incorporating portions of a pre-existing Moorish castle. Still greater prosperity came with the discovery of the New World, since Sevilla was the principal port for the returning treasure galleons. Commerce and the arts flourished during that Golden Age, which nurtured the native artists Velázquez, Zurbarán and Murillo. But the flame flared and died with the endless wars of Felipe IV and the slow erosion of control over the colonies.

Today Sevilla is the principal city of Andalucía, the region that runs across the bottom of the peninsula from Portugal to Murcia. Its canning and textile industries are still served in part by the Guadalquivir. The city straddles the river, with its major monuments, business offices and **Barrio de Santa Cruz** on the E bank, the fairgrounds and factories on the W bank.

Two of the most Spanish of folkloric events are held in Sevilla each spring. During **Holy Week**, there are nightly processions by the ancient brotherhoods (*cofradías*) associated with 52 neighborhood churches. These solemn parades are led by *pasos* — massive floats with images depicting saints or stages of the Passion in meticulous detail. In front and behind, penitents troop, wearing conical hoods, masks and robes in designated colors. Most of the men carry large candles, but some drag heavy chains or timber crosses along the entire route. For believer and nonbeliever alike, it is a profoundly moving spectacle.

Two or three weeks later is the **Feria de Sevilla**, the annual fair that began long ago as a simple livestock auction. Now, behind a great illuminated gateway at the edge of a large field on the W side of the river, 1,000 canvas *casetas* (little houses), some humble, others grand, are erected by families, unions, clubs and political parties. Men, boys and some women don traditional Andalucían riding habits with flat-brimmed hats, short snug jackets and tooled leather chaps. Other women and girls dress in brightly colored dresses with tiered ruffled skirts, fringed shawls around their shoulders, carnations or roses in their hair. In the late afternoon, the wealthy, the titled and the pretenders circulate in brightly polished carriages drawn by matched pairs and teams of horses with cockades and braided tails. Or a gentleman may choose to go instead on horseback, sometimes with a lady proudly riding pillion behind him, one arm around his waist. From dusk and far into the night, occupants of the *casetas* dance a type of choreographed flamenco called the *sevillanas*. Most of the tents are open to passers-by. The experience is unforgettable.

Basic information

Getting there and getting around

Iberia and Aviaco have frequent **flights** from Madrid and other Spanish cities. The expanded **San Pablo airport**, which has a new passenger terminal, is only 12km ($7\frac{1}{2}$ miles) from the city center, so a taxi ride into town isn't expensive. **Buses** meet some Iberia flights, taking passengers to the airline's downtown office (*Almirante Lobo 2*).

The national **railroad**, RENFE, offers more than 20 trains a day from Madrid, Málaga, Cádiz and other cities. An exceptionally high-velocity train called the *AVE (Tren de Alta Velocidad Española)* was introduced in early 1992. With a top speed of 250km/h (187mph), it covers the distance between Madrid and Sevilla in under 3hrs, a trip that used to take twice as long. The *AVE* operates between the refurbished Atocha station in Madrid and the very new **Santa Justa** station in Sevilla. Santa Justa replaces the two old stations, one of which is to be torn down, the other converted to other purposes.

Sevilla is a fairly compact city, most of its principal attractions being within walking distance of each other. For that reason, **taxis** should not be a sizable expense. The orange city **buses** follow complicated routes, due to the many narrow streets. One-way fares are inexpensive, and the ten-ride **Bonobus** passbook makes travel by bus still cheaper. There is as yet no functioning metro (subway) system, although one is under sporadic construction.

Horse-drawn carriages gather around the Plaza Virgen de los Reyes, E of the cathedral. Although they aren't too costly, it is nonetheless a good idea to bargain and set the fare *before* boarding.

Using a private **car** to get around Sevilla is not to be recommended. Most of its streets are clogged with traffic and narrow, and they are arranged in often confusing one-way patterns. Parking is extremely limited, and cars are favorite targets of street criminals, even when the vehicles are moving and occupied. For convenience and peace of mind, it is far better to park your car at the hotel and drive it again only when leaving the city.

Telephone area code

☎ The **telephone prefix (area code)** for Sevilla province is **95**.

Tourist information

☎423-4465. By mail: **Oficina Municipal de Turismo** (*Paseo de las Delicias s/n, 41012 Sevilla*). There is a walk-in visitor's office at **Avda. Constitución 21** (☎ *422-1404, map 11 C2*), where brochures and maps are handed out and questions are answered by harried, but multilingual, clerks.

Tour operators

Since most attractions are clustered together and easily visited on foot, bus tours aren't really necessary. Licensed guides are available at **Guidetur de Sevilla** (*Cuna 41, map 11 B3*) for walking tours. **Cruises** along the Guadalquivir leave from the wharf next to the Torre de Oro. Trips are 1hr in length, with commentary that is usually enlightening.

Emergencies

Police, fire ☎091

Sights and places of interest

ALCÁZAR 🏛 ★
Plaza del Triunfo s/n. Map 11C3 🖼 ✗ *Open 9am-12.45pm, 3-5.30pm.*

Only minor fragments of the earlier Almohad palace survive; most of what is now standing was commissioned by Pedro the Cruel in the 14thC. Evidently he admired the Alhambra in Granada, for his Mudejar architects clearly emulated that grand array of gardens and residences.

The entrance is on the s side of the Plaza del Triunfo. Immediately inside is a Moorish patio, but continue through an arched wall into the **Montería court**. Directly ahead is the facade of the Alcázar itself, and on the right is the **Cuarto del Almirante** (Admiral's Apartment), commissioned by Isabel to house the officers in charge of activities in the New World.

Inside, on the 1st floor, the **royal apartments** are notable for their tile murals, Mudejar details and *artesonado* ceilings. Return to the courtyard and enter the main building through the Puerta Principal, which leads into the **Patio de las Doncellas** (Courtyard of the Maidens), decorated with tiles, paired columns and arabesques. Most impressive is the **Salón de Embajadores** (Hall of Ambassadors), dominated by an intricately detailed dome. It is amusing to speculate whether the Christian kings knew that the scrollwork on the walls celebrated the glories of Allah. A banqueting hall and Felipe II's apartment follow, leading on to the tiny **Patio de las Muñecas** (Courtyard of the Dolls). Descend to the vaulted Arab baths and then follow passageways through the Montería courtyard to the **apartments of Carlos V**, for the superb 16thC Flemish tapestries. This tour also affords glimpses of the soothing gardens created for Carlos V.

AYUNTAMIENTO *(City Hall)*
Plaza Nueva s/n. Map 11B3.

The joyful Plateresque style of the 16thC is exemplified by the facade of this town hall. If the lengthy renovations are complete when you visit Sevilla, step into the lobby for a glimpse of the impressive interior.

BARRIO DE SANTA CRUZ ★
Map 11C3.

Just E of the CATEDRAL, whitewashed houses of the former Judería (Jewish quarter) crowd lanes that dip and twist beneath cascades of flowers and widen into squares with fountains ringed by orange trees.

Doors are purposely left open to allow passers-by to glimpse inner patios thick with greenery and decorated with colorful *azulejos* (tiles). Unplanned ambling along these constricted, often car-less streets is infinitely rewarding — a photographer's delight.

CASA LONJA AND ARCHIVO GENERAL DE INDIAS
Plaza del Triunfo. Map 11C2 🖼 ✗ *Open Mon-Sat 10am-2pm. Closed Sun. Enter from Av. Queipo de Llano.*

Originally an exchange designed by Juan de Herrera in the 16thC, this stolidly Classical building has a somber exterior but a memorable grand staircase inside. On the 1st floor are the **Indies Archives**, a large collection of maps and documents relating to the discovery and exploitation of the American colonies, including letters signed by Columbus and Magellan.

CASA DE PILATOS
Plaza de Pilatos 🔒 *Open summer 9am-1pm, 3-7pm, winter 9am-1pm, 3-6pm (but hours can vary).*
Reputed to be modeled on the house of Pontius Pilate in Jerusalem, this 15th-16thC Mudejar mansion took about 60yrs to complete, which partly accounts for the imposition of both Gothic and Renaissance elements. It boasts many fine tiles.

CATEDRAL 🏛 ★
Av. de la Constitución. Map 11C3. Open 10.30am-1pm, 4.30-6.30pm. Enter through main door in W facade.
Only three cathedrals in the world, including St Peter's in Rome and St Paul's in London, are larger than this. The mosque that originally stood here was used as a church from the Christian Reconquest in 1248 until it was razed to make way for the present building in 1401. Remaining from the original mosque are the GIRALDA and **Patio de los Naranjos** (Courtyard of the Orange Trees), on the N side.

The architecture blends Gothic and Renaissance, except for the principal portal, on the W side, which is modern but fortunately consistent in design. The interior is vast: almost 40 columns virtually disappear into darkness at the ceiling. They form the central nave with double aisles on either side, which are in turn bordered by chapels. There are 75 stained-glass windows, some of which date back to the early 16thC.

Turn left from the main entrance, then right along the N wall. The second chapel contains two Murillo canvases, *San Antonio de Padua* and *Christ's Baptism*. Continue (E) to see the magnificent choirstalls in the nave, with a 16thC *reja* (grille). At the door from the Patio de los Naranjos, turn right (s) along the transept for a glimpse of the *capilla mayor*, its sumptuous Gothic retable and a 16thC *reja*. Behind the *capilla mayor* is the domed Renaissance *capilla real* (royal chapel), where Alfonso X is buried. The highlight is a costumed wooden statue of the *Virgen de los Reyes*, allegedly given to Fernando III by Louis IX of France in the 13thC. King Fernando is entombed in the silver shrine below the altar, and stairs lead down to the tombs of Pedro the Cruel, who was largely responsible for the Alcázar, and his mistress María de Padilla, who lived there.

Returning to the main floor, turn left (s) from the *capilla real* into the vestibule of the Puerta de las Campanillas and continue into the **Sala Capitular** (chapterhouse). An elliptical room echoed by its dome, it contains a number of Murillos, including a large canvas of the *Conception* above the throne. Retrace your steps into the main part of the cathedral, then turn left immediately into the **Sacristía Mayor**, which houses the **treasury** and a lavish display of religious artifacts and paintings, including two representations of the Virgin by Zurbarán. The next chapel leads to the Gothic **Sacristía de los Cálices**, where there are two more Murillos and a Goya.

At the end of the s transept is a monument to Columbus, and in the floor by the main door, the tomb of his son, Fernando.

GIRALDA 🏛 ★
Plaza del Triunfo. Map 11C3 🔒 *Open Mon-Sat: summer 10.30am-1pm, 4-6.30pm; winter 10.30am-1pm, 4-6pm. Closed Sun.*
This pinkish square tower functions as an adjunct to the CATEDRAL, but began its life as a Muslim minaret. Hardy sightseers can climb to the top for a superb view of the city. The lower third

of the structure is of austere stonework typical of the Almohads; the 12thC central portion is of brick, employed in a decorative lattice scheme embracing horseshoe windows and pointed arches; and the comparatively florid 16thC upper stories include a large bell chamber, balconies and sculptures, surmounted by an angel weathervane representing *Faith*. What may sound like a painful hodgepodge is in fact a remarkably harmonious whole. At the foot of the tower is a portal that leads into the **Patio de los Naranjos** (Orange Trees), which is the only other remnant of the mosque that once stood here.

HOSPITAL DE LA CARIDAD
Temprado s/n. Map 11C2 🖼

The 17thC hospital for the indigent has a pleasing facade at the end of a small park that extends to the riverside Paseo de Cristóbal Colón. Inside there are paintings by Valdés Leal and Murillo; the latter also executed the tile murals on the front of the church.

MUSEO ARQUEOLÓGICO PROVINCIAL
Plaza de América s/n. Map 11F2 🖼 *Open Tues-Sun 10am-2pm, 5-8pm. Closed Mon.*

Two floors of sculptures, houseware, jewelry and related artifacts focus on archeological finds from the region, notably **Itálica**, the Roman city NW of Sevilla. There are also objects of the Paleolithic, Phoenician, Carthaginian, Greek and Moorish eras.

MUSEO DE ARTE CONTEMPORÁNEO
Santo Tomás 5. Map 11C2 🖼 *(🔲 to Spaniards). Open Tues-Sun 10am-2pm, 5-8pm. Closed Mon.*

Across the street from the CASA LONJA and near the entrance to the ALCÁZAR is an 18thC chapterhouse displaying the works of Spanish artists of the last 100yrs.

MUSEO DE ARTE Y COSTUMBRES POPULARES
Plaza de América s/n. Map 11F2 🖼 *(🔲 to Europeans). Open Tues-Sun 10am-2pm, 4-7pm. Closed Mon; Aug.*

The popular arts are represented by displays of costumes, farm implements, musical instruments, houseware, saddles, weapons, clothing and accessories. Some of the costumes are typical of those worn during festivals. Look, too, for the *trillo*, a wooden sled with an upturned tip and bits of flint and metal embedded in the bottom. At threshing time, the farmer stands on the sled while it is drawn by horse or mule across flattened piles of grain. It is a scene still witnessed in some rural districts.

MUSEO DE BELLAS ARTES
Plaza del Museo 9. Map 11B2 🖼 *Open 10am-2pm, 4-7pm. Closed Sun afternoon; Mon.*

The pride of this former 17thC convent is a collection of paintings by such Golden Age luminaries as El Greco, Zurbarán, Murillo and Velázquez. They are supplemented by works of lesser artists of the Sevilla school.

PALACIO DE SAN TELMO
Av. de Roma. Map 11D2.

On the E bank, just S of the San Telmo bridge, the former ducal palace has served educational purposes since its completion in 1796. Originally a naval college, now a seminary, its best feature is the Baroque main entrance.

PARQUE DE MARÍA LUISA
Map 11E2.
The park runs S along the river from the PALACIO DE SAN TELMO and was once part of the palace's estate. During the 1929 Ibero-American Exposition, it was the principal site for exposition buildings. Several of these remain, the largest of which is the massive semicircular government house on the E side of the park, in front of which is the **Plaza de España**, partially enclosed by moats. Boat rides are available, and the many paths are bordered by flowers and orange trees.

PLAZA DE TOROS
Paseo de Cristóbal Colón s/n. Map 11C2 ☒ *Open for bullfights.*
Bullrings rarely qualify as tourist attractions, for any reason other than their customary function. This *plaza* — **La Maestranza**, as it is known — is a showcase that equals or surpasses in grandeur any such arena in Spain, and, no doubt, the world. The 18thC structure esthetically enhances the events it hosts, with a perfect oval enclosed by a series of graceful arches. There isn't a bad seat in the house.

TORRE DEL ORO *(Tower of Gold)*
Paseo de Cristóbal Colón. Map 11C2 ☒ *Open Tues-Sun 10am-1pm. Closed Mon.*
The "tower of gold," so called because of the color of the tiles that once covered it, formed part of the 13thC Moorish fortifications. It now stands alone beside the river, at the E end of the San Telmo bridge. The balconied windows and decorative top were 18thC additions. In the past it has been used as a prison; now it is a maritime museum. There are good views.

UNIVERSIDAD
San Fernando. Map 11D2.
Sevilla is the city of Carmen, the fiery heroine of the novel and opera. Her prototype toiled in the mid-18thC *fábrica de tabacos* (cigar factory) that is now the university.

Where to stay in Sevilla

Sevilla has never been blessed with an abundance of superior hotels, a deficiency that only intermittently captures the attention of developers. The approach of the 1992 Expo did prompt enough interest to underwrite four large new hotels, several smaller ones and the renovation of some others. Considerable attention has been given to the **Príncipe de Asturias**, the only hotel on the Isla de la Cartuja, where the pavilions of Expo '92 were installed. Although it didn't open until late 1991, it was fully booked through 1992. Ironically, the lodging scene is otherwise dominated by two hostelries erected for the *1929* Exposition, the **Alfonso XIII** and the **Tryp Colón**.

Reservations must be made many months, even a year, in advance of the Holy Week and April Fair celebrations. Rates for those periods are nearly double, as they no doubt will be during the Expo. If arriving at the airport without a reserved room, an agency that might be of help is **Todohotel**. They also have an office downtown (*Imagen 8, map 11 B3*), and the service is free.

ALFONSO XIII
San Fernando 2, Sevilla 41004
☎ 222-850 ☏ 72725 ⊠ 421-6033.
Map **11D2** ⬛⬛⬛ 148 rms ▭148 ▦
🔟 🖼 ⊟ *AE* ⊙ ⊡ 🅥

*Location: Facing the Jardines del
Alcázar.* Built to house guests at the
1929 Exposition, the stately Alfonso
XIII simulates a Mudejar *palacio* in
the ham-handed manner of the time
in which it was built. Rooms are
uncommonly spacious. Much of the
furniture, however, looks like
original equipment. The people at
the front desk also need to be
advised that dealing with the public
is their function, not their travail.
Despite such shortcomings, the
tables around the courtyard fountain
are the cocktail-hour rallying point
for Sevilla's Establishment, and the
dream of many a young Sevillana is
to have her wedding here. Every
major attraction is within walking
distance. Still, the management has
work to do to justify its prices and
reputation.
🏠 ♨ ᴞ ☐ 🎝 🇾 🖼

LAS CASAS DE LA JUDERÍA
*Callejón de Dos Hermanas s/n,
Sevilla 41004* ☎ 441-5150
⊠ 442-2170. Map **11C3** ⬛⬛ to ⬛⬛⬛⬛
32 suites ▭32 suites ▦ *AE* ⊙
🅥

*Location: In the ᴇ end of the Barrio
de Santa Cruz.* Four attached
houses on an almost hidden
cul-de-sac off the Plaza Santa María
La Blanca were joined to create an
unusual hotel of exceptional charm.
Once owned by the Duke of Béjar,
Cervantes' patron, the houses have
been made into 1- and 2-bedroom
suites, most with patios or balconies
and equipped kitchens. Furnishings
are mostly 19thC reproductions:
pencil-post beds and Victorian
dining sets. All have satellite TV
with channels in several languages.
There is a large underground
parking garage.
🏠 ☐ 🖼

DOÑA MARÍA
Don Remondo 19, Sevilla 41004
☎ 422-4990. Map **11C3** ⬛⬛⬛ 61
rms ▭61 ▦ *AE* ⊙ 🅥

*Location: Near the central Plaza del
Triunfo.* Tucked into a side street
only steps from the CATEDRAL,
ALCÁZAR and the BARRIO DE SANTA
CRUZ, its public rooms are crowded
with semi-antiques and paintings.
Many regulars favor the place for its
inn-like intimacy. The bedrooms,
however, are cramped and need
sprucing up, although some have
4-poster beds. There is a wrap-

around nook of a lobby bar and a
rooftop pool (big enough for
plunges, but not for serious laps).
♨ ⍟ ᴞ ☐ 🎝 🇾

INGLATERRA
Plaza Nueva 7, Sevilla 41001
☎ 422-4970 ☏ 72244. Map **11B3**
⬛⬛⬛ to ⬛⬛⬛⬛ 120 rms ▭120 ▦ 🖼
🔟 ⊟ *AE* ⊙ ⊡ 🅥

*Location: A short walk from the
cathedral.* It droops here and there
from heavy use, but that can be
counted as testimony to the
desirability of its location. It is near
everything of importance, and
borders a park-like square. The
public and private rooms are
functional but dispirited.
‡ ☐ 🎝 🎴 🇾

LOS LEBREROS
Luis de Morales 2, Sevilla 41005
☎ 457-9400 ☏ 72954 ⊠ 457-9400
⬛⬛⬛ to ⬛⬛⬛⬛ 439 rms ▭439 ▦ 🔟
⊟ *AE* ⊙ ⊡ 🅥

Location: Near the soccer stadium.
Los Lebreros (the rabbit hunters)
presents a brisk contemporary face
to as many as 832 guests a night.
Echoing marble lobbies and
somewhat constricted bedrooms are
the rule. Soccer fans are happy with
proximity to the stadium, but
sightseers have long walks or short
taxi-rides in store.
♨ ᴞ ‡ ☐ 🎝 🎴 🇾

MACARENA SOL
Juan de Ribera 2, Sevilla 41009
☎ 437-5800 ☏ 72815 ⊠ 438-1803
⬛⬛⬛ 285 rms ▭285 ▦ ⊟ *AE* ⊙
⊡ 🅥

*Location: In the northern sector,
opposite the old walls.* This is among
the more stylish entries of the
ubiquitous Sol chain, with a lively
lobby emulating a Moorish patio, a
pleasant staff at the front desks, and
rooms equipped not only with color
TV but with satellite video. An
"English" bar and the snack-bar
beside the pool provide respite from
touring. The "executive floor"
promises special services and extra
touches of comfort, and a rooftop
pool has fine views of the city. It is
at some distance from the center.
ᴞ ‡ ☐ 🎝 🎴 🇾

PORTA COELI
*Av. Eduardo Dato 49, Sevilla
41005* ☎ 457-0040 ☏ 72913
⊠ 457-8580 ⬛⬛⬛ 243 rms ▭243
⊟ *AE* ⊙ 🅥

*Location: ᴇ side of town, near the
soccer stadium.* The management
like to think of this neighborhood as
the "Sevilla of the future." That

means it's a very long walk or medium taxi ride from the city's principal attractions, which is probably secondary to its business-minded clients. They have an executive floor, a heated pool, whirlpool, and the formal but unintimidating in-house restaurant, **Florencia**. Otherwise, the hotel is entirely conventional, with contemporary decor.

≈ ≉ 🗆 🖼 🐾 ⛆ 🖭

TRYP COLÓN
Canalejas 1, Sevilla 41001
☎ 422-2900 ☎ 72726 ☎ 422-0938.
Map **11B2** ▥▥ to ▥▥ 218 rms
▱218 ▦ ⇌ ⇌ AE ⊕ 🖭 VISA
Location: A short walk N of the bullring. The new owners of the old Majestic did everything their rivals at the **Alfonso XIII** should be doing. They closed to business for over 2yrs to undertake a total top-to-bottom renovation. It was needed, for this hotel too was built for the

1929 Exposition, and its age showed. Now, every room has the comforts and gadgets a luxury hotel should offer as the 21stC approaches. Baths are marble, with two sinks, hairdryer, separate toilet and an adjustable massaging showerhead. Rooms are in subdued tones, with touches of brass, and, for a change, truly comfortable settees and chairs in which to linger over breakfast. On the main floor, a stained-glass dome over the lobby was restored, and a small workout room with sauna was installed down below. The locally famous **El Burladero** restaurant and its bar are in the same building, also refurbished. And, the staff actually seems pleased to see you: the *conserjes* make it a point to hand over the proper room key before being asked. Until further developments, the Colón deserves to be considered the best in town.
🎺 🐖 ≉ 🗆 🖼 ⛆ 🖭

Where to eat in Sevilla

Dining isn't as important to Andalucíans as to other Spaniards, a fact borne out by their restaurants. That isn't to say that meals need be less than entirely satisfactory, rather that they are more often memorable for things other than what is on the plate.

While beer, red wine and cola drinks are increasingly the beverages of choice, the characteristic drinks of Sevilla are the sherries of Jerez de la Frontera and its nearby villages, an hour to the S. They range from the very dry to the cloyingly sweet, but the sherry most often chosen to accompany *tapas* or as an aperitif before meals is the style called *fino*, the driest of several grades. The similar but somewhat softer *manzanilla* is a strong second in popularity.

EL BURLADERO
Canalejas 1 ☎ 422-2900. Map **11B2** ▥▥ to ▥▥ ▦ ⛆ AE ⊕ VISA
Closed Aug.
Long one of Sevilla's favorite dining spots, El Burladero was closed for renovation along with the Hotel **Tryp Colón**, in which it was housed. Both reopened in 1988, and their anxious publics were reassured, or should have been. In truth, the food here was never more than slightly elevated country fare, uncomplicated and abundant. It is a manly, two-fisted environment. After all, many of its habitués are associated with the bullfighting game. (A *burladero* is the plank barricade behind which *toreros* escape charging bulls.) Women are in largely silent evidence, leaving

the stage to the stubby, big-shouldered men who hunker down together in clouds of cigar smoke. Their degrees of importance are signaled when the host summons the chef to discuss the meal directly with the customers. Outsiders are treated correctly, if not as warmly.

DON RAIMUNDO
Argote de Molina 26 ☎ 421-2925. Map **11C3** ▥▥ ▦ ⛆ AE ⊕ VISA
The former 16thC convent at the edge of the Barrio de Santa Cruz is crowded with antiques and folk art in delightful profusion. Truth to tell, it scores more points for ambience than gastronomy. That is not to suggest that the *sopa con almejas* or wild boar stew are less than

adequate, simply that eating with the eyes is at least as rewarding.

LA DORADA

Virgen de Aguas Santas 6
☎ 445-5100 *IIII* 🍽 ⊻ *AE* ⊙ *VISA*
Closed Sun; Aug.
All shadings of the piscatorial palette are explored, with marine creatures familiar and exotic undergoing every preparation that the Spanish love for seafood has inspired. Frying is in the airy style of Málaga, and it is as well not to examine too closely the identities of the ingredients — just enjoy. Among many other dishes, *dorada* and *lubina* are special when baked to moist tenderness in hard salt shells (which are broken apart and discarded when served). Look also for *sopa de mariscos, chanquetes, salmonetes, boquerones* and *rodaballo.* Service is fast and furious, with drink orders taken before guests are even seated, and waiters flinging themselves through the kitchen doors with reckless abandon. Only the bill comes slowly.

EGAÑA ORIZA △

San Fernando 41 ☎ 422-7111.
Map 11D3 IIIII 🍽 *AE* ⊙ ⊙ *VISA*
Closed Sat lunch; Sun; Aug.
One of Seville's two top restaurants and by far its most expensive, it does its best to live up to both its reputation and its prices. The window at the end of the 2-story room frames a garden enclosed by a fragment of ancient parapet. With the creamy walls, snowy napery and beige slipcovers on the comfortable tub chairs, a quartet of F. Scott Fitzgerald's idle rich can be imagined lounging the afternoon away at one of the ample tables. Disappointments are rare, and are to do more with personal taste than execution. As a rule, Spanish restaurateurs are more knowledgeable about fish than meat. Only in places of such high standards as this is beef given equal attention, both in quality and preparation. In a country where they don't quite believe you if you ask that your steak be rare, it arrives exactly as requested. If the prices for all this are beyond budgetary limits, at least stop in at the bar for one or two of the classy *tapas* — the fresh asparagus on toast, perhaps, topped with two shrimps and a dollop of caviar.

FIGON DEL CABILDO

Plaza del Cabildo s/n ☎ 422-

0117. *Map 11C2 IIII* 🍽 🐾 *AE* ⊙
VISA Closed Sun; July.
No culinary wonderment here, so settle for warmth and competence. To find it, locate the pedestrian passage opposite the main door of the cathedral. It leads to an enclosed plaza dominated by the restaurant. Beyond the busy bar in front are two floors of dining rooms, including an open-air terrace. Ingredients are market-fresh, prepared in largely traditional ways: garlic soup, artichoke hearts with baby eels, and tournedos with shrimp are good, but there are few disappointments in the balance of the card. It is the best of a local chain that includes **El Rincón de Curro** (below) and **Bodegón El Riojano** (*Virgen de las Montañas 12* ☎ 445-0682 *IIII*).

HOSTERÍA DEL LAUREL

Plaza de Los Venerables 5
☎ 422-0295. *Map 11C3 IIII* 🍽
⊻ *AE* ⊙ *VISA*
The atmospheric bar room is hung with serrano hams and bundles of herbs, befitting the surrounding BARRIO DE SANTA CRUZ. Stop in for a *fino* (sherry) or beer with a slab of cheese, or pick your way through the low tables and up to the more formal dining room on the 1st floor.

LA ISLA

Arfe 25 ☎ 421-5376. *Map 11C2*
IIII 🍽 *AE* ⊙ *VISA Closed Mon; Aug.*
A fish house in newly renovated quarters down a back street near the cathedral, it sustains its 40yrs of popularity. Heading the list of possible first courses is what amounts to a scaled-down *paella*, to be followed, perhaps, by the sea bass with clams and shrimp laid on a pond of silky *marinera* sauce. Chicken and pork are available for those averse to seafood.

MODESTO

Cano y Cueto 5. Map 11C3 IIII
🍽 *AE* ⊙ *VISA Closed Wed.*
Widely proclaimed the best *tasca* in town, eating is at least as important as drinking and talking. Make your way through the friendly crowd toward the multitude of *tapas* spread along the marble-topped bar. Point at *angulas*, the thumbnail-sized clams called *coquinas*, or the mysterious but tasty *pescado frito.* Patrons order one or more of these, chased by bread and wine, often in lieu of dinner. It is nearly impossible to avoid meeting the people pressing at either elbow. Upstairs is

a dining room, and tables are set out in front in warm weather.

EL RINCÓN DE CURRO
Virgen de Luján 45 ☎ *445-0238. Map 11E1* ⅢⅡ 🎫 ⒶⒺ ⒸⒹ 🈂️ *Closed Sun; Aug.*
Formal dinners of regional dishes — *frito Sevillano, cordero asado, almejas con langosta* — and occasional Franco-Italian detours are offered in a gracious setting only slightly marred by the ungainly decor. Little is likely to startle or disappoint in this, one of the better mid-level entries in the city, and from May-Sept the air conditioning is a blessing.

RÍO GRANDE
Betis 70 ☎ *427-3956. Map 11C2* ⅢⅡ 🎫 🈁 🍸 ⒶⒺ ⒸⒹ 🈂️
The dining terrace sprawls above the river, opposite the TORRE DEL ORO and adjacent to the w end of San Telmo bridge. That situation and the relatively elaborate interior trappings at Río Grande mean higher-than-usual but justifiable prices. The performance of the

kitchen can be uneven, the odds favoring good, if not superlative, selections. *Perdiz a la salsa castellana, sopa de ajo* and *paella* are among the house specialties.

SAN MARCO
Cuna 6 ☎ *421-2440. Map 11B3* ⅢⅡ 🎫 🈁 ⒸⒹ 🈂️ *Closed Sun; Aug.*
In the same culinary and esthetic league as **Egaña Oriza** (above), the San Marco charges considerably less. The lordly 19thC mansion has been given an Italianate cast, decorated with fluted columns, statuary, a Venetian glass chandelier and a prominent bust of Caesar.

The menu is part Basque, part Italian in influence, and the pasta is *al dente*, a skill yet to be mastered by most Spanish chefs. Ravioli stuffed with flaked sea bass and lasagna *frutti di mare* are winning examples. For even lower prices and a more casual atmosphere, try the owners' **Pizzería San Marco** (*Betis 68* ☎ *428-0310* ⅢⅡ) on the w side of the river, near the San Telmo bridge.

Nightlife

The Flamenco tradition long ago degenerated into choreographed prancing and the forced jollity of audience participation, all of which denies its improvisational vitality and innate eroticism. Able performers persist, however, and in Sevilla they usually congregate in two fairly reliable *tablaos* (as the clubs are called): **Los Gallos** (*Plaza de Santa Cruz s/n* ☎ *212-154*) and **Curro Vélez** (*Rodó 7*). Don't arrive before midnight: the early shows are for tourists, and the dancers and guitarists barely work up a sweat. Otherwise, prowl the alleys of the **Barrio de Santa Cruz**, along which are a number of friendly bars and clubs.

Shopping

Calle de las Sierpes (Street of the Snakes), running N from Plaza San Francisco to Plaza Campana, is a pedestrians-only shopping lane with many kinds of stores, including the leather goods for which Spain is famous. Among the remaining semibargains are handmade ceramics: plates, pitchers, tureens, bowls, vases, and the water jugs called *porrónes*. Sevillian designs are delicate, intricate floral traceries on white glaze.

Good selections are available at **Pascual Lázaro** on Calle Sierpes and at **Cerámicas Sevilla** (*Pimienta 9*), on a street that parallels the outer wall of the Alcázar. The owner of the latter shop speaks English. Unfortunately, neither store will ship purchases, but they will wrap them carefully for carrying by hand.

An excursion through Andalucía

Leave Sevilla by the Avenida de Kansas City (yes, that's the name), which becomes the NIV (a.k.a. EO5) heading E toward Córdoba. Continue 33km (21 miles) to **Carmona**, which possesses a Roman necropolis and crumbling Moorish walls.

☞ Within the walls is the modern **Parador de Carmona** (*Alcázar s/n* ☎ *(95) 414-1010* **ⅢⅡ**).

Head N of town on the C432 until it crosses the Guadalquivir, then turn E on the C431, near **Lora del Río**.

Up on the right (S), after about 50km (31 miles), stands the perfectly preserved castle of **Almodóvar del Río**. It can be visited, by those who are willing to face an uphill walk. After another 20km (12 miles), look for the turn left (N) toward **Medina Azahara**.

Once a Moorish palace complex of allegedly unimaginable splendor, the site now demands an active imagination to conjure its former dimensions, but there are exposed foundations and some structures to suggest its scope. Most of the significant artifacts discovered there have been removed to the archeological museum in **Córdoba**.

Return to the C431 and turn left (E) for that city and its singular, unmissable **Mezquita**. This mosque, which covers six acres and envelops a 16thC Baroque cathedral, is the second most important Moorish monument in Andalucía (see illustration on page 14).

Córdoba deserves at least one day to visit the mosque and explore the picturesque **Judería**, the old Jewish quarter, with its whitewashed houses and flower-bedecked patios. The modern city, on the opposite bank of the river, is of relatively little interest.

☞ Opposite the Mezquita is the very good **El Caballo Rojo** (*Cardenal Herrero 28* ☎ *(957) 475-375* **ⅢⅡ**), known for its fine Moorish recipes.

Leave the city by the Paseo de la Rivera, heading E along the N bank of the river, and on to the NIV. Continue as far as **Andújar** (77km/48 miles), a fortified town of prehistoric origin with a Roman bridge and, in the *plaza mayor*, Gothic and Renaissance buildings and a fountain.

☞ At **Bailén**, 27km (17 miles) farther E, is the **Parador de Bailén** (*Ave. Málaga s/n* ☎ *(953) 670-100* **ⅢⅡ**), at the intersection with the primary Granada-Madrid road. Essentially a motel, and in no way memorable, it is clean and inexpensive.

Still heading E, now on the N322, pass right through **Linares**, a mining town of little character. Wait until **Ubeda**, one of the first towns in Andalucía to be recaptured from the Moors. It has a monumental center of fine Isabeline and Plateresque structures.

☞ One of these is the **Parador de Ubeda** (*Plaza Vázquez de Molina 1* ☎ *(953) 750-345* **ⅢⅡ**).

On leaving Ubeda, find the N321 heading SW. Go through **Baeza**, another Renaissance town of less grand proportions, and on toward **Jaén**.

☞ Here, if it is lunchtime, there is the modern **Parador de Jaén** (*no street address* ☎ *(953) 264-411* **ⅢⅡ**), next to a ruined castle on a cliff high above the city.

Otherwise, turn S on the N323 E of Jaén and head for **Granada**, 90km (56 miles) away. After rising through blunted uplands, the road descends to a fertile plain and runs toward Granada, set against the blue-gray backdrop of the **Sierra Nevada**. The **Alhambra** rears above the city, the ultimate architectural achievement of the Moors. Not just a single building, as many imagine, the Alhambra is instead an extensive complex of gardens, palaces, fortifications and castles, ranking in near-mystical exuberance with the Taj Mahal, the Parthenon and Mayan Tikal.

✎ An overnight stay should be planned. The inn of choice for both lodging and meals is the **Parador de Granada** (*Recinto de la Alhambra* ☎ *(958) 221-443* ▥). The converted 15thC convent is actually in the grounds of the Alhambra, and therefore one of the two most popular *paradores* in the system (the other is at Toledo). Reservations must usually be made three or more months in advance.

The N323 continues S, skirting the W end of the sierra, passing sugar-cane fields and reaching the Mediterranean after 70km (44 miles).

Turn right (W) onto the N340 toward Málaga for the first of the popular Costa del Sol resorts, **Nerja**, on a promontory above the sea. Nearby are caves in which prehistoric artifacts have been discovered, and they are large enough for music and dance festivals every summer. **Málaga**, the largest city on the Costa del Sol and a major seaport, lies 53km (33 miles) to the W. Its attractions include a ruined Moorish Alcazaba and a Roman amphitheater.

✎ A further attraction is the **Parador de Málaga** (☎ *(952) 840-901* ▭), perched on a hill overlooking the port.

The almost continuous band of Costa del Sol resorts begins 5km (3 miles) SW of Málaga, with frenetic **Torremolinos**, tacky **Benalmádena** and tawdry **Fuengirola**. Numerous package tours disgorge into these artificial towns, filling them with two kinds of people — those who rarely stray from their national groups, and those sorts of mindless, besotted louts that have Spaniards rethinking their commitment to mass tourism. From Fuengirola, a road goes N to **Mijas**, a hill town too close to the coast to avoid commercialization but maintaining a measure of its former charm.

❧ ▨ There are several decent restaurants and a pleasant hotel, the **Husa Mijas** (*Av. México s/n* ☎ *(952) 485-800* **Ⅲ▯**).

Back on the coastal N340 road, head w to the stylish resort, **Marbella**, well w of whose center lies the concentration of chic bars and *boîtes* clustered around the yacht basin of **Puerto Banús**.

❧ Several fine luxury hotels include **Puente Romano** (*Ctra. Cádiz, km 176.7* ☎ *(952) 770-100* **ⅢⅢ**) and the **Marbella Club** (*Ctra. Cádiz, km 178* ☎ *(952) 771-300* **ⅢⅢ**).

At **San Pedro de Alcántara**, 10km (6 miles) farther, a right turn N points toward **Ronda** (on the C339). The once terrifying corniche road has been widened and straightened, and it is now possible to reach the town in under an hour. It occupies the flat top of a giant mesa, the sides falling away into cultivated valleys. A dramatic gorge almost 500ft deep cleaves the town in two, the sides stitched together by an 18thC bridge, which is far higher than it is long. One part of the old town maintains its Moorish character; the other has a bullring that may be the oldest in Spain. The present-day form of bullfighting is said to have been developed here.

Leave Ronda along the C339 heading for Sevilla. After 12km (7 miles), turn left (s) along an unnumbered road for **Benaoján** and the **Pileta Caves**. Prehistoric wall paintings are the most intriguing remnants of Stone Age inhabitants, pointed out by the guide in the several chambers, which are of cathedral dimensions. Return to the C339 and continue to its junction with the N342. Turn left (w) toward **Arcos de la Frontera**. From here, the jagged wilderness softens to rounded hills embracing quilted plains. Just as the land threatens to flatten completely, a granite ridge erupts from the valley. The attractive town of **Arcos de la Frontera** packs the summit.

❧ On the plaza at the very top is the **Parador de Arcos de la Frontera** (*Plaza Cabildo s/n* ☎ *(956) 700-500* **Ⅲ▯**). From its terrace, guests can look *down* at swifts sailing on the cliffside updrafts.

Leave Arcos by the N342 to **Jerez de la Frontera**, 24km (15 miles) to the w, where guided tours of the sherry *bodegas* are available. From Jerez, take the A4 *autopista* to **Sevilla**, 84km (52 miles) to the north.

Bullfighting

Although long ago eclipsed by soccer in the numbers of its devotees — *aficionados* — bullfighting remains popular. No attempt will be made here to justify or deplore the spectacle. It is a fact of the Spanish culture, to be sampled or ignored according to individual tastes and principles.

As an activity, bullfighting falls into an unclassifiable area between sport and ritual. The season is from late March to mid-October, although fights are occasionally scheduled during fiestas in winter. Every city and many towns have bullrings — *plazas de toros* — some of them centuries old and elegantly proportioned, others simple amphitheaters used only a few times a year. The major arenas schedule weekly fights during the season, usually on Sunday, often on one or two other nights, and every day of the longer fiestas. They begin promptly at the scheduled hour, usually 5 or 6pm, and last about $2\frac{1}{2}$ hours. Six bulls, all specially bred for this single purpose and weighing approximately 450kg (992lbs), comprise a standard card, with three *matadores* taking on two each, in rotation. (Bullfighters are also known as *toreros*, but never as "toreadors," which was an invention of a composer of operas.)

Once the opening parade of participants is over, the *corrida* has three distinct acts, or *tercios*. In the first, after the bull's release, the *matador* and his *peones* (assistants) attract his attention with capes, quickly taking refuge behind the stockade that encircles the arena. After observing the bull's movements for a few moments, the *matador* approaches the animal carrying a large flowing cape, magenta on one side, yellow on the other. The colors are traditional but have no effect on the bull, which is color-blind.

When the bull charges, the *matador* moves the cape in an often complicated series of maneuvers, intended both to display his artistry at such ritualized passes as the *verónica* and to test the bull's responses. Two men on horseback, the *picadores*, now enter the ring. They wear armored leggings and flat-brimmed hats with rounded crowns, and carry long lances with steel points. The bull is goaded into charging the right side of one of the heavily padded horses, while the *picador* thrusts a pike into his shoulders. The bull is encouraged to repeat the act once or twice more. Should the *picador* jab or pump the pike into the bull or take too long in making the animal back off, a predictable crescendo of derisive whistles comes from the audience, which rarely approves of the *picador*'s actions.

In the second *tercio*, men called *banderilleros* incite the bull into charging them. Running toward him, they dance out of the way of the horns at the last second while thrusting pairs of barbed *banderillas* (ribboned darts) into the beast's withers, where they are meant to stay. Three sets of *banderillas* are implanted, or at least attempted. Some *matadores* place their own darts to please the crowd.

Ten to 15 minutes have passed, and the final *tercio*, the *faena*, now begins. While the weakened bull waits, the *matador* ceremoniously salutes the *presidente*, the presiding official who sits in a special box above the ring. Then he dedicates the bull to a friend or to the crowd, into a microphone if the *corrida* is being televised. Finally, an assistant hands him a sword and a small red cape sewn to a stick, the *muleta*. He carries these toward his opponent. Weary from his wounds and exertions, the bull is panting heavily, his head down. Yet he remains very dangerous, and it is in this *tercio* that *matadores* are most often gored.

The *matador* approaches, presenting his body directly before the horns, *muleta* at his side. Again and again, the animal is made to charge. The *matador* is judged by the artistry of his capework and his daring in placing himself in ever greater jeopardy. After some minutes, he goes to the stockade, exchanges swords, and returns to the bull. With the *muleta* in his left hand, pointing down and to the side, he looks along the blade of the sword toward the hump of the bull's back. Catching the drama of the moment, the *matador* finally lunges forward, attempting to thrust the blade into the narrow space between the animal's shoulders and down into its heart. The bull coils at the same time for a last charge. Should all go as is hoped, the thrust is true and the animal collapses. That is rarely the case. Instead, the blade is poorly placed or bounces off bone, and further attempts must be made. Even when the sword is properly planted, the bull often refuses to go down and must be cajoled by capework into exhausting himself. Once in the sand, he is dispatched with a stab into his brain, with either a dagger or a special sword called a *verduguillo*.

A good performance by a *matador* is acknowledged by one of several degrees of symbolic award, signaled by the crowd waving white handkerchiefs in the direction of the *presidente*. If he responds by draping his own kerchief over the banister of his box, one of the bull's ears is cut off and presented to the *matador*. If the *aficionados* persist, the other ear is bestowed, and on very rare occasions, when it has been a spectacular performance, the tail as well.

The *matador* then makes a triumphal circuit of the arena, brandishing his trophies and dodging a barrage of flowers, hats, and the wineskins called *botas*. Most of these are thrown back by members of his entourage. In the meantime, a team of horses drags the bull from the ring, and the sand is raked over for the next fight.

There are variations of the *corrida*. A *rejoneo* features a *torero* in Andalucían riding costume who conducts the entire *corrida* singlehandedly, from horseback. He is often an additional attraction to the usual card. At a *goyesca*, named for the painter, Goya, the *matadores* are dressed in 18thC costume; and a *novillada* is for apprentice *matadores* against younger, smaller bulls.

Tickets are purchased at the bullring on the day of the fight, at booths and offices around town a day or two before, or — for an extra commission — the hotel hall porter can obtain them. Seats are in several categories and price ranges. The least expensive are those that are in sun throughout the *corrida*, the "*sol*" section. The logic of this is apparent on a Sunday in July. Next is "*sol y sombra*" — part sun, part shade — and "*sombra*," in the shade from the start and therefore most costly.

The relative proximity of seats to the ring makes a difference, too. The front row is the *barrera*, those immediately behind are the *contrabarra*, the lower grandstand is the *tendido bajo*, the upper grandstand the *tendido alta*, and highest up, the *andanada*. Ticket prices also vary according to the importance of the bullring, the box-office appeal of the *matadores*, and whether the *corrida* is part of a larger celebration. Front-row seats really aren't necessary, for most bullrings are small, and everything can be seen from the more distant rows, where the bloodletting seems a little less graphic. Seats are usually just cement steps or wooden benches, so rent a pillow from the vendors inside the arena. It is important to arrive on time, or the gates may be closed. Courtesy demands that no one leave in the middle of a fight, waiting instead until a pause between bulls.

Spanish wines

No country makes wines in a greater variety of styles. Among the best of a wide selection are the apéritif and dessert wines of Andalucía, the superb table wines of Rioja, and the excellent still and sparkling wines of Catalunya.

The name **sherry** is an early British corruption of *Jerez* de la Frontera, the Andalucían city that is the center of production of this distinctive wine. Sherry has been shipped from Spain since Sir Francis Drake's raid on Cádiz in 1587. Most popular varieties are the light, dry *finos*, which may be drunk chilled as an apéritif; the softer but still dry *manzanillas*; the amber, full-bodied *amontillados*; the *olorosos*, dark, fragrant and higher in alcohol; and the dessert wines, such as "Bristol Cream."

Rioja, an upland district lying along the Ebro valley on the fringes of the Basque country, makes the best-known Spanish table wines. Predominantly red, Riojas are fairly light in body, and resemble the wines of Bordeaux more than those of Burgundy.

The region has been making wines since pre-Roman times, but in their present style they date from the phylloxera epidemic of the late 19thC in France, when French vintners settled in the region and introduced the wine-making methods current in Bordeaux.

The largest group of *bodegas* — "wineries," in this context — is to be found in Haro, the capital of the subregion of La Rioja Alta, which produces the most delicate wines. Haro is the home of such famous firms as **Bilbainas**, **CVNE** and **Federico Paternina**.

Production of Rioja wines is strictly supervised. Of the select types, *vino de crianza* must be aged for not less than two calendar years. The red *reservas* spend a year in cask and two in bottle, while the *gran reservas* are matured for a total of seven years before leaving the *bodega*. Rioja also makes attractively fresh and fruity white wines. Very good to excellent recent vintages were 1978, 1981, 1985 and 1987.

The best of the still wines from **Catalunya** rival those of Rioja, and the region also produces most Spanish sparkling wine. Activity centers around the wine town of Vilafranca del Penedès, sw of Barcelona. *Bodegas* such as **Masia Bach**, **René Barbier** and **Jean León** make good wines, both white and red, but the best-known Catalunyan still wines are from **Bodegas Torres**, which exports world-wide. This family-owned concern has displayed great initiative, both in acclimatizing noble varietals from abroad, such as the Chardonnay and Cabernet Sauvignon, and in its technical methods (it was a pioneer in Spain of "cold fermentation"). Its red 1970 "Gran Coronas Black Label" was judged even better than Château Latour by an international jury in Paris in 1980. Top recent vintages were 1978, 1983, 1984, 1985 and 1987.

The sparkling wines from **Penedès** are made by the Champagne method and have become increasingly popular in world markets because of their very reasonable price and good quality. The largest concerns are those of **Codorníu** and **Freixenet**.

Other regions produce very drinkable wines. The small domain of **Vega Sicilia**, E of Valladolid, makes some of the most sought-after red wines of Spain, intensely fruity in bouquet and flavor, and obtainable only at the best hotels and restaurants. To the w of Valladolid, **Rueda** produces fresh young white wines, notably the widely distributed Marqués de Riscal. **Galician** wines have a slight bubble on the tongue resembling the *vinhos verdes* or "green wines" of neighboring Portugal. The great bulk of wine for everyday drinking comes from the vast central plateau of **La Mancha**, stretching s from Madrid toward Andalucía. Of the reds, the fresh and clear **Valdepeñas** is most often served in the *tabernas* of old Madrid.

A guide to Spanish

This glossary covers the basic language needs of the traveler: for pronunciation, essential vocabulary and simple conversation, finding accommodations, visiting the bank, shopping, and for eating out.

Pronunciation

Spanish is a phonetic language in which the spelling matches the pronunciation. Letters whose pronunciation is not obvious are the *b*, which is always silent, and *v*, which is pronounced like *b*. While *z* and, in certain circumstances, *c* are lisped in central Spain, about 70 percent of Spaniards don't observe that so-called Castilian accent.

Stress is on the next-to-last syllable in words ending in a vowel, *n* or *s*. Other words are stressed on the last syllable. Exceptions are indicated by a written accent, e.g., inglés.

Vowels

a	as the **a** in f**a**ther — e.g., pat**a**t**a**
e	as the **e** in l**e**t — e.g., p**e**s**e**ta
i	as the **i** in pol**i**ce — e.g., l**i**tro
o	as the **o** in **o**rgan — e.g., p**o**ll**o**
u	as the **u** in r**u**de — e.g., m**u**cho; before another vowel, as the **w** in **w**ell — e.g., c**u**ando
y	as the **i** in mach**i**ne, when it stands alone; as the **y** in **y**es when next to a vowel — e.g., va**y**a or **y**o

Consonants

b	soft, with the lips slightly apart — e.g., sá**b**ado;
c	hard, as in **c**at — e.g., **c**ator**c**e; or before **e** or **i**, soft, as in **c**ent — e.g., do**c**e
d	between vowels and at end of word, as the **th** in **th**an — e.g., come**d**or
g	hard, as in **g**et — e.g., **g**ra**c**ias; before **e** or **i**, soft, slightly guttural — e.g., **g**ente
h	never sounded — e.g., **h**otel
j	as a slightly guttural **h** — e.g., aba**j**o
ñ	as the **ni** in o**ni**on — e.g., maña**n**a
r	trilled — e.g., ta**r**de
v	like the Spanish **b** — e.g., **v**ino
x	like the **x** in bo**x** — e.g., pró**x**imo; between e and a consonant, as an **s** — e.g., e**x**portación
z	as the **c** in **c**ent — e.g., die**z**

Letter groups

ch	as the **ch** in **ch**urch — e.g., dere**ch**o
ll	as the **lli** in mi**lli**on — e.g., a**ll**í
qu	as the **c** in **c**at — e.g., **qu**eso
rr	strongly trilled — e.g., ce**rr**ado

Gender

Gender is indicated below where appropriate. Adjectives are given in the masculine form, with the alternative ending used when it accompanies a feminine noun.

Reference words

Monday	lunes	Friday	viernes
Tuesday	martes	Saturday	sábado
Wednesday	miércoles	Sunday	domingo
Thursday	jueves		

January	enero	April	abril
February	febrero	May	mayo
March	marzo	June	junio

July julio			December diciembre	
August agosto			First primero, -a	
September septiembre			Second segundo, -a	
October octubre			Third tercero, -a	
November noviembre			Fourth cuarto, -a	

1	uno	13	trece	32	treinta y dos
2	dos	14	catorce	40	cuarenta
3	tres	15	quince	50	cincuenta
4	cuatro	16	dieciséis	60	sesenta
5	cinco	17	diecisiete	70	setenta
6	seis	18	dieciocho	80	ochenta
7	siete	19	diecinueve	90	noventa
8	ocho	20	veinte	10	cien, ciento
9	nueve	21	veintiuno	200	doscientos
10	diez	22	veintidós	500	quinientos
11	once	30	treinta	1,000	mil
12	doce	31	treinta y uno		

1992/93/94 mil novacientos noventa y dos/tres/cuatro

...o'clock las...(la una)	Quarter to... ...menos cuarto
Quarter-past... ...y cuarto	Quarter to six las seis menos cuarto
Half-past... ...y media	

Mr señor/Sr	Ladies señoras
Mrs señora/Sra	Gents caballeros
Miss señorita/Srta	

Basic communication

Yes/no sí/no	With con
Please por favor	And y
Thank you gracias	But pero
I'm sorry lo siento	Very mucho
Excuse me perdone/perdóneme	All todo(s), toda(s)
You're welcome de nada	Open abierto, -a
Hello hola; oiga (telephoning)	Closed cerrado, -a
dígame (answering telephone)	Entrance entrada (f)
Good morning/good day buenos	Exit salida (f)
días	Free (unoccupied or of
Good afternoon buenas tardes	charge) libre
Good night buenas noches	Left izquierda
Goodbye adiós	Right derecha
Morning mañana (f)	Straight derecho
Afternoon tarde (f)	Near cerca (de)
Evening tarde (early) noche (after	Far lejos (de)
dark) madrugada (early hours	Above encima
after midnight)	Below abajo
Night noche (f)	Front delante (de)
Yesterday ayer	Behind detrás (de)
Today hoy	Early temprano
Tomorrow mañana	Late tarde
Next week la semana próxima	Quickly rápido
Last week la semana pasada	Pleased to meet you. Encantado,
Month mes (m)	-a; mucho gusto.
Year año (m)	How are you? ¿Cómo está usted?
Here aquí	(formal) ¿Qué tal? (familiar)
There ahí, allí	Very well, thank you. Muy bien,
Over there allá	gracias.
Big grande	Do you speak English? ¿Habla
Small pequeño, -a	usted inglés?
Hot caliente	I don't understand. No
Cold frío, -a	comprendo/no entiendo.
Good buen(o), -a	I don't know. No sé.
Bad mal(o), -a	More slowly, please. Más
Beautiful bello, -a	despacio, por favor.
Well bien	My name is... Me llamo...

Words and phrases

I am American/English. Soy inglés, -esa/nortamericano, -a

Where is/are...? ¿Dónde está/están...?

Is there a...? ¿Hay un/una...?

What? ¿Qué?

How much? ¿Cuanto?

Too expensive Demasiado.

Expensive caro, -a

Cheap barato, -a

I would like... quisiera...

Do you have...? ¿Tiene usted...?

Where is the toilet? ¿Dónde está el aseo?

Where is the telephone? ¿Dónde está el teléfono?

Just a minute. Un momento.

That's fine/OK. Está bien.

What time is it? ¿Qué hora es?

I don't feel well. Me siento mal/no me encuentro bien.

Accommodations

Making a reservation by letter

Dear Sir, Madam, *Muy señor mío, muy señora mía:*
I would like to reserve one double room *Quisiera reservar una habitación doble* (with bathroom), *(con cuarto de baño),* and one single room (with shower) *y una habitación sencilla (con ducha)* for 7 nights from 12 August. *por 7 noches desde el 12 de agosto.*

We would like bed and half board/full board. *Quisieramos media pensión/pensión completa.*

Please send me details of your terms with the confirmation. *Por favor envíeme sus condiciones y precios con la confirmación.*

Yours faithfully,

Le saludo atentamente

Arriving at the hotel

I have a reservation. My name is... Tengo una reserva. Me llamo...

A quiet room with bath/shower... Una habitación tranquila con baño/ducha...

...overlooking the sea/park/street/back. ...con vista al mar/al parque/a la calle/atrás.

Does the price include breakfast/service/tax? ¿El precio comprende desayuno/servicio/impuestos?

This room is too large/small/cold/hot/noisy. Esta habitación es demasiado grande/pequeña/fría/caliente/ruidosa.

That's too expensive. Have you anything cheaper? Eso es demasiado caro. ¿Tiene usted algo más barato?

Where can I park my car? ¿Dónde puedo aparcar?

Is it safe to leave the car on the street? ¿Se puede dejar el coche en la calle?

Do you have a room? ¿Tiene usted una habitación?

Floor/story piso (m)/planta (f)

Dining room comedor (m)

Manager director (m)

What time is breakfast/dinner? ¿A qué hora se sirve el desayuno/la cena?

Is there a laundry service? ¿Hay servicio de lavado?

What time does the hotel close? ¿A qué hora cierra el hotel?

Will I need a key? ¿Me hará falta una llave?

I'll be leaving tomorrow morning. Me marcharé mañana por la mañana.

Please give me a call at... ¿Puede usted despertarme a... por favor?

Come in! ¡Adelante!/¡Pase usted!

Shopping

Where is the nearest...? ¿Dónde está...más cercano, -a?

Can you help me/show me...? ¿Puede usted ayudarme/enseñarme...?

I'm just looking. Sólo estoy mirando.

Do you accept credit cards/travelers checks? ¿Acepta usted tarjetas de crédito/cheques de viaje?

Can you deliver/ship to...? ¿Puede usted enviar a...?

I'll take it. Me lo llevo.

I don't want to spend more than... No quiero gastar más de...

Shops

Antique store tienda de antigüedades

Bakery panaderia (f)

Bank banco (m)

Beauty parlor salón de belleza (m)

Bookstore libreria (f)

Words and phrases

Butcher carnicería (f)
Pastry shop pastelería (f)
Pharmacy/chemist farmacia (f)
Clothes store tienda de moda (f)
Delicatessen mantequería (f)
Fish store pescadería (f)
Florist florería (f)
Hairdresser barbería (men's), peluquería (women's)
Hardware store ferretería (f)
Jeweler joyería (f)
Market mercado (m)

Newsstand quiosco de periódicos (m)
Photographic store tienda de fotografía (f)
Post office oficina de correos (f)
Shoe store zapatería (f)
Stationer papelería (f)
Supermarket supermercado (m)
Tobacconist estanco (m)
Travel agency agencia de viajes (f)

At the bank

I would like to change some dollars/pounds/travelers checks. Quisiera cambiar unas libras esterlinas/unos dólares/unos cheques de viaje.

What is the exchange rate? ¿A cuánto está el cambio?

Can you cash a personal check? ¿Puede usted cobrarme un cheque personal?

Can I obtain cash with this credit card? ¿Puedo sacar dinero con esta tarjeta de crédito?

Do you need to see my passport? ¿Quiere usted ver mi pasaporte?

Some useful goods

From the pharmacy:

Adhesive bandage esparadrapo (m)
Antiseptic antiséptica (f)
Aspirin aspirina (f)
Bandages vendas (f)
Diarrhea/upset stomach pills píldoras (f) para diarrea/el estómago trastornado
Indigestion tablets tabletas (f) para indigestión
Insect repellant repelente (m) para insectos
Laxative laxante (m)
Sanitary napkins compresas (f)
Shampoo champú (m)
Shaving cream crema de afeitar (f)
Soap jabón (m)
Sunburn cream crema (f) para quemaduras del sol
Sunglasses gafas de sol (f)
Tampons tampones (m)

Tissues pañuelos de papel (m)
Toothbrush cepillo de dientes (m)
Toothpaste oasta de dientes (f)
Travel sickness pills píldoras (f) para mareo

Clothing:

Bathing suit traje de baño (m)
Bra sostén (m)
Coat abrigo (m)
Dress vestido (m)
Jacket chaqueta (f)
Pants (trousers) pantalones (m)
Shirt camisa (f)
Shoes zapatos (m)
Skirt falda (f)
Socks calcetines (m)
Stockings/tights medias (f)/leotardos (m)
Sweater sueta (f)
Underpants for women bragas (f), for men calzoncillos (m)

Miscellaneous:

Film película (f)
Letter carta (f)

Postcard tarjeta postal (f)
Stamp sello (m)
Telegram telegrama (f)

Driving

Gas/service station estación de servicio (f)
Fill it up. Llénelo.
Give me...pesetas worth. Déme...pesetas por favor.
I'd like...liters of gas/petrol. Quiero...litros de gasolina.
Can you check the...? ¿Puede usted mirar el/la...?
There is something wrong with the... Hay algo que no va bien en el/la...

Battery batería (f)
Brakes frenos (m)
Exhaust tubo de escape (m)
Fan belt correa (f) de ventilador
Lights luces (f)

Oil aceite (m)
Tires neumaticos (m)
Water agua (m)
Windshield parabrisas (m)

My car won't start. Mi coche no arranca.
My car has broken down/had a flat tire. Tengo un coche averiado/un neumático pinchado.
The engine is overheating. El motor se calienta.
How long will it take to repair? ¿Cuánto tardará en repararlo?

Words and phrases

Car rental
Where can I rent a car? ¿Dónde puedo alquilar un coche?
Is full insurance included? ¿Está incluido un seguro a todo riesgo?
Is it insured for another driver? ¿Es asegurado para otro conductor?
Unlimited mileage kilometraje ilimitado
Deposit depósito (m)
By what time must I return it? ¿Para qué hora debo devolverlo?
Can I return it to another depot? ¿Puedo devolverlo a otra agencia?
Is the tank full? ¿Está lleno el depósito?

Road signs
¡Alto! stop
Ceda el paso yield/give way
Centro ciudad town center
Cuidado caution
Despacio slow
Desviación detour
Dirección única one way
Obras road works
Peaje toll
Peligro danger
Prohibido aparcar no parking
Salida de emergencia emergency exit

Other methods of transportation
Aircraft avión (m)
Airport aeropuerto (m)
Bus autobús (m)
Ferry/boat ferry/barco (m)
Railroad station estación (f)
Train tren (m)
Ticket billete (m)
Ticket office taquilla (f)
One-way/single de ida
Round trip/return de ida y vuelta
Half fare medio billete
First/second class primera/segunda clase
Sleeper/couchette coche-cama (m)/litera (f)
When is the next...for...? ¿A qué hora sale el próximo...para...?
What time does it arrive? ¿A qué hora llega?
What time does the last...for...leave? ¿A qué hora sale el último...para...?
Which track/platform/quay/gate? ¿Qué andén/muelle/barrera?
Is this the...for...? ¿Es éste el...para...?
Is it direct? Where does it stop? ¿Es directo? ¿Dónde para?
Do I need to change anywhere? ¿Tengo que hacer transbordo?
Please tell me where to get off. ¿Me diría usted cuando tengo que apearme?
Take me to... Lléveme a...
Is there a buffet car? ¿Hay un coche-comedor?

Food and drink
Have you a table for...? ¿Tiene usted una mesa para...?
I want to reserve a table. Quiero reservar una mesa.
A table near the window. Una mesa al lado de la ventana.
Could we have another table? ¿Nos puede dar otra mesa?
The menu, please. El menú, por favor.
I'll have... Tomaré...
Can I see the wine list? ¿Puedo ver la lista de vinos?
I would like... Quisiera...
What do you recommend? ¿Qué recomienda usted?
I did not order this. No he pedido esto.
The check/bill, please. La cuenta, por favor.
Is service included? ¿Está incluido el servicio?
Breakfast desayuno (m)
Lunch almuerzo (m)
Dinner cena (f)
Hot caliente
Cold frío, -a
Glass vaso (m)
Bottle botella (f)
Half-bottle media botella (f)
Orangeade/lemonade naranjada/limonada (f)
Mineral water agua mineral (m)
  carbonated con gas
  noncarbonated sin gas
Beer/lager cerveza (f)
Draft beer cerveza de barril
Ice hielo
Fruit juice zumo de fruta (m)
Carafe jarra (f)
Red wine vino tinto (m)
White wine vino blanco
Rosé wine vino rosado
Dry seco
Sweet dulce
Salt sal (f)
Pepper pimienta (f)
Mustard mostaza (f)
Oil aceite (m)

Vinegar vinagre (m)
Bread pan (m)
Butter mantequilla (f)
Cheese queso (m)
Milk leche (f)
Coffee café (m)

Tea té (m)
Chocolate chocolate (m)
Sugar azúcar (m)
Well done muy hecho
Medium regular
Rare poco hecho

Menu decoder

Aceitunas olives
Ahumado, -a smoked
Ajillo, ajo garlic
Alcachofa artichoke
Almejas clams
Almendras almonds
Anchoas anchovies
Angulas baby eels
Arroz rice
Asado roast
Atún tuna
Azafrán saffron
Bacalao cod
Brochetas skewers
Buey beef
Cabrito kid
Calamares (en su tinta) squid (in their ink)
Caldereta lamb or fish stew
Callos tripe
Camarones shrimp
Cangrejo crab, crayfish
Caracoles snails
Carne meat
Caza game
Cebolla onion
Cerdo pork
Champiñones mushrooms
Chipirones small squid
Chorizo spiced pork sausage
Chuleta chop, usually veal
Cigalas crayfish
Cochinillo suckling pig
Cocido stew of meat and vegetables
Conejo rabbit
Cordero lamb
Crema cream
Dulces sweets, desserts
Ensalada salad
Espárragos asparagus
Espinacas spinach
Faisán pheasant
Fideos pasta, noodles
Flan caramel dessert
Frambuesas raspberries
Fresas, fresones strawberries
Frío, -a cold
Frito, -a fried
Fruta fruit
Gambas large prawns
Guisantes peas
Habas broad beans
Helado ice cream
Hígado liver
Horno baked
Huevos eggs

Jamón ham
Judías beans
Jugo juice
Langosta spiny lobster
Lechuga lettuce
Lenguado sole
Limón lemon
Lomo loin (usually of pork)
Lubina sea bass
Mantequilla butter
Manzana apple
Mariscada mixed grill of seafoods
Mariscos shellfish
Mejillones mussels
Morcilla blood sausage, black pudding
Naranja orange
Nécoras small crabs
Ostras oysters
Parrillada grilled or broiled seafood
Patatas potatoes
Pato duck
Pavo turkey
Perdiz partridge
Pescado fish
Pez espada swordfish
Pichón pigeon
Pimientos sweet peppers
Piña pineapple
Pinchitos kebab
Plancha grilled
Pollo chicken
Pulpo octopus
Queso cheese
Rape anglerfish, monkfish
Relleno, -a stuffed
Riñones kidneys
Salchicha sausage
Salmonete red mullet
Salsa sauce
Sesos brains
Setas wild mushrooms
Solomillo tenderloin
Sopa soup
Surtido assortment
Ternera veal
Tortilla potato and egg omelet
Tostado, -a toasted
Trucha trout
Trufas truffles
Uvas grapes
Venado venison
Verduras vegetables
Vieiras scallops
Zanahorias carrots
Zumo juice

Index

Bold page numbers refer to main entries. *Italic* numbers refer to the illustrations and maps. See also the LIST OF STREET NAMES for the three cities on pages 159-160.

Index

154

Index

156

Index

Index

List of street names

All streets mentioned in the book that fall within the area covered by our maps are listed here. Map numbers are printed in **bold type**.

Barcelona

Amadeu Vives, C., **5**B3
Ample, C., **5**E3-6D4
Angel, Pl. de, **5**C3
Antonio López, Pl., **6**D4
Aragó, C., **4**C4-B6
Aribau, C. de, **3**B3-D3
Augusta, Via, **3**A1-B3
Avenir, C., **3**B2-3
Avinyó, C. d', **5**D3-E3

Balmes, C. de, **3**A2-4D4
Baluard, C., **6**E5-F6
Banca, Pge. de la, **5**E2
Bergara, C., **5**B1-2
Bisbe, C. del, **5**C3
Bonavista, C., **4**B7
Born, Pg. del, **6**D4-C5

Canaletes, Rbla., **5**B2
Canonja, Bda. de la, **5**C3
Caputxins, Rbla., **5**D2
Cardenal Casañas, C., **5**D2
Carme, C. del, **5**C1-2
Casanova, C. de, **3**C3
Castella, Pl. de, **3**D3
Catalunya, Pl. de, **5**B2
Catalunya, Rbla. de, **3**C3-4C4
Catedral, Av. de, **5**C3
Colom, Pg. de, **5**F2-6E4
Comtes, C. dels, **5**C3
Comtes Frenerता Dagueria, C., **5**C3
Comtessa de Sobradiel, C., **5**D3
Consell de Cent, C. del, **4**C4-5
Copons, C., **5**C3

Diagonal, Av., **3**B1-4B6
Diputació, C. de la, **3**D2-4B6
Drassanes, Av.de les, **5**E1-F2

Ensenyança, Pas de l', **4**E4
Espanya, Pl. d', **3**D2-E2
Estudis, Rbla. dels, **5**C2

Ferran, C. de, **5**D2-3
Flors, C. de les, **3**E3
Francesc Macià, Pl., **3**B2
Freneria, C., **5**C3

Gelabert, C., **3**C2
Gràcia, Pg. de, **4**C4
Gràcia, Trav. de, **3**B2-4A5
Granada del Penedès, C.

de la, **3**B3
Gran de Gràcia, C., **3**A3-B3
Gran Via de les Corts Catalanes, Av., **3**E1-4C6
Gravina, C., **4**D4

Isabel II, Pg. d', **6**D4

Jerusalem, C., **5**C1-D2
Jonqueres, C., **5**B3

Laietana, Via, **5**B3-6D4
Lincoln, C. de, **3**B3
Lleida, C. de, **3**E2
Llibreteria, Bda. de la, **5**C3
Lluis Companys, Pg., **6**B5
Loreto, C. de, **3**C2

Mallorca, C., **3**D2-4B4
Marc Aureli, C., **3**A2
Marià Cubí, C. de, **3**B2-3
Marina, C. de, **4**B5
Marquès de Comillas, Av., **3**E1-2
Mercaders, C. de, **5**C3
Montcada, C. de, **6**C4
Montjuïc del Bisbe, **5**C3
Montseny, C., **3**B3
Montsió, C., **5**B3
Muntaner, C. de, **3**A2-D3

Neptú, Pl., **3**F2
Nou de Rambla, C., **5**E1-D2

Palla, C. de la, **5**C2-3
Paradis, C. de, **5**C3
Paral-lel, Av. del, **3**E2-4E4
Paris, C. de, **3**C2-B2
Pau Claris, C. de, **4**C4
Pelai, C. de, **4**D4
Pintor Fortuny, C., **5**C1-2
Portaferrisa, C., **5**C2-3
Portal de l'Angel, Av., **5**B2
Portal de la Pau, Pl., **5**F2
Princesa, C. de la, **6**C4-5
Provença, C. de, **3**D2-4B6

Rambles, Les, **5**B2-E2
Rech, C. del, **6**C4
Rei, Pl. del, **5**C3
Reial, Pl., **5**D2
Roger de Flor, C. de, **4**B4-C5
Roger de Llúria, C. de, **4**C4
Rosselló, C. del, **3**C2-4A6

Sagrada Família, Pl. de la, **4**B5

Sant Carles, C., **6**F5-6
Sant Felip Neri, Pl. de, **5**C3
Sant Iu, Pl. de, **5**C3
Sant Jaume, Pl. de, **5**D3
Sant Joan, Pg. de, **4**B4-C5
Sant Josep, Rbla. de, **5**C2-D2
Sant Pau, C, de, **5**D1-2
Sant Pere Més Alt, C., **5**B3-6B4
Santa Clara, Bda, de, **5**C3
Santa Madrona, Pg. de, **3**E2
Santa Madrona, Pl., **3**E2
Santa Monica, Rbla., **5**E2
Santaló, C., **3**B2
Sarrià, Av. de, **3**B1-C2

Tallers, C. dels, **5**B1-2
Tapineria, C., **5**C3
Trinitat, C., **5**D3
Tuset, C., **3**B3

Universitat, Rda., **4**D4

Valencia, C. de, **3**D2-4B6
Valldonzella, C., **3**D3-4D4
Verdaguer i Callis, C., **5**B3

Madrid

Aduana, C. de la, **10**C-D4
Alcalá, C. de, **10**D4-C6
Alcalá, Pta. de, **10**C6
Alfonso XII, C. de, **10**C-F6
Amador de los Rios, C. de, **10**B5
Angel, Pl. del, **10**D4
Arenal, C. del, **9**D3
Arrieta, C. de, **9**C2
Atocha, C. de, **9**D3-**10**E5
Atocha, Rda. de, **10**F4-5

Bailén, C. de, **9**C-E2
Barceló, C. de, **10**B4
Bilbao, Gta. de, **9**A3-**10**A4
Bola, C. de la, **9**C2

Callao, Pl. de, **9**C3
Castellana, Po. de la, **10**A6-B5
Cava Baja, C., **9**E2-3
Cerrada, Pta., **9**D2
Cervantes, C. de, **10**D4-5
Cibeles, Pl. de la, **10**C5
Colón, Pl.de, **10**B5
Conde de Barajas, Pl. del, **9**D3
Cortes, Pl. de las, **10**D4
Cruz, C. de la, **9**D3-**10**D4
Cuchilleros, C. de, **9**D3

159

Street names

BARCELONA & MADRID

LEGEND

Environs Maps

=O= Autopista (with access point)

─── Main Road

─── Secondary Road

─── Other Road

N11 Road Number

═══ Railroad

✈ Airport

✦ Airfield

▓▓ International Boundary

- - - National Park Boundary

⌂ Monastery, Church

∴ Ancient Site, Ruin

♜ Castle

𝒳 Good Beach

■ Other Place of Interest

City Maps

▓ Major Place of Interest

� Other Important Building

▢ Built-up Area

▢ Park

† † Named Church, Church

✚ Hospital

𝑖 Information Office

⊠ Post Office

✋ Police Station

← Parking Lot

𝐎 Railroad Station

Ⓜ Metro Station

++++ Funicular

→ One Way Street

▥▥▥ Stepped Street

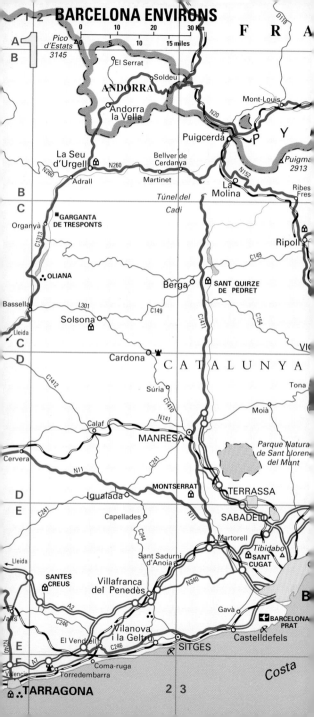

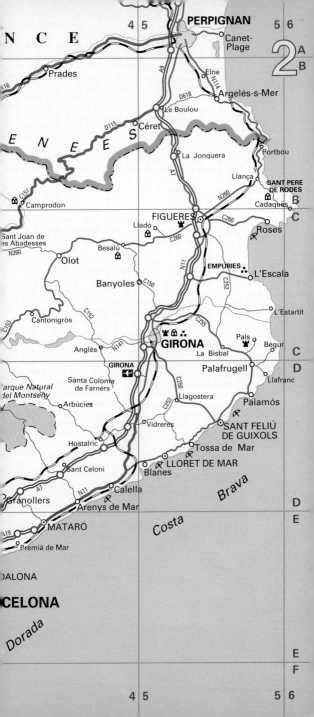

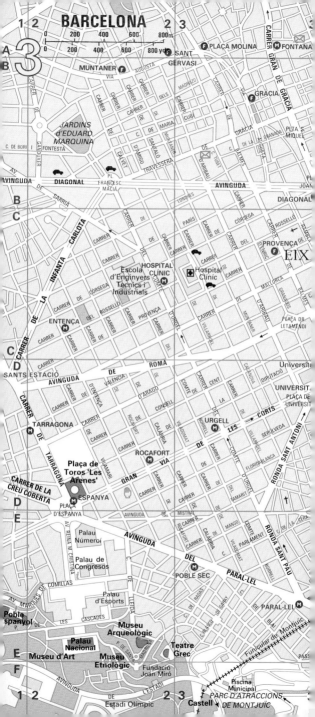

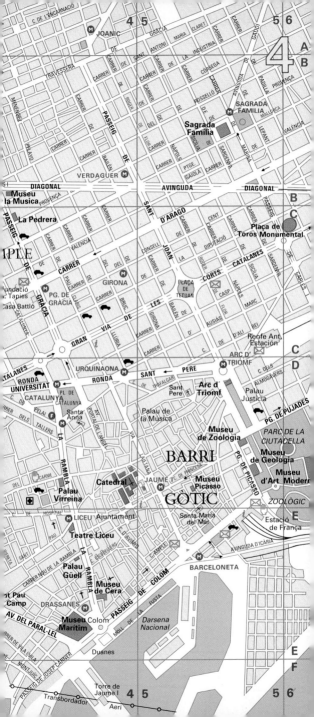

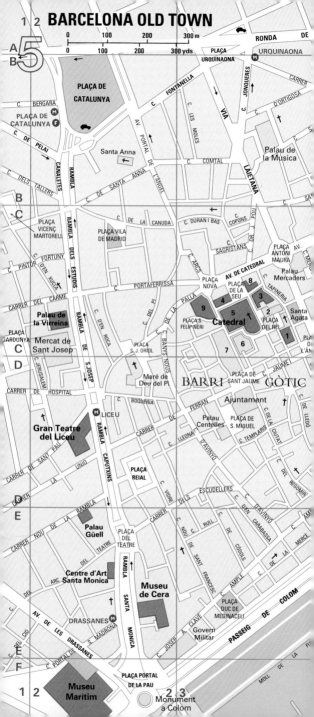

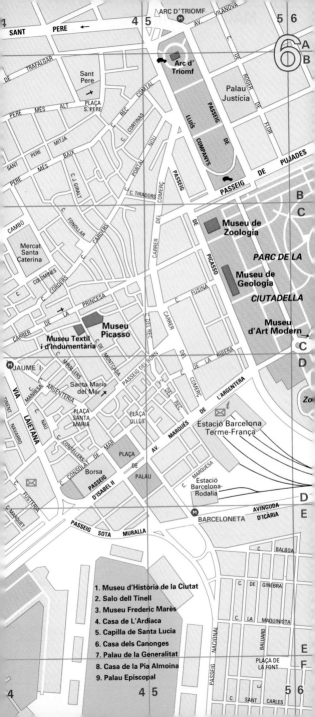

SANT   PERE ←

ARC D'TRIOMF   VILANOVA

DE   TRAFALGAR

Sant
Pere

PLAÇA
S. PERE

Arc d'
Triomf

Palau
Justicia

PASSEIG   DE   LLUÍS   COMPANYS

PASSEIG   DE   PUJADES

PASSEIG   DE   PASSEIG

A
B
C
B
C
D
D
E
F

6 5
5 6
4 5
4 4

Mercat
Santa
Caterina

Museu de
Zoologia

PARC DE LA

Museu de
Geologia

CIUTADELLA

Museu Textil
i d'Indumentària

Museu
Picasso

Museu
d'Art Modern

JAUME I

Santa Maria
del Már

PLAÇA
SANTA
MARIA

PLAÇA
OLLES

L'ARGENTERA

Estació Barcelona
Terme-França

VIA   LAIETANA

Borsa

PASSEIG
D'ISABEL II

PLAÇA
DE
PALAU

MARQUES   DE

Estació
Barcelona-
Rodalia

Zo

BARCELONETA

AVINGUDA
D'ICÀRIA

PASSEIG   SOTA   MURALLA

BALBOA

C.   DE   GINEBRA

C.   LA   MAQUINISTA

PLAÇA DE
LA FONT

C.   SANT   CARLES

1. Museu d'Història de la Ciutat
2. Salo dell Tinell
3. Museu Frederic Marès
4. Casa de L'Ardiaca
5. Capilla de Santa Lucia
6. Casa dels Canonges
7. Palau de la Generalitat
8. Casa de la Pia Almoina
9. Palau Episcopal

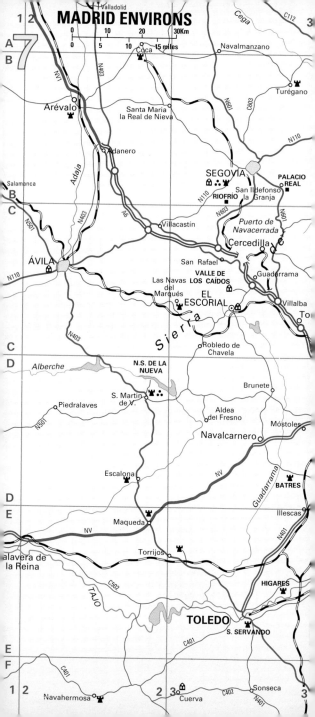

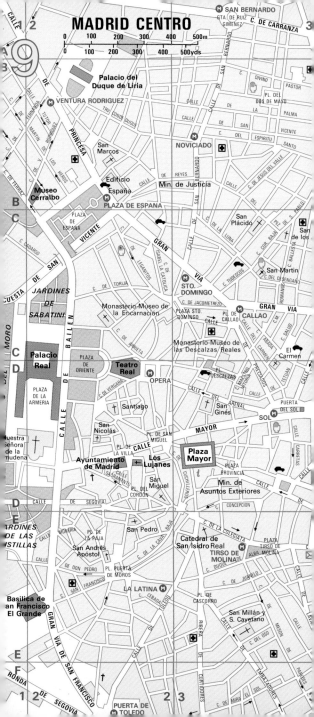

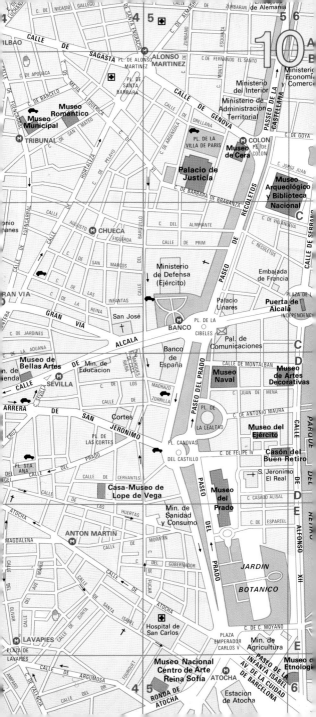